Hegel's Preface to the *Phenomenology of Spirit*

GEORG WILHELM FRIEDRICH HEGEL

✦

Translation and Running Commentary by

Yirmiyahu Yovel

PRINCETON UNIVERSITY PRESS · PRINCETON AND OXFORD

Copyright © 2005 by Yirmiyahu Yovel
Requests for permissions to reproduce material from this work
should be sent to Permissions, Princeton University Press
Published by Princeton University Press,
41 William Street, Princeton, New Jersey 08540
In the United Kingdom: Princeton University Press,
3 Market Place, Woodstock, Oxfordshire OX20 1SY
All Rights Reserved

Library of Congress Cataloging-in-Publication Data
Hegel, Georg Wilhelm Friedrich, 1770–1831.
[Vorrede, Phänomenologie des Geistes. English]
Hegel's preface to the Phenomenology of spirit / Georg Wilhelm Friedrich Hegel ;
translation and running commentary by Yirmiyahu Yovel.
p.   cm.
Includes bibliographical references and index.
ISBN 0-691-12052-8 (alk. paper)
1. Hegel, Georg Wilhelm Friedrich, 1770–1831. Phänomenologie des Geistes.
2. Knowledge, Theory of. 3. Spirit. 4. Consciousness. 5. Truth.
I. Yovel, Yirmiahu. II. Title.
B2928.E5Y68   2005
193—dc22   2004044514

British Cataloging-in-Publication Data is available

This book has been composed in Dante

Printed on acid-free paper.∞

pupress.princeton.edu

Printed in the United States of America

1   3   5   7   9   10   8   6   4   2

In memory of Yaakov (Eugène) Fleischmann

✦

Contents

✦

Preface
ix

Introduction
1

Text and Running Commentary
63–198

Works on Hegel
199

Index
213

Preface

><

THE *Phenomenology of Spirit* is the mature Hegel's first systematic work, which practically laid the ground for the rest of his system. It is also his most original work. The thirty-six-year-old Hegel, then teaching at Jena, finished the book around the time of the historic Battle of Jena, in which Napoleon crushed the Prussian army in the vicinity of Hegel's university town. At that time Hegel, not a nationalist like Fichte, saw the French emperor as the propagator of the French Revolution, who was to institutionalize its abstract ideas in concrete European laws and institutions.

Hegel wrote the Preface after finishing the book. In it he exposed his unorthodox ideas and revolutionary new approach to philosophy in succinct, intense terms, which made this text a much-admired classic, perhaps the best introduction to his general thought (and not specifically to the *Phenomenology*). Hegel himself, however, was uncomfortable writing a preface. Philosophical ideas, he says, derive their justification and very meaning from their context of development. Severing them from this living context (and, in addition, trying to frame the generalizations in ordinary, "predicative" language) is doomed to miss or distort their message.

This is a strong objection, which might count as Hegel's critique of the present book, too (and of any other introduction to his work). But in the end, Hegel himself bowed to necessity and, fortunately, gave us the celebrated Preface. The result is an enlightening (and tacitly ironic) text, which seems to negate performatively its own claim (namely, that truth lies exclusively in its full evolution). Hegel came to this decision because he considered that the Preface could work as a *pre*philosophical preparation to actual philosophizing. Well, so does any good introduction; and with this pontifical dispensation, the present book cheerfully adds its own voice to the company of "Introductions to Hegel," trying to be helpful to the growing audiences who face the Hegelian texts in a mixture of perplexity and despair.

Hegel's Preface contains a number of passages which are hard to digest, because of either syntax or content. At the same time it offers several short, pointed proverbs (like "the true is the whole," and "the absolute is a result") which mislead the reader into believing they hold their meaning within themselves, when in fact they require a development to be properly grasped. Even so, this Preface is a remarkably valuable introduction to Hegel, written by him at the height of his energy and original powers. Many thousands of students and Hegel scholars, in various periods and many languages, have discovered the special value that can be drawn from this text, provided one invests in it the necessary attention and, when needed, uses an appropriate interpretation.

THE TRANSLATION

After some hesitation, I decided to undertake my own translation of the text, for two reasons. One is that the extant translations (of the whole *Phenomenology*), by Baillie and Miller, are not sufficiently accurate for the magnifying glass that must be used in a close reading and commentary. (Baillie's winding sentences have a certain Victorian charm but not enough precision; and Miller takes more liberties with paraphrase and style than a running commentary can allow.) Another reason was that translations, even when they try to be as close to the original as I wished to be, often embody the translator's understanding of the text; so it made more sense to offer a unified introduction to Hegel in which the translator and commentator are the same person.

I followed the letter of the original Hegelian text (edited by J. Hoffmeister, Meiner, 1952), using straightforward contemporary style and avoiding literary embellishment. Often I broke Hegel's long sentences, or simplified their structure. I also omitted his italics. My aim was to make the translation work in conveying the German original even where it is ambiguous: the place for clarification is the commentary.

"Dear reader, study Latin and commit my translation to the fire" is the best advice ever given to readers of translations, though not the most practical. I do not claim to have produced an easy text. But whoever has read the original knows it is also not easy to read (and in this the translation agrees with the original). I hope the commentary, written in my own manner, succeeds in making intelligible both itself and Hegel's important and fascinating text. In any case, to me the two are integral parts of a single "introduction to Hegel's philosophy," which this book offers.

THE COMMENTARY

The commentary evolved in various seminars I have given over the years at the Hebrew University of Jerusalem, and in several institutions abroad. It contains an explication of the letter of the text together with its philosophical interpretation, given in a single sequence. Therefore, the beginner may encounter two levels of difficulty in understanding the commentary. Since the purpose of the commentary is to introduce the reader to basic Hegelian concepts, it often expands on an issue beyond what is strictly said in the text. For this reason, the volume of the commentaries is quite large at first, when one is entering Hegel's world, and diminishes later, when the reader has already been acquainted with important concepts.

As I explain in the introduction, my interpretation tries to be faithful to the historical Hegel and reconstruct his ideas within their own context. I abstained as much as possible from mixing my own philosophical preferences with my reading of Hegel. Approaches differing from mine, and works by other interpreters, are broadly illustrated in the section entitled "Works on Hegel."

ACKNOWLEDGMENTS

An earlier Hebrew version of this book was published by The Magness Press of the Hebrew University of Jerusalem (1996). For help in preparing the original version, and now the English-language version, I owe thanks to many people, above all my students in Jerusalem, and also at Princeton university, the Sorbonne, and the New School University. I have learned from them all. Colleagues and friends from whom I learned include Charles Taylor, Dieter Henrich, Werner Becker, Nathan Rotenstreich, Axel Honneth, Richard Bernstein, Richard Schacht, and, during my student days, Jean Hyppolite, Jean Wahl, Paul Ricoeur, and also Walter Kaufmann, with whom I had my differences, but I appreciated the differentiating freedom in which he criticized authors he held in esteem. Above all I should mention Yaakov (Eugène) Fleischmann, my teacher in the early Jerusalem days, through whom I first encountered Hegel and discovered the power of life and thought hidden in the Hegelian text that looks at first so opaque and academic. Fleischmann later emigrated to France where he wrote two books on Hegel (see "Works on Hegel"), but above all he was a charismatic teacher, ironic and piercing, who passed to his students the sense that philosophy in general, and dialectical thinking in particular, can matter to their lives. Fleischmann himself was a dialectical person, restless, without a synthesis between his many contradictions. I cannot think of anyone more suitable to whom to dedicate this work.

My thanks go to the Israel Science Foundation, whose grants assisted this work at different stages, and to the New School University in New York (Graduate Faculty), in whose friendly and unique intellectual atmosphere I was able to work on the expanded English version. Thanks are due to three of my doctoral students and former assistants in New York and Jerusalem, Howard Ponzer, Dr. Pini Ifergan, and Dr. Aaron Garrett, who helped in revising the text or completing the bibliography. I thank Michael Forster and an unnamed reader for Princeton University Press, whose remarks helped clarify important points in my text and approach. And, as in all my works, I am warmly indebted to Ms. Eva Shorr, the managing editor of the Jerusalem philosophical quarterly *IYYUN*, for her devoted help and advice. My thanks go also to Kathleen Cioffi of Princeton University Press, who helped improve the text, and to David Luljak, who prepared the index, and special thanks to Ian Malcolm, my wise Princeton editor.

Yirmiyahu Yovel

Hegel's Preface to the *Phenomenology of Spirit*

➤✦

Introduction

>+<

THIS INTRODUCTORY essay is not intended to replace the commentary, but to complement it. Its main purpose is to lay the ground for reading the text and commentary, by elaborating on two famous aphorisms in Hegel's Preface—*"The true is the whole,"* and *"The true [the absolute] is subject"*—and by offering a short interpretation of the Hegelian dialectic and its dual direction, which I call "dialectic as journey" and "dialectic as science." Another purpose is to explain my hermeneutical approach in relation to other Hegel interpretations.

ONTOLOGY, SOCIETY, AND RELIGION

First, a few words about my approach. Every commentary involves a standpoint and a choice of emphases. Different readers see different things in Hegel. Many interpreters tend to identify the whole of Hegel with that aspect of his philosophy which they consider valid or important today. I tend, however, to view Hegel in his own context and his variety of aspects, without suppressing elements of his thought that were crucial to him only because they can no longer be so to us. A good example is the "social Hegel." Many current scholars treat Hegel's innovative social and political theory as separate from his ontology (or even interpret his ontology as social philosophy), an approach I cannot share. Philosophy in Hegel does not climax in social praxis: this was Marx's view, which he voiced *against* Hegel, who put philosophical knowledge and comprehension at the top. In Hegel's own self-understanding, the social world and its evolution, while crucially important, are embodied within a larger project, in which being itself is supposed to attain a more actual and manifest state. The changing networks of social relations, built upon the human striving for recognition and selfhood, make possible diverse modes of reflective experience, that is, of knowledge and self-knowledge; and through the historical evolution of all these forms—cognitive, practical, and aesthetic—something is going on that, to Hegel, transcends the purely social domain—namely, *being is made actual and known to itself.* Therefore, one cannot adequately grasp the meaning of Hegel's social philosophy in separation from the specifically Hegelian ontology, according to which being is not given at the outset as finished and actual, but rather *evolves* toward actuality.

Moreover, this was a modern project for Hegel, not a residue of the metaphysics of the past. His ultimate interest in cognitive ontology defined a modern task for Hegel—the task of reconstructing—through philosophy, rather than religion or social praxis merely—the meaning of being that modern philosophy itself, working as abstract intellect, has irreversibly undermined when working as Enlightenment.

Other interpreters, especially in Europe, attribute to Hegel an overriding religious (Lutheran) outlook, and even a tendency towards mysticism. I cannot share this outlook, although I do recognize—indeed, stress—a religious substrate in Hegel, which calls for careful definition no less than the social. Hegel views religion as inferior to philosophy, a kind of metaphoric expression of it. The inferiority is due to the medium employed by each of them (which is a crucial consideration to the conceptually oriented Hegel). With respect to content, however, religion and philosophy share the same goal and general subject matter. The latter view is quite exceptional in modern philosophy, which has, for the most part, taken care to distinguish religion from philosophy, assigning a different, and usually more modest, role to philosophy. To understand Hegel's thought we must, therefore, recognize both its religious background, and the fact that Hegel *transcends* this background in two major respects.

First, philosophy stands on a higher level than religion because it is capable of conceptualizing religion's spiritual content: Reason is superior to image and metaphor. Although these elements (reason, image, metaphor) do not mutually exclude one another, the rational concept encompasses them all. And this also means that the concept is rational only in so far as it contains the essence of the experiences of imagining, feeling, and real being, and links them to a historical tradition. Hegel rejects the rationalism of the Enlightenment, which excludes imagining, feeling, and history from reason. Hegel calls such thinking Understanding (*Verstand*) as distinguished from Reason (*Vernunft*). Yet, in the final analysis, within the synthesis which all these elements are supposed to constitute, it is the rational form that reinstates itself as supreme. In this way the Enlightenment is essentially preserved in Hegel's philosophy, but only after it has reappropriated and encompassed its opponents rather than exclude them.

Second, even within the world of religious imagery, Hegel takes a heterodox position. Absolute being, God himself, does not exist as absolute from the outset. God rather develops, evolves in stages, mediated by the temporal becoming of the world-spirit, that is, by human history. Herein lies the essence of Hegel's dialectical version of Christianity: God does not only become man (in the image of Jesus), he also becomes *God* through the mediation of his becoming man. Human history is the phenomenal manifestation of absolute spirit's process of becoming, and consequently of God's own becoming. These are certainly metaphors, not concepts, but religious metaphor carries philosophical weight for Hegel, since it expresses absolute truth in images.

This is also true of Hegel's personal itinerary.[1] Religion remained a foundation of his mental world, but as the object of critique, transformation, *Aufhebung*. To reach the deeper truth to which religion points, one needs to go beyond it—that is, leave it, and do something else with it, something which religion itself, when duly understood, is found to be calling for. But what? The young Hegel found the answer in Kant's Enlightenment critique of religion, which draws the moral kernel of religion and disposes of its historical shell. The mature Hegel, on the contrary, turned to the history of religion as a substrate (along with social history) of the evolution

---

[1] For a vast panorama of the young Hegel see H. S. Harris's *Hegel's Ladder* (Indianopolis: Hackett Publications, 1997). For a succinct analysis of Hegel's grappling with the spirit of Christianity and Judaism see chapters 2 and 6 of my *Dark Riddle: Hegel and Nietzsche on the Jews* (Cambridge: Polity Press; University Park: Penn State University Press, 1998).

of Reason and absolute spirit. Hegel's two opposite answers were linked by a common goal: to inform philosophy with religion's essential content, while using philosophy's conceptual truth to reinterpret religion and raise it to a higher form of life.

Uniting the two issues, we may say that Hegel's distinctive social theory, while most important, is dependent upon his view of history, which must be understood in relation to ontology and with background reference to—the same thematic as treated by—religion. Religion, as a system of images, endows philosophy with experiential and historical depth. Yet Hegel transcends religion in the two ways mentioned above: he goes beyond religion to the higher, philosophical Concept; and he interprets the religious (Christian) tradition itself in a sharply heterodox way.

My reading of Hegel thus gives priority to universal thought— the *Logos*—though in a dialectical manner, which incorporates history, life, social relations, the imagination, and existential experiences as integral dimensions of the rational Concept. Hegel is not a mystic, quite the contrary, but the life-experience he calls "absolute Knowing" is supposed to provide in a *rational* manner that which mystics have always sought and promised to provide through irrational means like enthusiasm, concentration, or indeterminate *feeling*—namely, a dialectical union with the absolute, which encompasses one's whole existential experience and is not confined to one's intellectual consciousness alone. This also distinguishes Hegel from other rational philosophers—Plato, Aristotle, or Spinoza—for whom such union can only occur through the intellect, and by a separate, extraordinary mental act. *The Hegelian "absolute Knowing" is supposed to evolve and take shape within ordinary, secular life*—through work, family, social concerns, practical engagements, political participation in the state, and so forth—and also through ordinary religious practice: only thus can it attain a pure, Conceptual expression.

The Worldly Embodiment of Spirit

As I read it, then, Hegel's absolute Knowing is not merely an intellectual event but a living experience and a mode of life. As such it arises from concrete life-forms located in some definite historical time and in a social and geographical place. This is how we are anchored in the universe, immersed in a social life and a cultural milieu, and tied to our ordinary, earthly existence. In Hegel's philosophy, the highest spiritual state needs to be realized in and through worldly life. It is not an ascetic ideal aspiring to purity and dependent on mere intellectual concentration.

It should be noticed that the worldly dimension of the spirit does not manifest itself primarily in economics, as in Calvinism, but in more solidary forms of social life like the family and civil society, leading to citizenship and the state. Economics per se is for Hegel the domain of particular interests fighting a war of all against all, and therefore lacks spirit. Still, the state in Hegel is based on civil society (as its sublation), and civil society presupposes the interplay of economic interests; in this respect the state's universality permeates economic life as well and gives it a universal significance beyond itself.

In a word, Hegel's thought assigns weight and importance to worldly secular life (social and personal), while viewing it as embodying a meaning which extends beyond itself, a "rational" meaning in Hegel's sense, which translates (or sublates) a religious meaning. Spirit is realized in our world, but for Hegel (as for Luther, though not in the same Christian sense) our world—this world—is not merely an inferior, contingent being: our world is the embodiment of Spirit with a capital S. Even absolute Knowing, the top intellectual and existential state, is not severed from the rest of this worldly life, but is realized through it.

Modernists and Alienation

As I mentioned above, a central concern of Hegel, especially in the *Phenomenology*, was to reconstruct, and thereby redeem, those areas of modern life that have been damaged and undermined by modern rationality—community, family, custom, work, the sense of a well-anchored self, of political and social belonging, the assurance of meaning in life and the universe—and in doing so, to make *reason itself* restore the broken unity on a different and higher plane. The goal was, in other words, to transform modern self-conscious rationality from a destabilizing and alienating element into a constructive and invigorating force: the same reason that had produced the rift must repair it from its own resources. It was obvious to Hegel that the new unity could not be as compact and immediate as the lost unity had been—there is no turning back from modernity in Hegel, no romantic, conservative nostalgia toward the past. The modern unification had to be more complex, mediated by difference, built on tension and opposition, and therefore requiring a "dialectical" rationality.

As Hegel foresaw it, a successful modernity would make possible an autonomous—that is, truly free—individual, at home in society and the universe, and provide a self-sustaining ("absolute") meaning to human life and the world's existence: the love of wisdom (*philo-sophia*) would turn into actual *sophia*. By autonomy Hegel did not only mean enjoying abstract political rights and the freedom to choose between alternative options, but using universal rationality, as embodied in the historicized products of one's culture, in constructing one's individual self and singularity in the world.

To put it differently: the problem of severance and alienation is not unique to the social domain in Hegel. It runs through all parts of his system, including (indeed, primarily) the questions concerning the meaning of life and the universe, to which absolute Knowing—or wisdom, when attained—was to provide an adequate response, one that no longer undermines itself dialectically and is therefore "absolute," or self-sustaining. This problem has become particularly pressing in early phases of modernity, and must be resolved by high modernity. With the decline of the religious worldview, the individual finds herself cut off from the vindicating, meaning-generating elements she possessed in the past; the universe has undergone *désenchantement*, and lost, as Hegel says in our text, "the thread of light that links it to heaven" (p. 78, below). So the modern individual turns to philosophy for new insights, to philosophy as a mode of "Knowing" (*Wissen*) and not as a social doctrine merely. Speculative philosophy, which rides on a substrate of religion but transcends it toward a secular, conceptual wisdom, is expected to overcome this theoretical and existential alienation, a task which the doctrine of "ethical life" (*Sittlichkeit*) cannot achieve *in itself*, although it is a necessary condition for it. Ethical life—the modern reconstruction of social and political relations and institutions, and thereby of a concrete human subjectivity—prepares and makes possible the redemptive element in philosophical Knowing, but cannot replace it. To view the social domain, with its outward-looking activity and business, as substitute for the ontological and existential concerns is to escape or repress the issue rather than face it; and repression, which splits the self further, cannot be the solution.

This said, we should nevertheless remember that absolute Knowing is not a *detached* intellectual activity. Hegelian self-knowledge rides on a substrate of a socially engaged and affective life, and always involves the intermediation of theory and practice. At all levels, we know ourselves (and our environment) through a "lived" experience embodied in actual life-forms. This is due in part to the social dimension of the human self, whose individuality is mediated by intersubjective relations, and partly to the affective character, that of a lived experience, which rationality has in Hegel. The Hegelian self is gradually constituted and known to itself through involvement and interaction with other selves within a common world of work, language, conflict over recognition, love, shared beliefs, social institutions, religious symbols and cult, and other forms of concrete life which, by nature, are entwined with affective elements: emotions, drives, and moods.

This distinctive Hegelian outlook, which is foreshadowed by some elements in Aristotle and even Luther, evolved from Hegel's Jena lectures preceding the *Phenomenology*. There, Hegel had stressed the practical basis of cognitive reason, as a kind of ethical self-understanding that mediates the theoretical.[2] The conceptual essence of philosophy, and of absolute Knowing, is distilled through practical forms of experiencing oneself, others, and the world. But this does not indicate the primacy of practical reason, as in Kant or

---

[2] These lectures were particularly emphasized by Siep, Habermas, and Honnet. Recently, Pini Ifergan's doctoral thesis (The Hebrew University of Jerusalem, 2003) richly elaborates this issue.

Fichte. Indeed, practical experience itself is important also from a
cognitive standpoint, and not only from that of reason's socializa-
tion; for there is in Hegel a *practical* form of self-knowledge (or self-
understanding). It is a kind of prereflective reflection that occurs
through the experience of living, working, entering into social conflict and intercourse, and so forth. But then, a reflective, philosophical comprehension is said to grow from this soil. To use Hegel's
proverb, it is over this practical terrain that the owl of Minerva
spreads its wings at dusk: from here the genuinely cognitive reflection of philosophy arises and is distilled when the day's work is done.

All this does not exclude the possibility of dealing sensibly with
Hegel's ethics and social philosophy per se, as long as we do not
see them as standing alone, but recognize their role within a higher
and broader Hegelian project. Social philosophy can have this relative independence because it cannot be *derived* from ontology, although it cannot be fully *understood* without it.

An Ontological Journey

Let's take a cursory look at the road traveled by the *Phenomenology.*
By almost all accounts, the first part ("Consciousness") describes different cognitive modes, in which the mind pictures what is actually
real, and what it takes to be a concrete individual being. At first we
believe the actually real (the concrete individual) is a sense datum;
then a pack of properties we call "thing"; then an abstraction we call
"force," and its even more abstract counterpart we call [natural]
"law." Yet all these interpretations collapse because of inner deficiencies. With them, collapses our broader initial attempt—to capture
the actually real *directly,* and through a cognitive (and representational) attitude merely. To try again, relying on the knowledge we
have gained from those failures, we must turn from cognition to
desire, and from the natural object to the other human *subject,* to
whom we relate through the *will*—the will that wills another's will.
This turn, which results in a struggle for recognition and a dialectic
of subjugation and liberation, leads me to seek the actually real (and
individual) in my own self, which, however, turns out to be equally
abstract, split from itself (alienated), and not given immediately.

Self-consciousness, as we discover, is far from being Cartesian, or even Kantian; its dynamic of being makes it depend on its own social and cognitive evolution. And this opens a vast new domain—practical, social, *and* cognitive history—whose evolution is the terrain that allows self-consciousness, including philosophical self-knowledge, to arise in several levels and degrees. Through this process, new forms of interpreting the real arise and are replaced, until a Knowing of the actually real—and the true, individual self, both in the social and the ontic sense—is made possible, a Knowing whose dialectic no longer undermines its results but reinforces them, and thereby becomes self-sustaining, or absolute.

This is an ontological journey—toward the constitution and recognition of the transperspectival (the no-longer-relative, or absolutely true) meaning of the real (i.e., to God, in a nontheological, immanent sense)—that uses a social turn as its necessary medium and condition. In taking this crucial turn, we express a tacit recognition that the question, What does it *mean* to actually be? must assume the form, What does it *take* to actually be—to which a shorthand answer is: It takes living and being involved in a society, one that, despite inevitable regressions, eventually leads to freedom and mutual recognition. Yet this evolution is not the answer itself, only a prerequisite to it.

Similarly in Hegel's *Science of Logic*, which is not a formal science, the tacitly underlying query is, What is actually there, and what is the meaning of that which is? Here, too, we go at first through a failed immediacy and abstraction. We start from general, indefinite "being" which, as such, is uniform and meaningless; we move on to specific, one-dimensional (positivistic) entities, which on that account are unreal and abstract; then we move to complex entities, things with an "inner" and "outer" dimension—an "essence" and an "appearance"—which, in their duality, are dogmatically considered to be there in themselves. To this extent we have traversed (reenacted in thought) the history of the thing-like interpretations of the real which Kant called "dogmatic metaphysics," and whose final collapse, after a climax in Spinoza, calls for Kant's Copernican revolution (see p. 17 below). Here again, discovering subjectivity entails, beyond Kant, the discovery of sociality and the other subject as mediating our relations with the object; but this is a dimension of the search for actuality and not a substitute for it. The logic of the Concept, or rather the Idea, is mediated by the natural and the social dimensions of the Idea but, for Hegel, transcends them both.

Absolute Spirit

No less distinctive of Hegel than the intimate link of theory and practice is the claim that the institutional anchors of the self he calls *"objective* spirit" serve to realize *"absolute* spirit." In its narrow technical sense, absolute spirit denotes the self-reflective ways in which every historical period and culture—and eventually, humanity at large—affirms itself, and articulates its self-understanding and experience of the world in its art, religion, and philosophy. As mentioned earlier, Hegel sees something greater going on in human history than merely contingent societies and cultures expressing and justifying their modes of life in their reflective creations (philosophy, art, religion): there is an encompassing rational, even divine, principle that is actualized through their combined theory and practice. This encompassing principle, Spirit writ large—in its universal sense[3]—transcends (*aufhebt*) the objective (socialized, institutional) dimension of spirit toward the realization, and manifestation, of the absolute meaning of being.[4] The result is a heterodox Hegelian version of a self-revealing immanent deity: neither the transcendent creator-God of Christianity, nor the immanent substance-God of Spinoza, but an immanent synthesis of substance and subject that becomes manifest to itself through human history and knowledge.

A full explication of absolute spirit (or, also, of "world-Spirit") is impossible to give in an introduction, especially as Hegel's account

---

[3] In the sense of spirit that transcends its confinement to a certain culture or *Zeitgeist*. (These particular periods have also, so to speak, "perspectival" shapes of absolute spirit, expressed in their religions and dominant philosophies.)

[4] If this recalls Heidegger, it is no accident; Heidegger had appropriated Hegelian ideas more than he cares to admit. But let me also note the crucial difference between them: in Heidegger's terms, Hegel's question is inauthentic, because at every stage he drowns the issue in a scholastic "metaphysical" apparatus of terms and categories that hopelessly conceal it.

is not univocal. It is easier to start by stating what Hegelian spirit is not: it is neither a separate "world-soul," nor a superperson, nor the world seen as "a large, single intentional subject," as some contemporary scholars still write dismissively.[5] These images are typical of a misunderstanding that led to much derision and Hegel-bashing in the twentieth century, but cannot be anchored in the logic of Hegel's own system, which rejects the transcendent status of the divine, and stresses spirit's necessary inherence in the empirical world—in nature, history, and actual, empirical persons. There are *only* empirical persons in Hegel—only people like Plato, Solon, Rembrandt, Luther, Napoleon, Newton, or Kant—as well as ordinary members of society, like Hegel's wine-supplier in Jena and the lord-mayor of that provincial town. Spirit (in one of its basic senses) is the underlying element of their conscious, preconscious, and self-conscious activity, in which such actual men and women reshape (or, "subjectivize") nature by generating history and the products of culture, including the artifacts of *technē*, social and ethical attitudes, political institutions, scientific knowledge, as well as the public products and mental experiences of art, religion, and philosophizing. Spirit writ large, the immanent Hegelian divinity, is the unifyng, or totalizing, principle of all these developments, their underlying and self-displaying *meaning*, which informs the process and, at the same time, is also *constituted* and *revealed* by it.

As such, spirit is not foreign to nature—to the seemingly inert, thing-like being of the world—but is its dialectical outgrowth and evolution. As the human mind transforms (*aufhebt*) nature into historicized culture, it also constitutes *itself* as self-conscious spirit, and, so to speak, "humanizes" and "spiritualizes" the world—that is, causes the world's objective texture to manifest human goals and meanings. This does not occur, as in Kant (and later in Marx and in Sartre),[6] by the incursion of a foreign (human) teleology into nature, but by an immanent process, whose conflicts and resolu-

---

[5] Paul Redding, *Hegel's Hermeneutics* (Ithaca, NY: Cornell University Press, 1996), p. 15.

[6] On Marx's different approach to the humanization of nature—and its Kantian antecedents—see my *Spinoza and Other Heretics*, vol 2, *The Adventures of Immanence* (Princeton: Princeton University Press, 1989), chapter 4.

tions develop a latent structure in nature itself, and drive nature towards its higher mode of being.

Hegel thus assigns to human history an ontic role. This role is made possible by Hegel's specific brand of idealism, which not only claims to have uncovered a subject-like (i.e., a dynamic and self-differentiating) structure in what seems to be an inert natural substance, but goes on to interpret this structure as tacitly teleological.[7] This semi-Schellingian view was laden with many consequences for Hegel. Among other things, it drove him beyond the Kantian limits in performing his own "Copernican turn" in the philosophy of history. Hegel's extended Copernican turn consisted in assigning to human agency—to the socialized human subject, conceived as *embodied will* rather than as pure intellect—a determining role in the shape and career of the ultimately real. What human history is said to promote are not human goals only, *but the inner telos of being itself*: this, no less, was Hegel's expectation of modernity (at least before his more sobering Berlin years). When *philo-sophia* turns into *sophia*, spirit would have achieved a centuries-long project of realizing and making manifest the overall meaning of existence, its self-understanding and vindication.[8]

All this was frightfully ambitious (and hopelessly optimistic), a symptom of the exuberant hopes of budding modernity.[9] But there

---

[7] Kant had also looked for an ontological ground for explaining man's capability to "moralize" nature and further the goal of history; but his radical dualism excluded an immanent common ground, and forced Kant to postulate God's existence as a transcendent mediator. In Hegel, his immanent ontology supplies this ground by attributing to nature itself a dynamic, self-differentiating (subject-like) mode of being.

[8] At the same, absolute spirit also has relative phases as long as the historical process goes on, for then it serves to assert and vindicate the self-experience of specific cultures and periods.

[9] It is not, however, as harmonious and optimistic as it may superficially sound. The Hegelian dialectic remains cruelly sober and realistic to the end. Neither war, nor evil, suffering, violence, irrationality, or metaphysical contingency can ever be totally eliminated, because negativity remains constitutive of the positive result, even in its absolute form. Yet the rational principle has the upper hand. The intermediation of the rational and its opposite yields in Hegel a "concrete" rational (which also means, a realized, and therefore impure and nonuniform, rationality).

is no personification of the revealed meaning of being, or of the underlying principle that makes its emerging possible. Hegelian spirit, even at its highest point, remains embodied in empirical persons, societies, books, cults, works of art, and the like. There is no transcendence even at the end.[10]

Analogies and Incorporations

Hegel is so many-sided—often in the same body of text—that there is no univocal single key to his doctrine. Nor is there a valid way to peel off one aspect of his thought as the "true" or "actual" Hegel. Of course, the structural parallels in the system make it easy to identify the marks of one issue in another, and from here to claim that what goes on in one area of the system is "in truth" a discussion of the other. Thus, religious interpreters have argued that Hegel gives theology precedence over philosophy because of the structural analogy between dialectical logic and the Christian Trinity (or the Gospel); and socially oriented philosophers were tempted to read Hegel's *Logic* as a social treatise, noticing parallels between the evolution of the subject/object relation in ontology and in social philosophy. But such hermeneutical moves are dubious. The *Logic*, as a "kingdom of shadows," is meant to contain the conceptual skeleton which nature and spirit flesh out in their diverse subsystems; therefore, observing analogies between these domains should not impress us as a "discovery"; we should rather be surprised if we noticed no such analogies.

The Hegelian happy end is neither messianic nor scripted à la Hollywood, but preserves a tragic element, a bitter taste even at the accomplished end, and, as Kierkegaard realized, cannot satisfy the individual's particularity in full.

[10] Absolute spirit, when accomplished, is considered a subject but not a world-encompassing person. A subject has certain ontological characteristics and modes of beings, including a self-differentiating identity that exists only as return-to-self. This applies to the absolute (no-longer-relative) totality, which can be said not only to be subject-like, but also to know itself, in so far as its understanding arises in human culture and philosophy, which constitute an integral element of the same (absolute) totality. But this does not make it a superperson with particular thoughts and intentions. The absolute-as-person (as distinguished from the absolute-as-sub-

In the next section we shall see how Hegel incorporates elements from earlier philosophies into the Copernican ontology he inherited from Kant—above all, Spinoza's immanent monism, and Aristotle's view of being as a self-actualizing process. This illustrates a typical spiral (progressive/regressive) movement by which Hegel's dialectic progresses: once a higher level of knowledge and being has been attained in principle, one must turn back to earlier stages and elevate their sound kernel to that new level, so it can be further explicated and transformed by it. Kant had launched the higher phase of "Subjective Logic"—the subject-based ontology; now, crucial elements from Spinoza, Aristotle, and other past systems must be transformed and reinterpreted in terms of the new principle, so as to become integral components of the new system, as essential as the Kantian revolution itself. And just as Kant has served Hegel to criticize and overcome the flaws of those "dogmatic" metaphysics, so *their* essential contribution serves him to criticize Kant's shortcomings no less severely, and greatly modify his teaching.

With these background remarks in mind, let me now turn to the two main aphorisms of the Preface. But first, a word about their role in discourse.

The Paradox of Aphorisms

It is ironic that Hegel should use aphorisms to explain his ideas, he who, in the same text—indeed, in those very aphorisms—denies the possibility of saying anything significant about philosophy in a single generalized statement. Such a statement, in addition to lacking truth, fails to contain the meaning that it claims to convey. Truth and meaning require an evolving context; hence, they can arise only at the end, as a result of the full explication and self-tranformation of the idea that the general statement purports to enounce, but inevitably misses. Nevertheless, Hegel happily uses those inadequate means of philosophical communication as intro-

---

ject) is strictly speaking a *metaphor*, a (Judeo-Christian) religious *Vorstellung,* produced by the imagination, which represents the philosophical Concept in images.

ductory devices, in prefacing both the *Phenomenology* and the *Philosophy of Right* ("what is rational is actual and what is actual is rational"). Hegel seems to believe that the initiation to a "speculative" (i.e., dialectical) mode of thinking requires a surprising shock, a sense of paradox or enigma that puzzles ordinary rationality (*Verstand*) and calls for the *Aufhebung* of its customary ways of thinking, by which alone the paradox can be resolved. Neither an argument nor a "deduction," this shock treatment is an auxiliary device—call it "Socratic"—serving the process of philosophical *Bildung*.

No less important, Hegel has a general problem with philosophical language. On the one hand he has a strong systematic reason for denying the propriety in philosophical discourse of using the predicative proposition (which is built as a unilateral dependence of a predicate on a subject); yet on the other hand, he has an equally systematic reason against devising a special, nonnatural language for philosophy. Philosophical discouse, being rooted in society and its history, cannot be severed from the actual historical languages in which philosophy has evolved, and these are all predicative in character (and thereby captive of *Verstand*, abstract rationality). Since no theoretical resolution of this antinomy is possible, Hegel turns to practical solutions, like using the whole paragraph, and even larger portions of a chapter or an oral explication. This technique allows for the back-and-forth movement, the looping, the undermining of what has just been said, so as to progress to a higher viewpoint that Hegel's dialectic requires and for which it is both famous and notorious.

Using blatantly predicative aphorisms may be another device of coping with the antinomy of language. These aphorisms are fundamentally self-refuting; what they say contradicts what they are and seem to perform; so they must either explode (when taken at face value), or their indicative appearance must be bypassed, so that, as merely evocative proverbs, they will serve to allude to what officially they must fail to convey. Either way, these aphorisms are meant to do a preparatory *rhetorical* work, in helping clear the way for the dialectical mode of thinking.

This will have occurred if the newly initiated learner proceeds to a detailed systematic explication of these ironic dicta that, despite their dialectical sterility and illusory form, nevertheless point to an important objective that the learner will have conquered when he or she overcomes the temptation and false promise of learning *from* those dicta.

As given, then, these ironic dicta have a real, important reference and a delusive, vacuous meaning. They bear from the outset a false and a true promise at the same time, which clash at first, creating puzzlement, yet can and must be separated for actual knowledge to proceed.

The view above creates a problem for an interpreter who wishes to explicate the historical Hegel as faithfully as possible, yet does not share his organistic view of philosophical discourse. Inevitably, I shall use the good old predicative language, knowing that an orthodox Hegelian (if any is left) will call my text a mere *konversation* about Hegel rather than expressing the *Sache selbst*.

The Absolute as Subject

The single most important sentence in the Preface reads:

> According to my way of seeing . . . everything depends on comprehending and expressing the true not as substance, but equally also as subject. (p. 95)

This aphorism has several meanings, on different historical and ontological levels of the Hegelian philosophy.

Historically, this dictum calls for a synthesis between Spinoza's concept of substance and Kant's (and Fichte's) concept of subject. Each of these poles will thereby be liberated from one-sidedness, and the road to "absolute Knowing" will at last be opened. Hegel declared this synthesis to be the final goal of his philosophy, and viewed it as a task defining philosophical modernity in general. Indeed, at least in Germany, this project stood at the center of the philosophical, cultural—even political—interests for almost a century after Kant's *Critique*. The attempt, in various and sometimes opposing ways, to establish a union between Kant and Spinoza is visible in the work of Fichte, the early Schelling, Hegel himself, Schopenhauer, some of the Left Young Hegelians, and, in a less obvious way, Marx.[11]

The central place this attempt held in Hegel's philosophy is attested by several main texts beside the *Phenomenology*. In the *Logic*, Hegel sees Kant's idealism as the foundation of modern philosophy, because it asserted the role which the knowing I plays in the constitution of the reality which it knows. This revolutionary discovery led philosophy away from the long phase of dogmatic metaphysics (which Hegel calls "Objective Logic") on to the so-called "Subjective Logic." Henceforth, the mind no longer views the world-*logos* as a kind of substance or thing (*Ding, res*)—that is, as object only— but starts viewing it also as subject. This decisive turn leads philosophy from dogmatic metaphysics (culminating in Spinoza) to the critical, idealist metaphysics initiated by Kant; and in what concerns the ontological categories we thereby pass from the category of "actuality," centered on Spinoza's concept of substance, to Hegel's own category of the "Concept," which takes its paradigm from Kant's "I think." Thus a clear parallel exists between the structure of the *Logic*, and what Hegel says programmatically in the Preface to the *Phenomenology*.

The same idea in different version recurs in Hegel's *Lectures on the History of Philosophy*. Hegel praises Spinoza's doctrine as the necessary basis of all true philosophy, but says it must be transcended—by presenting the absolute not as substance only but also as spirit. God is immanent in the world, and identical with its totality, yet he is not therefore a mere thing, not substance or nature only, but a spiritual process, as well. Moreover, God as spirit is not external to men and women; he is not some separate, sublime subject over and above them, but is embodied in human history and human culture, and evolves within and through them. This means, in essence, that God is realized through man, and that God's subjectivity is mediated by the consciousness of particular men and women and the social culture which unites them.

[11] See note 6 above.

From an ontological standpoint, asserting that "the absolute is subject" means, in the first place, that *being itself exists as a process*— it is not given in its perfect state from the outset, but has to be actualized. For this reason, absolute being is a result—of its own movement and process of self-becoming. It is therefore also a purposive process, which has itself—in its actualized essence—as the immanent goal of its movement. This already says that the movement of mediation—philosophical knowledge—is not external to being but is being's own motion. Being-as-subject knows itself, and this knowledge *actualizes* being according to its true essence.

To grasp this profound and difficult idea we must note that the movement in question is not only the movement of something in being, but the movement of being itself—its development toward higher levels of actuality. In its lower stages, being's subjective character, that is, its self-actualizing movement, is manifest in the organic domain: the phenomenon of life. In its higher stages it is a historical movement—the movement of culture, practical life, social forms, and institutions, and of the consciousness they express or embody. And at still a higher stage this is the movement of self-consciousness, pure contemplative cognition, and absolute Spirit.

An Aristotelian idea is hiding in the background of this Hegelian view. There are several degrees of being, and reality evolves from one to the other until it attains *energeia*, actuality, or "entelechy."[12] But, in keeping with his strictly immanent and historical approach, Hegel introduces deep and far-reaching changes into this Aristotelian view. For Aristotle, God as the unity of the knower and the known exists outside man and even outside the universe, or at least at its limit. Also, the Aristotelian God enjoys his perfect state from eternity to eternity, with no relation to time and the particular items of existence. For Hegel, however, God is immanent; he exists only in time and within the world, and attains his perfect state through human culture and its evolution.

The subjectivity of being thus has two complementary senses in Hegel: (a) the self-*actualizing* movement of being; and (b) the self-

---

[12] Cf. also medieval views, as in Maimonides, of the "unity of knowledge, the knower and the known."

knowledge of being. The second sense is the climax of the first, its "entelechy" of sorts. Both senses are united at the highest stage, where being is fully actualized through Knowing itself. This occurs through human philosophy, religion, and art. Thus, it follows from the idea of the absolute-as-subject that human culture (with its necessary social and historical frame) is not some external, contingent relation into which being happens to enter, but is *a state of being's own development.*[13]

This also affects Hegel's philosophical notion of truth, as distinguished from the truth of a formal or an empirical statement. In philosophy, truth is not the Concept's adequacy with external reality. Truth is, first of all, the adequacy of reality with its own inner Concept, that is, its end. Truth is therefore an ontic state, and not a state of consciousness merely. It is linked to the process of the actualization of being and its several degrees. In this sense, Hegel often says of a higher stage that it is the "truth" of the one beneath it. He means that the higher stage does not only disclose what is contained in the lower one, but thereby also actualizes it.

The Subject and Self-Negation

Another important way of viewing the absolute as subject concerns the structure of the movement by which being is actualized, and the role negation fulfills within it. This has direct relevance to the logic and method of philosophy.

To be a subject is to exist according to a certain ontological structure (or "logic") which differs from that of a substance or mere thing. The difference lies in the subject's characteristic activity, which is to negate, or produce negation. This negation is first directed at the subject itself, and at any content or definite state with which the subject seems initially to be identified. The subject therefore exists as distinguished from itself, it transcends its own particular states and negates any immediacy that exists within it or is attributed to it. True, in the last analysis, the subject has also a positive activity in which it recognizes certain stable contents as "its own," identifies

---

[13] Herein seems to lie one of Heidegger's Hegelian roots.

with them, and reconstitutes its own identity through them. Yet even this positive activity is performed through another negation. It presupposes a series of negations which do not return the process to its point of departure, but rather each negation constitutes a new state of affairs, and a new state of consciousness. As a result, the subject attributes to itself a diversity of states and contents which are seen in retrospect as expressing its selfhood, and one even considered as the subject's own particularization. Yet this is a selfhood in the process of becoming, a selfhood which will not actually exist until it reaches the end of the road. In other words, as long as the process is still ongoing there is no *actual* subject.

Self-Identity

Hegel makes a crucial distinction between the identity of a substance and the identity attributed to a subject. A substance or mere thing is considered as directly identical with itself: its self-identity is conceived as a simple primary datum: A = A. A subject, however, does not have this sort of simple identity (I = I). Its self-identity must be understood as *an activity of self-identification*, which takes place through the mediation of otherness and is attained only at the end of the process. Therefore, as mentioned above, the subject is not immediately self-identical, but acquires and constitutes its identity both through the complete process and as its result.

This idea is pertinent to today's debates concerning the subject: does the subject have identity and ontological status in itself? Hegel's innovative answer as just described had its origin in the "Transcendental Deduction" of the *Critique of Pure Reason*, where Kant explicates the structure of "I think" while tacitly polemicizing against Descartes. Descartes presented "I think" (a) as a simple, primary datum; (b) as substance; and (c) as a thinking *thing* (*res cogitans*). And Spinoza, following Descartes, presented God himself as substance and as thing (*res*), which does not think and has no I. Opposing Descartes, Kant tried to show that "I think" is neither a substance or thing nor a simple datum, but rather a complex structure whose self-identity presupposes a set of preconditions. Put succinctly (and somewhat simplified): the identity of the I is made possible because the I refers to a manifold of sensible data, unites it according to patterns of connection (called "categories") supplied by the understanding—which follow from the I itself—and attributes those connections to the unity of an objective world and temporal sequence which is separate from the I and faces it. Only through this complex process can the I eventually return to itself as identical, say "I think" to itself, and thus constitute, or actualize, that self-identity which is lacking at the outset.

From this it follows (already in Kant's philosophy) that (a) the subject's self-identity occurs as the result of a set of relationships, or process, and is not primordially given; (b) it is an activity of self-identification, not an inert fact; and (c) the pure subject is identified with itself through the mediation of its opposites—the sense impressions opposing the understanding, and the outer world opposing the I.[14]

Hegel adopts this Kantian model, but extends its application from the finite I to infinite, comprehensive reality. Absolute being itself has the structure of a subject. It, too, is not from the outset that which it will ultimately become, but *proceeds towards itself through its opposites*—namely, through multiplicity and otherness. In addition, multiplicity and otherness are now considered to be the subject's *own* particularization. Thereby, Hegel breaks away from the boundaries of the Kantian critique of reason—which requires the subject to have an external source for all its particular contents—and gives the subject a daring ontological (and also theological) interpretation. The subject discussed in Hegel's theory is not only the I of a finite individual—of this or that man or

---

[14] At the background is also a distinction between the self, the object, the consciousness of self, and the consciousness of the object's relation to the self. In Reinhold and Fichte, following Kant, these constituent elements of consciousness seem to be simultaneous; in Kant—and certainly in Hegel—some of them are preconditions to others. (The consciousness of the external object's relation to the self, and the tacit, not necessarily explicit awareness of the self's own role in setting up this relation, are in Kant preconditions for the self being conscious of itself and able to say or think, "I think." For a slightly different analysis see Michael Forster, *Hegel's Idea of a Phenomenology of Spirit* [Chicago: University of Chicago Press, 1998], 116–17.)

woman—but also God as immanent in nature and history, that is, the Spinozistic substance become subject-object. Thus, Hegel uses the Kantian model of the subject—with a crucial change—in order to explicate not only the ontology of finite, conditioned beings, as Kant did, but also the ontology of the infinite, absolute Being. This forces us to stress the religious, albeit heterodox, background of Hegel's thought.

The Enigma of Self-Particularization

Hegel's readers are often puzzled by an apparently mysterious problem. Against Kant, Hegel demands that the multifold particulars which the subject ascribes to itself be seen not as utterly external but, in a certain sense, as the subject's own particularization. This idea is hard to understand, and even harder to accept, when considering the particular I in separation from the broader context of the spirit; in other words, when trying to understand the issue in purely epistemological terms. Who in his or her right mind would agree that, for instance, the particular contents of our sensation, or the contingent facts which face us and lie beyond our control, have their material source in our own consciousness? Many interpreters struggling with this problem have attributed to Hegel a mystical position, according to which consciousness spontaneously particularizes itself into the rich, manifold system of the world. I think we might better understand Hegel by realizing that his philosophy is not primarily concerned with epistemology of the individual mind, but with the ontology (and history) of the universal spirit. From this perspective we shall see the following:

(1) The particularization in question does not concern contingent particulars in the empirical world like facts or sense perceptions (not Professor Krug's pen),[15] but primarily the ontological categories: Being, Being-there, Quantity, Essence, and so forth. Only *they* are said to derive from the absolute subject, and their derivation in the *Logic* indeed follows a structured dialectical devel-

---

[15] Professor Krug was a philosophy professor who challenged Hegel to "deduce" his pen from the absolute subject.

opment rather than being a mere assemblage, which Hegel says both Aristotle and Kant have offered.

(2) All the other contents which eventually appear in the system of philosophy—"matter," "family," "passion," "Stoicism," "civil society," or "magnetism"—are indeed first borrowed from historical experience; but since that experience has been philosophically shaped and is the unfolding of the universal spirit, these contents can all be seen as spirit's own self-particularization in the process in which it is realized; and from this viewpoint they are neither contingent nor external. To be sure, the particular individual will always see such contents as contingent and external; but here the process of philosophy comes in, whereby the individual sets out to understand herself, her history, the formation of her consciousness, and thereby reaches the point where she views these ingredients as belonging to her own identity and not as contingent and imposed by accident. For this to happen, the individual must attain a self-consciousness which grasps her connection to the whole of spirit; and she must be living in a period that is not completely alienated, and within circumstances that allow the individual, in great measure, to rationally identify with the basic ingredients of her social, political, and cultural environment.

In such a case Hegel would say that the particular contents of reality are not external and contingent even for the individual. They are rather a particularization of her own spirit which constitute the individual's self (at least partially)—in so far as the self can identify with the universal spirit as embodied in the individual's time and place. In a word, the question of "particularization" must not be dealt with in epistemological terms mainly, but in social and historical ones. (See also the commentary on "recollection," pp. 86ff., 123ff. below.)

The Absolute as a Totality-in-Becoming

As we have mentioned above, absolute being, because it is a subject, is not immediately identical with itself, nor is it a static, finished totality—as it is for Spinoza—but exists as a *becoming* totality. This means that the entirety of being—the immanent God—constitutes its self-identity by becoming other than itself, and by rediscovering itself both in its otherness and as the result of its own development. More specifically, the hidden rational—indeed divine—essence of the whole of being externalizes itself in the empirical world, and exists in a variety of empirical shapes and degrees in nature and history. These shapes diverge from the rational essence in ways which cause them to oppose it and cause the essence to be alienated from itself. The result is that the essence seems to have been lost in its contradictions. Actually, however, the essence remains present and active within its contradictions, and through them continues to structure the movement of the evolving reality. That process continues until reality itself reaches a stage at which the rational essence can rediscover itself in and through the empirical world and adequately actualize itself. The three major stages in this process involve many intermediary processes, each of which again manifests the structure of negation and re-negation: they are spelled out in detail both in the *Phenomenology* and in Hegel's later works.

The self-actualization of spirit is equally a process of *liberation*. Freedom has both an ontological sense and a sociopolitical sense in Hegel, which mediate one another. It is both freedom from political oppression and the autonomy of self-realization—of the subject's becoming a true individual through political rights and standing, and through the awareness that her natural, social, and political environment is not an alien (or even alienating) "substance" but an active expression (and enhancing externalization) of her own rational self; this too is a central aspect of substance becoming a subject.

Seen from the human standpoint, the process ends at the stage of *Reason* or *freedom*. From the standpoint of being it ends with the actualization of absolute being, when the totality reaches self-understanding through human culture and philosophy. This event fully actualizes the subjective character of substance and makes it into a subject/object. Thus, according to Hegel, the emergence of absolute Knowing—and of human freedom—is a crucial event, not only in the history of the human race, but in the history of being itself.[16]

---

[16] Heidegger drew the idea of "the history of being" from the Hegelian tradition, but did away with its teleological character, including the goal of freedom.

Society and Politics as Conditions for Knowledge

A central feature of Hegel's philosophy is that both the ontological process (the actualization of being) and the process of knowledge which serves it are carried out through social and historical evolution—the evolution toward human freedom. Philosophical knowledge can only arise as the conceptualization of a certain social and political reality, and therefore presuppose the latter's existence. Hence the crucial importance of human *practical* history as a precondition for realizing the subject/object. The subjectivity of the absolute indicates, among other things, that social and cultural life, with their various forms of private and public consciousness, are genuine modes in which *being itself* exists and develops. Although the *climax* of this development is cognitive, its major body is historical and resides in social and cultural life: in the family, the community, civil society, state institutions, religion and art, collective mentality and the psychic life of the individual within her time and sociocultural environment. Hegel makes these the necessary substrates and conditions for the evolution of knowledge.

Herein, as I already mentioned, lies a major Hegelian novelty. Philosophical knowledge does not occur within a separate logical space of its own, but is the conceptualization of various forms of life—social, political, mental, and so on—as they have already been realized in the world. Knowledge depends on its own history, and also on the history of other, practical forms of culture, which are embodied in the objective world and which philosophical knowledge explicates. This is the Hegelian notion of *Zeitgeist* ("the spirit of the times"), which philosophy is said to explicate and which expresses the inner meaning of the forms of human culture in a certain era—up to and including the last epoch.

Special importance in this context is given to civil society and politics. Hegel sees the social and political institutions as the spirit's outer (objective) shape, through which alone—by its *Aufhebung* (sublation)—the spirit can be actualized and know itself in its inner dimensions, too. This, to use a different Hegelian idiom, means that the domain of lived and embodied ethics (*Sittlichkeit*)—social norms and customs, contractual relations, the family, law, politics, and the state—are the necessary presupposition of philosophy, and also of art and religion, the three shapes of absolute spirit. Hegel is not satisfied with stating this major thesis in the abstract, but spells and works it out so significantly in the *Phenomenology* and other works that it can be said to be the most extensive, or at least the most visible, domain in which Hegel's idea of the "absolute as subject" is realized. Social, practical, and political life is based on both the external and the internal shapes by which consciousness relates to itself and to other consciousnesses. Even its relation to nature is mediated by its relation to another consciousness, since both knowing nature and using nature are socially mediated activities. And because all of these stand in a network of mutual interrelations, it can be said that "objective spirit" has a *subjective* substrate, in the sense that social institutions are outer configurations of intersubjective relations. As such, objective spirit provides the medium and underlying structure for the evolution of the subject/object, and of the philosophical system that explicates it.

Conceiving the absolute as subject also has direct implications with respect to philosophical method. Before we begin to discuss this topic, however, three further remarks are required.

(1) Hegel's position involves a dialectical monism. Being is conceived as a single totality whose unity emerges from a synthesis of all those ontological poles and dimensions which philosophy usually regards as mutually exclusive. The Hegelian philosophy sees these poles as reciprocally constitutive of each other: unity and plurality, universality and particularity, thought and being, spirit and nature, theory and practice, intellect and will, the inner and the outer, and so on. In viewing the absolute as subject, the philosopher avoids the splitting of reality into disparate, unmediated regions, as happens in dualism, and understands each of these regions as an abstract sector, or aspect, of the one absolute being.

(2) The view of this overarching One as a single, animated individual, expresses a quasi-pantheistic tendency which is found in some of Hegel's contemporaries from Goethe to Schelling. Nature was conceived as a living entity, a global organism endowed with

inner animation, rather than as an inert mass of matter in motion. Hegel shares this tendency but makes spirit rather than nature into the comprehensive One. Spirit is the overall living principle, of which nature is but a dimension or "moment." Nature is inferior to spirit and to history (spirit's appearance in time), but is also included in spirit as substrate and base. Hegel thereby opposes the naturalism of Spinoza, from whom he nevertheless takes the principle of immanent philosophy. The overarching immanent being for Hegel is not *natura* (nature) but *Geist*, self-conscious spirit. In consequence, Hegel rejects Schelling's romantic philosophy of nature and its foundations in Goethe. Nature as such has no spirituality and is certainly not divine: Hegel would consider this to be paganism. Nature is primarily an aggregate of items in space and time, each located outside the other in an inert relation which endows them with quantity and disposes them to measurement. True, nature in its deeper dimension also discloses an organic, subject-like structure and thereby the potentiality for spirit; yet realizing that potentiality will take us outside of nature and into the domain of human culture and thought, of which, as mentioned, nature is a mere substrate. Thus, even when he transcends Christian orthodoxy towards a kind of pantheism, Hegel does so in a genuinely Christian way: namely, by insisting on the superiority of spirit over nature and on God's identity with his human embodiment in history.

(3) If overall being attains self-knowledge through human knowledge, it is because it contains human knowledge as one of its integral constituents. Hegel insists that this is internal knowledge, namely, knowledge which contemplates its object because it belongs to its very constitution. As such, it is knowledge by "Reason," and not the ordinary scientific "Understanding" which contemplates its objects from the outside while maintaining the barrier between itself and the object. Philosophical contemplation is not only knowledge *about* reality, it is, so to speak, reality's contemplation *of itself*. Therefore, from the viewpoint of the individual philosopher, the act of philosophical Knowing involves her dialectical unification with the whole of being. Hegel here offers his own, rational and nonmystical version of the achievements which mysticism falsely leads its followers to

expect. The finite human being, when engaged in the philosophical
act of knowing and in the social and political activity which makes
that act possible, is contemplating true being from within, and is an
inner moment of it. This person is thereby not only united with
absolute being but, in a small way, even helps to constitute it. Philosophy is not a detached, analytical contemplation through the intellect only, but a mode of being, a living experience of the person
who contemplates being from within. Yet this is no vague, isolated,
romantic event, because its medium is conceptual thinking, and because the thinker is equally a practical agent involved in the society
and practical life through which philosophical Knowing is actualized.
This sociopractical involvement "secularizes" the act and deroman-
ticizes the experience.

Thus again, the phase of absolute Knowing involves a sublation of
religion and mysticism, which preserves their underlying interests.
It radically differs from mysticism while pursuing similar goals. The
difference lies, first, in the rational character of the Hegelian
method, which translates everything into the level of the Concept;
and, second, in that the experiential element retained in Hegel's
absolute Knowing is largely nourished by practical concerns—the
individual's immersion in social, political, and worldly affairs; it is
not a privileged mental event confined to a person's interior world,
or a form of contemplation which takes her beyond this world to
a transcendent domain. Even at the highest stage, the individual
goes on living an ordinary life in the external world, in society, in
her daily work and occupation, as an active member of the polity,
in the privacy of the family and the public arena of politics, without
retiring into a closed inner world or being carried away by romantic
enthusiasm. This is Hegel's version of Spinoza's "intellectual love
of God," and more broadly, Hegel's substitute for the mystical notion that knowing God is union with him.

Consequences for the System and Method of Philosophy

The subjective nature of the absolute also has far-reaching effects
on the system and method of philosophy. Because reality itself has

a subject-like structure, Hegel concludes that philosophical logic, which has to express that structure, must likewise have a subject-like character. From a methodological point of view, therefore, to say that "the absolute is subject" amounts to saying that actuality is shaped by dialectical logic rather than by ordinary, formal logic.[17]

We have seen that subject and substance obey different ontical logics. The logic of substance is the logic of entities which are directly and tautologically self-identical ($A = A$), and therefore obey the law of noncontradiction. Also, within this domain, the negation of negation is a tautology which simply reverts to the point of departure ($\sim\sim p = p$). Such items in Hegel's judgment are not, however, actual beings but, as we shall see later, abstractions. True actuality is governed by another kind of *logos*, that of evolving, subject-like systems, which are not self-identical at the outset, and therefore do not obey the law of noncontradiction, and in which double-negation produces something new.

Another consequence of viewing the absolute as subject is that philosophical logic must derive from the structure of the subject matter which it is investigating, rather than being imposed upon ("applied to") it externally. Hegel uses the term "logic" as a derivative of *logos*, the principle the Greeks understood as structuring reality. Hegel does not mean a formal calculus, nor an a priori method whose norms precede its subject matter. Hegel insists that dialectical, subject-like logic cannot be formalized, not even by the famous formula "thesis-antithesis-synthesis" (which is Fichte's, not Hegel's).[18] All we can learn in advance from this logic are a few general characteristics: for example, that every domain of actual being will have a subject-like shape; that it will thereby have an evolving, organic nature which must be actualized through oth-

---

[17] Incidentally, the term "dialectical logic" is more common in the secondary literature than in Hegel himself. I use it because of its wide acceptance.

[18] Fichte constructed his system by triads of the form "thesis-antithesis-synthesis," which repeat themselves throughout his systematic work, *The Theory of Science*, as an a priori formula. Though Hegel refrains from using this formula, it has nevertheless been ascribed to him in many textbooks and in the public's mind. It is true that Hegel's system, in its broad lines, also advances a triadic form, but it is different, freer, and without a priori formulaic limitations.

erness; and therefore it can be expected to return to itself as the result of a three-stage process. But, beyond those generalities, it is impossible to formalize a set of mandatory a priori rules which must be followed at all times and in all particular cases. One must rather depend on some intellectual immersion—or "phenomenological insight" in the modern sense—which permeates the philosophical subject matter and follows its movement "from within."

As to formal logic, it is valid in such areas as mathematics, the natural sciences, and daily discourse, areas which Hegel sees as abstract because they peel off a single aspect of being and grasp it one-sidedly, as if it were the whole. These areas deal with allegedly simple, self-identical units of discourse, which are dominated by the form of identity of a substance, not a subject, and therefore must obey the law of noncontradiction. Hence formal logic is the supreme canon (or legislation) of the "Understanding," though not of "Reason," of *Verstand* but not *Vernunft*. The entities treated in these areas (simple data, numbers, symbols, facts, self-identical arguments, inert systems, and objects built as aggregates of such entities) are abstract, imaginary beings in Hegel's ontology—not complete nothingness, to be sure, but an inferior aspect of reality, that is, impoverished reflections of being similar to Plato's "appearances."

It is ironic that both Hegel and the positivists make the same criticisms of each other. The positivist believes the concrete world to be constructed from allegedly "simple" units (sensible and logical), and will see a dogmatic metaphysician in any philosopher who, like Hegel, regards the empirical particulars as expressing an inner conceptual "essence." For Hegel, however, the dogmatic metaphysician is the positivist, because he takes such abstractions and imaginary entities ("the simple") to be actual beings.

Subject-like dialectical logic is appropriate to all areas which express the movement of self-actualizing systems: the philosophy of mind, of being (ontology), of society, culture, and history. Above all, it is the way philosophy itself is to construe and relate to its objects. Philosophy, too, is a mode of being's movement and actualization; therefore, dialectical logic, with its subject-like shape, must come to bear on the structure of philosophy and the way its specific areas are organized. The chief methodological demand implied here is that philosophical truth be shaped as an organic totality, which maintains itself through its own negations. Since philosophy must express the structure of reality from within, and that structure is subject-like, true philosophy must share that structure, as well. Hence the second famous dictum of our Preface, "the true is the whole."

The True Is the Whole

The dictum, "the true is the whole," is usually understood as a principle of method only. It is said that Hegel holds a coherence theory of truth, and therefore requires that all the system's ingredients be given in order to be reciprocally verified. This reading is only partially correct. It ignores the ontological basis of Hegel's view, and also the developmental character of truth in his system.

When Hegel asserts that the true is the whole, he immediately adds his own explanation:

> The true is the whole. Yet the whole is but the essence which brings itself to fulfillment through its development. Of the absolute it must be said that it is essentially a result, that only at the end is the absolute what it is in truth; and herein consists its nature—to be actual, subject, or becoming-its-own-self. (p. 102)

This passage links together all three dicta—the true is subject, the absolute is a result, the true is the whole—which are here disclosed as ingredients of the same idea. Therefore the claim that the true is the whole says more than the ordinary coherence theory. First, Hegel is speaking of an organic, or dialectical, coherence, not of external links of inference connecting static, self-identical items. Second, the "whole" in question includes its own generation as one of its elements. The philosopher cannot therefore abstract the result from its genesis and view the process of development as a scaffold to be disposed of when the goal is reached, as can be done with mathematical demonstrations and analytical arguments. This is true not only of the history of philosophy, but also of a special kind of process which affects the conceptual system from within. In the finished system of philosophy, every member will point to all of the others in a process of negation and negation-of-negation, so that our thought cannot rest until it runs the whole course of the system; and even then it will not hold on to it as something static and finished, but rather as a self-repeating conceptual movement.

In this sense the history of philosophy is preserved (as *aufgehoben*) in the pure system of philosophy. The diachronic process that has generated the system is sublated (negated but preserved in new form) within the synchronic movement of the system of philosophy that emerges from it. If we forgo that movement and make do with a simple list of concepts and principles which make up the final system, like Kant's list of the categories, we shall lose the dynamic structure of their mutual negation, and thereby their truth. And if we offer some general proposition or formula as a concluding summary, again we shall have an abstract and unrealized universal which cannot, as such, be true; rather, in so far as it is abstract and only part of the story, it is false.

An ironic illustration of this is given by our own dictum, the true is the whole. Because it stands in the Preface as an abstract generality severed from its systematic context—namely, from the remainder of the book which demonstrates its meaning by carrying it out—the dictum fails to convey its own purported meaning and is, dialectically speaking, untrue.

Thirdly, the true is the whole not only in the sense that its diverse elements form a unified system of discourse, but also in that knowledge is therein unified with its object. The system of philosophy does not reflect the world from the outside; it expresses in the subject's domain the same structure that has successfully realized itself in the objective world. Hence the ontic character of truth, by virtue of which it *is* truth. As we have remarked, the term "truth" does not denote the property of a sentence or a statement but a certain mode of being, which is revealed to itself in philosophical knowledge. It is therefore the ontic nature of truth from which its methodological conditions are also derived, including the principle of coherence.

Truth has been traditionally, and notoriously, defined as *adequatio rei et intellectus*—the conformity of the thing and the intellect (or the concept). This definition views the thing and the concept as two foreign elements which share nothing in common. There is a world of things on the one hand and a world of thoughts on the other, and the latter must conform to the former. Hegel has no problem accepting the nominal definition (because it is so broad and says so little), but rejects the dualism inherent in it. If the concept agrees with reality, it is because reality itself has evolved until it agrees with its concept (which includes its self-knowledge through philosophy). Or putting it conversely, they agree because the concept is latent in reality as its essence, and drives reality to develop and agree with it (that is, in the final analysis, to agree with itself, with its own essence). These two, reality and the concept, are not foreign elements but two complementary moments within a single dialectical process. Hegel expressed this by another famous proverb, "what is rational is actual, and what is actual is rational."[19] Hegel does not intend to confer the adjective "rational" (or, for that matter, "actual") on any contingent existence, but only on existence that has been actualized and reached its rational *telos*. The rational and the actual are united only at the final, culminating stage of being's evolution. This peculiar, speculative view can be called "an ontic theory of truth."

Hegel rejects the pre-Kantian ("dogmatic") metaphysics, which holds that the concept corresponds to reality because it copies or represents it as it is *in itself*. This view presupposes that being does not change but is forever static, only our concepts about it evolve until they correspond to it. Yet Hegel maintains there is evolution and self-actualization in being itself, mediated by human action and knowledge. He also rejects an important element in Kant: the thesis that Concepts are external to reality and injected into it (or imposed on it) by human self-consciousness. This "subjective" idealism, as Hegel calls it, gives priority to the subject over the object, and makes reality a function of knowledge. By contrast, Hegel claims that the Concept—in his sense—does not reside in our knowledge alone, but is implicitly at work in the *object* of our knowledge, that

---

[19] Preface to the *Philosophy of Right*; I have interpreted this proverb in Yirmiyahu Yovel, "Hegel's Dictum that the Rational Is Actual and the Actual Is Rational," in *The Hegel Myths and Legends*, ed. Jon Stewart (Evanston, IL: Northwestern University Press, 1996), 26–41, from which the present lines are taken.

is, within reality. And as reality evolves towards its Concept, it enables knowledge, too, to evolve ever more clearly and to consciously explicate that implicit Concept.

In summary, the true is the whole, but this whole includes the process of its own genesis, as well as the moment of being with which it stands in a dialectical relation. Only in this way does the system of philosophy form an organic, self-grounding whole which, like Spinoza's *causa sui*, bears witness to its own truth.

Consequences for the Theory of Discourse

This leads to several consequences concerning Hegel's theory of discourse (which could also have arisen independently). First, philosophical statements are only true within their *total* dynamic context, which is the system as a whole. It should therefore be impossible to cut off a proposition from the overall context and still ascribe a truth value to it, as the analytic understanding tends to do. Every singular statement, even those which merely summarize the system's conclusions, must miss those conclusions and function as an "abstract universal" whose form opposes the content it purports to express.

Second, the same applies to the *meaning* of a philosophical statement. Just as singular statements have no autonomous truth value, so they also lack an autonomous meaning. They fail to express adequately what they are meant to state. Hegel views meaning as dependent upon intention (*meinen*), yet every partial statement or sentence is marked by a dialectical opposition between its meaning and what is intended by it: that which the statement says in actuality must fall short of what it says (or "intends saying") implicitly.[20]

[20] The dialectical relation between intending ("to mean," *meinen*) and linguistic expression (*ausprechen*) starts with the mind's most primitive stance—its grasp of allegedly simple particulars here and now (which Hegel calls "sense certainty"; see chapter 1 of the *Phenomenology*). The tension takes different forms in other mental attitudes. In a more general way, *every* stage in Hegel's dialectic involves an opposition between what this stage is implicitly *meant* (intended) *to be* and the incongruent form it assumes in realizing that meaning. Incidentally, Hegel plays with the potential of the verb *meinen* in other ways, too, linking it to

This opposition explains the need for further development of the statement and serves as the drive for it. As long as such an inadequacy persists, it indicates that the explication has not attained its goal and must move on to further stages. Only when the end is reached can it be expected that the circular totality will lack nothing. At this stage we can finally explore the full meaning—and each category will only then express its meaning adequately, that is, within the framework of the attained totality.

Thirdly, the same can be said of the process of the pupil's *subjective process of understanding*. The issue now is no longer the logical relations between the elements of discourse, but the learner's ability to grasp the philosophical meanings which they express. And here again, Hegel argues that philosophical understanding requires the complete system: a person who has carefully gone through the system's detailed stages will grasp a single sentence (a generalization) very differently than someone hearing the same sentence for the first time. For the latter person the sentence is an indeterminate, out-of-context generality, whereas for the person who already knows the system, it compresses and summarizes an entire set of interrelations which are present in her memory. Even generalizations like "the true is the whole" or "the absolute is a result" will have a completely different value at the end of the road than they did at the beginning.

THE DIALECTIC: A FEW GENERAL CHARACTERISTICS

In light of what has been said, it is clearly impossible to give a formal definition of Hegel's dialectic or to explain it adequately in an introduction. In order to grasp its nature, one must follow its actual denouement in one of Hegel's major works, such as the *Phenomenology* or the *Logic*. Keeping this caveat in mind, we may still offer a tentative preview of some of the main features of the dialectic, hoping that the reader will remember that the true is the

---

Meinung (opinion), and even to *meinen* in the sense of "making mine." (I owe the latter point to Michael Forster.)

whole, and will use this preview to enter the substantive matter on his own.

In the *Phenomenology,* the dialectical structure of truth and history displays the following interrelated characteristics:

(1) Spirit's rational essence needs its "other"—empirical existence, appearance, contingency, error, suffering—as a necessary medium through which alone that essence can develop and be actualized. The rational essence must become other-than-itself in order to be able to eventually return to itself on a higher level, that is, as actualized.

(2) In consequence, the rational essence exists actually only at the end of the road—as its own result. At the outset it is not actual, but abstract and latent. It needs a long, arduous, and diversified process of development in order to actualize itself and become what it is.

(3) Thereby, Hegel's so-called dialectical logic follows the dynamic structure of mental, or rather subject-like, systems. In a subject-like system, self-consciousness and self-identity are attained only at the end. This result presupposes a process in which consciousness ascribes to itself a multitude of predicates, stages, mental states, and the like and recognizes them as its own, while at the same time recognizing, and thereby realizing, itself as the subject of that manifold. Dialectical logic is the dynamic structure—the *logos*—at work in this kind of system. And since absolute being itself has that structure, it follows that dialectical logic must be the logic of philosophy and of "Reason," as distinguished from mere analysis and the "Understanding."

(4) In a system expressing the life and evolution of consciousness, the act of negation does not erase its preceding stages but retains them in the next stage as a kind of "recollection." The collapse of a given mental stage drives the process on, towards a new position that serves as the specific, if tentative, answer to the particular flaw which has arisen in its predecessor and caused its collapse. Thus all the affirmations, negations, and negations of negations, all the foregoing ups and downs, the rises and falls, are retained in spirit's organic memory—that is, in the texture of every new stage.

(5) Hegel's dialectic views the evolution of spirit as a *teleological* process, made of circles or rather spirals, in which "the end is the beginning." In other words, the purpose which is actualized in the end is also the abstract beginning of the process. Between that beginning and the actualized end there is a whole sequence of shapes and forms which spirit assumes and in which it is partially, and therefore always inadequately, realized. Because of its limited, one-sided character, each partial stage is affected by contradictions and inadequacies which drive the process forward through further contradictions, incongruities, alienations, and further partial realizations. But this is not an open-ended process: Hegel conceives it in Aristotelian fashion, as a potentiality moving toward entelechy. The movement is supposed to finally cease when all contradictions have been reconciled within the fully actualized end.

(6) From a dialectical perspective, therefore, opposing positions in the domain of spirit are not mutually exclusive; they rather complement and modify each other within the framework of a higher totality. Truth and falsity are not a binary pair, not an either/or relation. There is a latent kernel of truth in all conflicting religions, in all systems of philosophy, in all diverse political institutions, and all rival artistic schools. Some of these cultural forms are higher than others (Hegel's is a hierarchical, not an egalitarian multiculturalism), because they express truth in a less fragmentary way, or in a more adequate form and medium; but none are utterly false. Falsity resides in the claim of a partial form of culture to exhaust the whole truth and to exclude its opponent (its own other), when actually it needs that other—and all the others—in order to be itself, to complement and modify it within the overall system of truth.[21]

(7) Unlike formal logic, the dialectic has no a priori rules. In particular, its subject-like dynamic rejects the rule which says that

---

[21] In terms of a contemporary discussion, Hegel's dialectic expresses—indeed is—a logic of multiculturalism, although in a hierarchical, not an egalitarian form. Hegel's multiculturalism is not based on relativism or skepticism, but on an absolute truth that is made possible by dialectical diversity and by recognizing the other as medium for the self. But that is a purposive process with higher and lesser degrees of achievement.

double-negation returns the process to its initial point of departure, together with the attendant laws of noncontradiction and the excluded middle. These laws are fit for inert systems in which unchanging, self-identical items (like mathematical propositions, or sense data) are organized by external rules of order. They are inappropriate in a system which has the capacity of interiorizing its past experiences ("recollection"), and has the subject-like structure of a dynamic totality existing as a movement of self-actualization.

DIALECTIC-AS-JOURNEY AND DIALECTIC-AS-SCIENCE

The above ideas will be worked out in the commentary. Meanwhile, we might distinguish two different directions in the dialectic, which I label *dialectic-as-journey* and *dialectic-as-Science*. Both these directions already existed in Plato's dialectic. The first direction is basically negative: Socrates puts questions to his interlocutors (for example, Theaetetus) in order to undermine their dogmatic beliefs. As a result, they adopt a new position which resolves, so they believe, the flaws in their previous position. But this is only a tentative pause, because the second position is eventually also undermined and calls for a third to overcome it, and so forth. In this process of negative dialectic, each new stand is nourished by the failure of its predecessor(s), and draws its new positive content from their specific inadequacy, that is, negation. For Plato this process is an ascent, a journey towards knowledge and true being, which climbs a preestablished ladder, described in the *Republic* and elsewhere; whereas for Hegel the process traces its own way and builds, as it were, its own ladder. Also, in Plato the road is undergone by an individual pupil, Glaucon or Iheaetetus, whereas Hegel historicized Plato's process of education: the pupil or apprentice undergoing the process of dialectic-as-journey *is the entire human race*. Correspondingly, the single individual is limited by his times, and cannot advance beyond the constraints of his or her contemporary culture and the new, if limited, perspective opened up by the *Zeitgeist*. The Platonic trainee, however, is free of such limitations and depends solely on his individual talents and those of his teacher.

Taking a retrospective look, Hegel reviews this process in the *Phenomenology* as it had led to the modern era and made it possible. Human consciousness has experienced all the important positions and standpoints which it might take, and has transcended them because of the one-sided and limited character which undermines each partial position from within, and exposes its immaturity. Dialectic-as-journey—a journey to truth, or to "Science" (*epistēmē*)[22]—with its successive negations and transcendings, cannot cease before consciousness finally rises to a comprehensive standpoint. At this stage, all the partial perspectives of earlier stages are *aufgehoben* and retained in the higher synthesis, where they do not exclude each other but rather mutually constitute a common result. At this point, dialectic-as-journey becomes dialectic-as-Science. The sequence of negations which links the partial standpoints is interiorized into the system of absolute Knowing in which they function as a positive, constructive factor.

The Platonic philosopher, too, after he has gone through all the stages of dialectic-as-journey, finally arrives at the vision of the Ideas (Forms). Henceforth he becomes a "dialectician" in a new, positive sense (discussed in the *Republic*, the *Parmenides*, and the *Sophist*)—the one who knowingly moves within the realm of ideas and truth. For Hegel, at least in his middle period, this is the stage at which the *Phenomenology* turns into the *Science of Logic*—the foundation of absolute Knowing. The appearance of positive dialectic does not abolish negative dialectic, but reverses its result. Within dialectic-as-Science there is also a permanent transcending of each position—or category—but the sum total of these negations and transcendings now upholds the positive system of truth. In a Dionysian image which he takes from the Greek mystics, Hegel draws an analogy with the Bacchanalian dance, where no dancer remains in his or her place; all are whirling in an intoxicated ecstasy (*extasis*—a transcending of oneself), yet their repeated mutual motion creates a stable, transparent, and circular structure. Similarly, dialectic-as-Sci-

---

[22] The term "Science" (*Wissenschaft*) has in Hegel the sense of *epistēmē*. It does not refer only to the natural or so-called exact sciences, but to philosophy as absolute Knowing. (I therefore capitalize it.)

ence is a system of negations and transcendings that have been interiorized and now maintain the system from within.

Dialectic-as-Science is thus the "synchronic" movement within which the universe of absolute Knowing is achieved, while dialectic-as-journey is the "diachronic" movement towards it. From a textual point of view, we might say that the *Phenomenology* corresponds to dialectic-as-journey,[23] and the *Logic* represents dialectic-as-Science.[24]

In its first (1807) edition, the *Phenomenology* was subtitled the "first part" of a projected two-part work called *The System of Science* (*System der Wissenschaft*). As first part, the *Phenomenology* was meant to study spirit's outer, phenomenal existence, and follow its dialectical transformations from sensual knowledge to absolute Knowing. The second part was supposed to contain three divisions: logic, philosophy of nature, and philosophy of spirit. With certain amendments, a similar project was carried out many years later under the title *The Encyclopedia of Philosophical Sciences*. Meanwhile, Hegel had abandoned his original conception and regarded the *Phenomenology* as a preparation for the philosophical Science rather than an organic part of it. (In the edition of the *Phenomenology* he published in 1831, shortly before his death, Hegel omitted the subtitle "first part" altogether). The relation between the *Phenomenology* and the rest of Hegel's system, especially the *Logic*, has since become a subject of much debate. From the standpoint of the *Phenomenology* itself, however, and of the present preface, there is no doubt that the genesis of absolute Knowing must be considered an integral part of its system. We can see this also by viewing the *Phenomenology* (as was suggested before) as the historicization of Plato's process of philosophical education. In Plato that process, which is at first a dialectic-as-journey, is replaced by a dialectic-as-Science, in which the Platonic dialectician moves among the Ideas in the state of *theoria* (intellectual intuition). By analogy, we might say the *Phe-*

---

[23] Later supplanted by the various philosophical histories on which Hegel lectured: world politics, religion, art, and philosophy.

[24] Later supplanted by the philosophies of nature and spirit (i.e., the philosophy of right), and the discussions of the essence (not the history) of politics (objective spirit), religion, art, and philosophy contained in the lectures mentioned in the previous note.

nomenology represents Hegel's dialectic-as-journey, and the *Logic* (more generally, his full system) is Hegel's dialectic-as-Science. And since, in Hegel's philosophy, one understands the process in retrospect, it follows that the structure of the journey—the *Phenomenology*—is grasped and exposed from the same standpoint of *theoria*, and thereby belongs to Science's own context.

In addition, the *Phenomenology* is needed in order to provide the metatheory of the *special* philosophies of history contained in the system—of religion, politics, art, philosophy, and world history in general. These special philosophies of history belong to the system not as separate blocks, but rather as the necessary dimension of becoming which permeates the system throughout; and the *Phenomenology* is their underlying systematic structure.[25]

DIALECTIC-AS-SUBJECTIVE EDUCATION

The *Phenomenology* also has a second, educational and subjective task: to offer the individual a ladder by which he or she can be liberated from the standpoint of naïve consciousness and attain philosophy. This, too, is an aspect of dialectic-as-journey, now seen from the standpoint of the philosophizing individual. The need for a ladder arises from a recognition that rational truth cannot be externally imposed on the individual. Consciousness must be able to recognize truth as *its own*—an expression of its selfhood. Yet, philosophical truth at first is alien to the individual and extremely remote from her. The *Phenomenology* offers the individual that same ladder which universal human consciousness has been climbing up to that time, and helps the individual personally to mount it. It starts from the point where the nonphilosophical individual stands at present—sense certainty, perception, passion, the familiar world, and so forth—and is supposed to ascend step by step, stage by stage,

---

[25] The fact that Hegel delivered them only orally, and that the Berlin system does not set a rubric for the *Phenomenology* in its original dimension of spirit's historical becoming (there is only a limited section dealing with philosophical psychology, or the subjective mind) do not pose an essential difficulty; they stem rather from more technical and academic-didactic considerations, which also distinguished the older, Berlin Hegel from the more innovative thinker he had been at Jena.

even if by spiral, roundabout moves, towards absolute Knowing. The evolution of the *Phenomenology* is therefore the development of a personal, subjective mind which experiences the dialectical contradictions arising within it as a *personal* problem and malaise, and is driven beyond them in search of new positions. Within this subjective journey, the *Phenomenology* is meant to play the role of the Socratic educator, who serves as "midwife" to his pupil and helps draw dialectic-as-Science from the pupil's own mind.

EVIDENCE AND TRUTH

Also implied here is the modern principle formulated by Descartes: the individual subject rightfully demands that universal truth not oppose his consciousness, but be *derived* from it. Descartes, however, *identified* universal truth with subjective certainty ("evidence") and made that identity the starting point of philosophy, whereas Hegel sets a distance between certainty and truth. Each of these two stands at an opposite end of the *Phenomenology*. The process begins with subjective certainty which, because it is a direct, unmediated personal experience, is not yet truth; truth is attained only at the end, when the subject's consciousness has fully overcome its merely particular standpoint and adopted the standpoint of the whole as a development of its (the subject's) own self.

It must be stressed that overcoming particularity does not entail that subjectivity has been abolished. On the contrary, the actual subject—the thinking, feeling, willing, desiring subject—is present in all the positions which he or she attains and adopts, including the most universal standpoint. In this respect, all the standpoints the subject undergoes over the course of his mental career are his own, they express his subjective self and identity, and are not imposed upon him by external coercion, brainwashing, or manipulation.

RATIONALITY CANNOT BE IMPOSED (NOR CHOSEN ARBITRARILY)

This is a crucial point. It preserves the modernity of Hegel's position in stating that *rationality cannot be imposed*. When the individual cannot recognize the universal standpoint as an expression of her own self a fundamental condition of rationality is broken and the position *is not* rational. As with Kant, rationality for Hegel is a union of a subjective recognition and an objective, universal point of view. Both of these ingredients are equally necessary for rationality to exist. From this it follows that it is impossible to coerce a person or a society to be free, as Rousseau wanted; one can only help them to evolve toward freedom and rationality. It is likewise impossible to become rational by mere choice or decision, because rationality, again, must arise from the subject's evolution and self-explication. It is neither an automatic outcome—a position which can be deduced analytically—nor is it an arbitrary existential choice. Rather, rationality must emerge from and through the mind's self-evolution, as a kind of novelty, an *Aufhebung* that both depends on what went before and cannot be merely reduced to it. Rationality is attained neither by coercion nor by choice, but by a self-educational process which draws all its levers and shapes from the philosophizing individual's own mind and, when mature, allows rationality to emerge as an outcome, that is, as the expression of that mind and the culture which embodies it. There is neither an "algorithmic" necessity here nor an arbitrary occurrence. Hegel sees this rather as a "historical" necessity, meaning that although its outcome can be accounted for by reasons, it can neither be predicted in advance nor recur in precisely the same way. And this also explains the historical boundaries which, unlike for Plato, limit the individual's capacity to jump ahead and attain full rationality when the rest of the *Zeitgeist* has not yet reached its threshold.

HEGEL AND KIERKEGAARD

Hegel thereby addresses a famous existentialist objection raised by Kierkegaard, who complained that Hegel's philosophical "Science" may be beautifully constructed, yet he, as this particular individual, cannot find himself in it. Though Hegel did not know Kierkegaard, he had fully concurred with his demand. Indeed, the individual must be able to rediscover himself within the universal philosophical truth, or else the latter will not be rational. Hegel's original answer is to construct the *Phenomenology* as an educational bridge by which the individual can gradually cross into the absolute standpoint, and thereby be actualized as a genuine individual, rather than existing as an unreal individual—that is, as a merely particular entity.[26]

One can criticize or reject Hegel's account ("narrative") of this journey, but one cannot say that he ignores the demands of the particular consciousness or bans it from his system. True, Hegel does not allow for an absolute or "bare" particularity, the kind which Kierkegaard and other existentialists start from. This is to him as illusory a metaphysical notion as Descartes' disembodied I, or the "bare simples" on which the positivists build their world. The shape which the historical "universal" (culture, tradition, language, political institutions, rational claims and aspirations, and so on) has taken in the individual's lifetime plays a role in constituting that person's very individuality; it is the "spiritual substance" which nourishes each person's self and defines the range in which, as individual, he is able to move, either identifying with the historical situation, or dissenting from it, or seeking to transcend it towards some reformed shape. In this respect, a "bare" or "absolutely particular" individual is a figment of the imagination, and if *he* demands to find his most particular and personal traits expressed conceptually in thought and in spirit, he would indeed find no satisfaction in philosophy, neither in Hegel's nor in anyone else's.[27]

Just as the Socratic midwife educes dialectic-as-Science from his pupil's mind, so the *Phenomenology* claims to offer the individual the same ladder which universal human consciousness has been ascending up to his or her time, and helps him to personally ascend it, while also reliving its deficiencies as a call to go on.

---

[26] In Hegel's *Logic*, a true individual (as "singular") is a synthesis of particularity and universality. A merely particular entity is not a true individual—it does not have "singularity" (*Einzelheit*). It is an unreal individual, only appearing as such. Individuality (like actuality) is not given but *gained*: when the particular rises to a universal standpoint and recognizes it as her own.

[27] Just as, ontologically, Professor Krug could not find satisfaction when asking Hegel to "deduce" his pen.

The Polemics in the Preface: Hegel, Fichte, Schelling, Hölderlin

The *Phenomenology* is not only the founding work of Hegel's mature system, but also—and for the same reason—a document of divorce. The Preface has a trenchant polemical dimension. In coming into his own, Hegel had to break away from leading figures and fashions, and, more important, to suffer the pains of an inevitable (and self-inflicted) severance from some of his most intimate personal and intellectual friends, especially Schelling and Hölderlin. The three of them had been classmates and close friends at the Tübingen *Stift*; they matured, dreamed, and argued together. All had been to some extent influenced by Fichte. Schelling, though younger than Hegel, made his name as philosopher before him; the two friends debated common problems and collaborated in publishing a philosophical journal. And Hölderlin, before he submitted to mental illness, had not only been a towering young poet but also a promising systematic philosopher. At a certain point he got the young Hegel a tutor's job in Frankfurt, and their reunion in that town seems to have significantly marked Hegel's future evolution.[28]

The Preface to the *Phenomenology*, without mentioning names, censures all three men: Schelling, Fichte, and Hölderlin. The mature Hegel, as often happens, poured more sarcasm on those closer

---

[28] This thesis is defended by Dieter Henrich who devoted many years of study to the two young men's relationship. His conclusion, which sounds convincing in what concerns the main point, is based on several documentary fragments, a rigorous philosophical analysis, and some intuitive speculation bridging over the gaps. Although Hölderlin left very little written philosophy, Henrich makes it plausible to maintain that he had influenced Hegel no less, and perhaps more pointedly, than Schelling and Fichte. See Dieter Henrich, *The Course of Remembrance and Other Essays on Hölderlin* (Stanford, CA: Stanford University Press, 1997). The evidence, however, does not seem to warrant overstatements, like saying that "Hegel's system emerged *uninterruptedly*" (my emphasis) from his adoption of Hölderlin's concept of love "as the central term in his thought" (see "Hölderlin and Hegel," ibid., p. 131). (I am grateful to Howard Ponzer for his help in working on this topic).

to him than on complete intellectual strangers. Schelling is so cut-tingly criticized that his consequent break with Hegel could never be repaired. Hegel's insincere excuse, that he had only targeted Schelling's cruder disciples, did not help. Hölderlin, by then a sick man, is treated more mildly and indirectly in the Preface, yet his basic claim—that the absolute must be ineffable—is forcefully and repeatedly rejected. Above all, Fichte is made the target of an exten-sive and particularly acidic attack. (He seems to be taking the blame also for faults which Hegel attributes jointly to him and Schelling.) Fichte was neither a friend, nor a direct teacher of Hegel's. Hegel looked with irony on the older philosopher's vagaries, his bombas-tic public claims (the Preface pokes fun at Fichte's famous title: "A Sun-clear Account . . . An Effort to Force the Reader to Under-stand"), and the ardent German nationalism to which Fichte was soon to become a spokesman. Fichte, nevertheless, was a philo-sophical stepfather to Hegel, the first modern thinker who tried to fuse Kant's self-consciousness and Spinoza's absolute substance into an overall system of idealism. But since Hegel had adopted the standpoint of idealism from early on (perhaps since his Frankfurt days with Hölderlin), he was more acutely aware of his differences with Fichte than of their common ground.[29]

Among other things, Hegel rejected Fichte's "subjective" brand of idealism; his attributing primacy and absolute identity to the I; his placing self-consciousness (or the "I am I") at the center of philosophy; and the abstract formalism by which he applied a single a priori formula—thesis-antithesis-synthesis—to all domains of re-ality. (Ironically, a current view attributes the same abstract formula to Hegel himself.)

Hegel's break with Schelling, and indirectly with Hölderlin, had a different nature. Its wider target was the romantic school in phi-losophy and art, which sought to grasp absolute reality by special nonrational gifts—intellectual intuition, poetic vision, an unspeak-able act of faith and the like—rather than by reason. Hegel shared the goal of overcoming the shortcomings of the formal Under-

---

[29] In an early work, *The Difference between Fichte's and Schelling's Systems*, Hegel analyzed the evolving systems of idealism as an immanent critic.

standing—not, however, by poetic or mystical means, but through a higher and richer mode of rationality he called the Concept or speculative Reason, which unfolds systematically, and cannot be an esoteric gift, but must be open to everyone undergoing a philosophical formation.

Hölderlin's Impact

Hölderlin had studied under Fichte and criticized him. In an early fragment (later known as *Judgment and Being*) Hölderlin argued that the transcendental subject is not the source of unity, but rather of separation and distinction. Hence, Fichte's "I am I" cannot be the absolute principle because, as consciousness and self-consciousness, it entails self-*separation* and is constituted by it. "The I is possible only through its separation from the I," Hölderlin argues, so it is a principle of distinction, not unity.

Now distinction and separation are the domain of judgment (*Ur-teil*, which implies *Ur-Teil*—original division), whereas being is absolute unity. Identity therefore falls under judgment, whereas the absolute principle must be prior to judgment and immune to it; it must be original unity without original division. And that, Hölderlin argued, can only be Being, construed as lying altogether beyond the domain of consciousness and rational discourse—namely, as *ineffable* being. In consequence, philosophy must start not with the "I think" but with Being (as Spinoza had started, opposing Descartes, and as Hegel was to do later, opposing Fichte).

Hölderlin's adoption of Spinoza was modified by Jacobi's critique of Spinoza. The absolute which underlies everything cannot be a rationally demonstrable substance, as in Spinoza, but must precede rational knowledge. To give a rational argument for the absolute is not only invalid but unnecessary, because the absolute is always already there as an ultimate certainty, which one needs to assume rather than prove or search for. Whereas Jacobi construed this act as a leap of faith, Hölderlin placed his expectations on poetic expression as the privileged access to Being. (This explains Heidegger's fascination with Hölderlin, and repeated exegesis of his work.)

When Hölderlin met Hegel in Frankfurt he was, as Henrich suggests,[30] equally preoccupied with the broader project of "unification philosophy"—the need to unify not only life's various and conflicting powers, but especially the opposing human craving—for individuality and finitude, on the one hand, and for the absolute and the infinite, on the other. Again, Hölderlin sought the ground of these unifications in a primitive unity prior to consciousness and selfhood, namely, in that ineffable Being he had already opposed to Fichte.

The evidence may be too scarce to prove that Hegel's philosophical course was decisively and lastingly revolutionized by Hölderlin in Frankfurt. But it stands to reason that, as Henrich suggests, their encounter impinged upon Hegel the agenda and part of the terminology of unification philosophy,[31] as well as the need to cope with the failures of idealism in its Fichtean version. The mature Hegelian system, with its dialectical reconciliation of diversity and opposition, contains an original and far-reaching answer to the problem of unification, including the idealist attempt to unite being and reason.

Hegel agreed with Hölderlin that philosophy can neither start with the I nor be centered around it, and unlike Fichte (and like Spinoza), started his own system (in the *Logic*) with being rather than consciousness. Yet Hegel forcefully denied that being is ineffable and prerational, or that it underlies knowledge without being submitted to it. The being with which Hegel starts is, on the contrary, mediated in itself, immanently leading to its opposite (nothing) as its own condition, and producing the self-reflective "for itself" which is the nucleus of all selfhood, and eventual subjectivity and consciousness. No wonder that the notion that the absolute is opaque being which must be intuited, felt, approached by poetic means, and so forth, is one of the most debunked in the Preface before us—and with it, not only Schelling, but Hölderlin, too, is strongly censured.

Absolute immediacy is a myth to Hegel, an incoherent concept. Idealism, he says in the *Logic*, maintains that everything is both im-

---

[30] This is inferred from the papers of another friend, presumably echoing Hölderlin.

[31] On the evolution of his thought at this time, and use of love, see also chapter 2, in my *Dark Riddle: Hegel, Nietzsche, and the Jews.*

mediate and mediated at the same time—that immediacy (existence, definiteness, being) owes itself to a complex of mediations. All aspects and levels of being are pervaded by a movement of self-mediation, which is another way of saying that being has a subject-like structure even before it is expressed as self-consciousness. Therefore being is, to some extent, intelligible on any level of its evolution, up to—and most of all—the level of the realized absolute, which results from its evolution rather than preceding it as ineffably given. In declaring the absolute to be a result—and a subject—Hegel therefore implies a total rejection of Hölderlin's chief idea.

Note on the Meaning of "Speculative"

This polemics pertains also to the meaning of the term "speculative" in Hegel's special sense. Having several times used this term, let me pause for a brief explanation.

"Speculative" derives from Latin *speculare*, to see. In Hegel's use the term contains an allusion to Plato's vision of the Forms (Ideas), the highest stage in Plato's philosophy, which rises above scientific understanding (*dianoia*) and reaches to true being (*ousia*). This mode of thinking directly grasps the particular by thinking the universal, and vice versa. It thereby is capable of grasping the true shape of a totality, which is a condition for conceiving the absolute. Closer to home, the term "speculation" also alludes to Kant's (and Schelling's) notion of "intellectual vision" (*intellektuelle Anschauung*, often translated into English as "intellectual intuition"), which Kant denied to man, and to which Schelling gave an irrationalist interpretation. Hegel wants this kind of vision to be given a *rational* interpretation—albeit in terms of Reason rather than Understanding; and this calls for a dialectical mode of thinking that overcomes the habits of formal thinking and of ordinary predicative language (see pages 107–9 and 181–85, below). Hegel's use of "speculative" (and also "*truly* speculative") thus addresses the demand, raised by Schelling and others, of restoring to philosophy something analogous to intellectual intuition—and reinterprets this something as a nondiscursive logic, that of subject-like systems—in which conceptual Reason replaces mystical visions. Intel-

lectual intuition is a romantic illusion in so far as it is understood
as a direct mental event, a semimystical gift; but when converted
from a privileged mental *experience* into a logical *structure* (the
structure of dynamic totalities, in which particulars and their universals inherently lead to each other), then its notion is compatible
with conceptual Reason and, indeed, as dialectical logic, is the
moving principle of philosophy.

Post Scriptum: Hegel and Kant—Continuity in What?

A reader who wished to know where I stood with respect to a
dichotomy he called "post-Kantian versus traditionalist" was puzzled to discover that my reading of Hegel did not fit into this
matrix. The so-called post-Kantian reading, despite its merits, is
too restrictive to do justice to Hegel's many-sided complexity and,
in any case, depends on how one interprets Kant. I, too, insist on
essential continuities between Kant and Hegel (some of which are
not generally recognized);[32] but my Kant is not quite the Kant of
current Anglo-American epistemology and philosophy of mind.
Moreover, I see implicit in Kant, both at the core and in pregnant
peripheral texts,[33] the roots of ideas that are usually considered
distinctly Hegelian.

The Ontological Import of Kant's Copernican Revolution

The post-Kantian reading denies, or plays down, Hegel's interest
in ontology. This is because it equates ontology in general with
pre-Kantian metaphysics, which Hegel indeed rejected (or rather,

[32] Especially in *Kant and the Philosophy of History* (Princeton, 1980, 1986; second
ed. forthcoming), and in *Kant and the Renewal of Metaphysics* (Heb., Jerusalem,
1973, 1986).

[33] Such as, in the first *Critique*, the two prefaces, "The Architectonic of Pure
Reason" and "The History of Reason"; also the first part of the *Lectures on Logic*;
the "Final End of Creation" in the third *Critique*; "The Idea of Universal History";
and other programmatic texts concerning the nature and goals of philosophy
and of rational human action.

transcended). However, I see no dichotomy between continuing Kant's enterprise and being deeply versed in ontology. Kant, in my reading, had not demolished metaphysics in general but only what he called *dogmatic* metaphysics, which sees actual being as a thing-like domain, facing human subjectivity from an unreachable Beyond. Metaphysics as such, however, was to Kant an inalienable requirement inherent in human rationality. In his words, it is an "essential interest of human reason," which must, therefore, be reconciled with reason's equally essential interest in self-criticism and the recognition of its own finitude. As Kant reiterated several times in his programmatic texts, his project was to create a new, valid "metaphysics-as-science,"[34] conforming to critical demands, and thereby give metaphysics "a new birth." This, he maintained, became possible for the first time through his Copernican revolution, which locates the structure and grounds not only of knowledge, but also of the *objects* of knowledge—the actual entities existing in nature—in the productive structure of human subjectivity (the "I think").

The Copernican revolution states that the subjective-universal conditions of *knowing* real objects in the world are the same as the conditions for those objects *to be* what they are, and what our description claims they are.[35] Thereby, Kant's transcendental idealism established an ontology no less than an epistemology, since it explicates what it means for something *to be* an actual entity in the world, and not only the conditions of enouncing true propositions about it. Kant regards the result as "scientific" metaphysics. At the same time, he restricts the positive import of his new metaphysics to finite or "conditioned' entities only: conditioned by the boundaries of sensual experience, and, within those boundaries, conditioned by each other in causal chains. No valid metaphysics

[34] See for example the two prefaces to the *Critique of Pure Reason* and the first sections of the *Prolegomena*.

[35] That is, to be actual, through being numerically quantifiable, causally determined, open to sense perception, subject to mutual interaction, and so forth, and, in the second degree, by having the *particular* qualities and quantities they do.

is allowed of infinite, unconditioned elements, at least not as a cognitive theory.[36]

The ontological significance of Kant's Copernican revolution is manifest also in the novel concept of "transcendental logic," which stands at its center (and which Hegel appropriated and tranformed in his own *Logic*). Kant distinguished between formal logic and a logic of actual entities—that is, a logic of being. Formal logic sets the conditions for thinking anything at all—any intentional object, whether existing, fictional, or an empty symbol, whereas transcendental logic—Kant's system of a priori categories and principles—sets the conditions for thinking *actual entities in nature* (= the world of experience); it is thereby a logic of being derived from the structure of the subject—in other words, it is a subject-like ontology.[37]

Hegel followed the Kantian distinction between the two logics even to the point of dethroning formal logic from its role of supreme legislator and limiting its grasp of truth and its scope of application. Hegel's *Logic* treats the history of dogmatic metaphysics as finished, irreversibly overcome by Kant's principle of idealism, according to which the deep structure of reality is the same as the structure of the subject. At the same time, rejecting Kant's radical dualism of the rational and the sensual, Hegel carried the new interpretation of objecthood and actuality beyond the limitations set by Kant. Most notably, Hegel refused to confine the subject-centered ontology to finite entities only, and claimed that absolute Knowing was possible, both in principle and as a looming historical event. Furthermore,

---

[36] The unconditioned is attainable only by moral action, which produces it through the will. This is where the surplus metaphysical interest of reason that is frustrated by knowledge is transformed in Kant, who duly calls the moral-practical domain a *"metaphysics* of morals."

[37] Some interpreters deny that the *Logic* is an ontology on the grounds that it is but a "Science of pure thought" (understood as a transcendental structure). Thus John Burbridge, *On Hegel's Logic: Fragments of a Commentary* (Atlantic Highlands, NJ: Humanities Press, 1982) supported by E. H. Harris, *The Philosophical Review* 93, no. 1 (Jan. 1984): 138–40). They seem to follow Hans Friedrich Fulda's general reading. Yet to followers of Kant's idealism like Hegel, there cannot be a contradiction between a science of "pure thought" and ontology, since according to the Copernican turn, the structure of objective reality is the same as the structure of subject's "pure thought."

Hegel attributed subject-like dynamics and self-individuation not only to the "I think," but to other systems—organic, social, and cultural—as well, and even to the whole of being, which he conceived as a single totality that generates its self-knowledge through human culture and history.

In these respects, Hegel used Kant's wings to take off to regions that Kant had declared out of bounds. Yet Hegel believed he remained faithful to the new critical metaphysics, because (1) he abolished the pre-Kantian metaphysics of *substance*, and (2) he negated all metaphysics of *transcendence*. In Hegel there is only the *immanent* world, spiritualized by *itself* (through human action), on the basis of the *subject*-like dynamic he attributed to being in the *Logic* and elsewhere.[38]

Hegel's *Logic* is about the *logos* that articulates both the mind and the world. As such, it is linked at every level to some aspect of the real, from the most indefinite to the most concrete. At first the unformed mind conceives this *logos* in a mode that has persisted from the Greeks to Spinoza—namely, as a thing-like entity, or substance, existing externally in itself; but then, following Kant, the *logos* is conceived as a subject-centered system of forms, expressing the subject's dynamic. Thereby, the *Logic* at its peak understands itself as having all along been *egaged in explicating the pure structure of subjectivity*. This is what Kant has done paradigmatically (and on a smaller scale) in the Transcendental Logic. Or, using a post-Kantian comparison, Hegel's *Logic* can also be seen as having reworked and translated the mentalist "absolute subject" of Fichte and Schelling into *structural* terms as a system of dynamic categories. Moreover, Hegel's *Logic* understands the absolute subject as a result. This implies that although the *Logic* is a metaphysics, as Hegel expressly claims, it cannot serve as *"first* philosophy" (or a priori foundation), but must be the *last*, the summary of all our other cognitive and practical enterprises.[39]

[38] For a more extensive analysis of Hegel's philosophy of immanence, see chapter 2 of my *Spinoza and other Heretics*, vol. 2, *The Adventures of Immanence*.

[39] Even as such it is still a "realm of shadows," because the actual subject is also mediated by forms of social intercourse and recognition that are only sketched in the *Logic* itself.

Furthermore, the *Logic* also assumes an implicit historical dimension. It tacitly describes our diverse philosophical *images* of the real, as they change in relation to the partial levels of reality captured by each dominant logical category. This implied history of metaphysics significantly breaks into two distinct parts (the only such division in the book), *and the break between them marks the rise of modernity*. It separates the object-centered pre-Kantian metaphysics from the new view of the world stemming from the Copernican revolution, which not only created the modern, subject-centered ontology, but also revolutionized our understanding of logic itself.

Hegel also followed Kant in maintaining that the self is not a primary given, as in Descartes, but a constituted result, whose identity depends on confronting otherness.[40] But Hegel completed this Kantian strategy by advancing the powerful argument that the self's confronting its Other cannot be limited to the world of natural objects, as in Kant, but must, even primarily, include the *other subject* and the world of intersubjective relations and institutions built upon this encounter. In this way, the social world gains ontological import in Hegel, not only as the substrate of being's historical evolution, but also as the condition for the emergence of selfhood and singular individuality as such.

The Will and History

I cannot here discuss all the dialectical continuities between Kant and Hegel. But I should briefly mention the will, history, the "cunning of nature," and the construal of reason as a motivating force.

---

[40] I read this view as implied in the "progressive" argument of the Transcendental Deduction. The argument starts from the "I think" as given, and searches for the conditions that make it possible. It concludes that these preconditions include the application of the categories to sense materials in a way that constructs a world of experience distinct from the constructing subject, who then, and only then, is capable of the self-reflection expressed in the thought (or enunciation), "I think." Thus objective reality and subjective identity are mutually dependent in Kant's idealism; they enable *each other* in a benign circularity; and the structure of the ego is, already in Kant, that of a *result* of its own world-objectifying activity.

Kant understood human rationality not as calculus merely, but as a goal-oriented activity which he explicitly calls "interest."[41] Kantian reason is a system of rational interests, all directed toward the realization, in different domains, of rationality as an end in itself. This accounts, *inter alia*, for Kant's construal of practical rationality as *will*; his concept of "the *history* of reason"; and the demand—indeed, imperative—that the moral will become a world-shaping power. This task defined world history for Kant: the human will projects itself in objects of moral civilization. In so doing, the will transforms the naturally given, and strives to rediscover *itself* in its products: to see its own norms and moral vision embodied in new laws and institutions, including a "republican" polity; a reformed religion of reason (understood as an "ethical community"); enlightened educational methods; a world confederation ensuring peace; and—no less important (because "morally deserving")—the *material* benefits which such reforms justify and make possible.

This merger of universal morality and prosperity, to which Kant shifted the title of "Highest Good,"[42] was envisioned as an offshoot of the Copernican revolution and its principle of autonomy: The subject, as will, has the self-imposed task of reshaping the naturally given into cultural objects—a moral civilization—that bear the marks of the will's own structure. At the same time, anticipating Hegel's "cunning of reason," Kant himself recognized a semidialectical natural dynamic which promotes political progress through ambition, exploitation, and violence rather than the moral will. Even more important, Kant's "unsociable sociability," his main thesis in social philosophy, according to which all egos stand in a nonutilitarian conflict over the prestige and acknowledgment each refuses to grant others, recurs grandly in Hegel's philosophy as the struggle for recognition that drives all human affairs.

An even less-recognized continuity between Kant and Hegel concerns the goal of the world as a whole. At the end of the *Critique*

---

[41] The term "interest(s) of reason," which many Kant scholars find odd, is so genuinely Kantian that it recurs several hundred times in his writings.

[42] The shift occurred in the third *Critique* and in the political and religious writings. At first however (notably in the *Critique of Practical Reason*), the "highest

of Judgment Kant inquires about "the ultimate end of Creation it-self,"[43] a metaphor by which he means all there is, empirical and noumenal alike; and Kant, like Hegel, gives a future-oriented an-swer, grounded in human action. The meaning-endowing goal which justifies the world's existence cannot be found in anything given beforehand or already existing; it is a *moral task*, which the human race must accomplish by the gradual "moralization of na-ture."[44] In the first *Critique*, the metaphysics of the unconditioned collapsed into antinomies because it claimed to know (attribute specific features to) the world as a single whole. Now Kant declares there *is*, after all, a valid critical way of making the world intelligible and justified *as a whole*, not cognitively but morally, by centering on the world's final end rather than beginning. In other words, while avoiding idle metaphysical speculations about the world's ori-gin, or global features, or concerning a *natural* teleology allegedly inherent in it, Kant introduces instead a human-projected *moral* teleology, which determines what the world *ought to become* through the moral action of the will. In this way, the justifying meaning of being is not metaphysically given "in itself" (it defies essentialism and a "metaphysics of presence," as one might say today), but *constitutes* a moral Ought (Kant also calls it "vocation") to be realized in history.

Similarly in Hegel, the meaning and justification of being do not exist beforehand. They are generated by transforming nature into spirit. Yet Hegel judges Kant's position as one-sided, because (among other reasons) Kant shrinks the specifically human input to pure morality alone, and considers this input to be an obligation extraneous to nature, a foreign teleology imposed upon it. This makes Kant's theory not only narrowly moralistic, but hopelessly utopian, and, in addition, requires him to postulate a transcendent God to mediate between the two disparate domains of nature and freedom. In Hegel no external God is needed, because an imma-

good" had a narrower personal meaning, the combination of personal virtue and happiness. (See my *Kant and the Philosophy of History*, part 1.)

[43] *Der Endzweck der Schöpfung selbst.*

[44] See the *Critique of Judgment*, paragraphs 82–84, 87, as well as my analysis in *Kant and the Philosophy of History*, pp. 70–80, 175–78.

nent teleology takes his place. The historical process realizes a possibility that inheres in nature's own, semisubjective structure.

Hegel: A Critical Philosopher?

If Hegel saw no possibility of return to pre-Kantian metaphysics, was he then a critical philosopher? Yes and No: yes, if to be critical means to reject the "naïve" view of objects in themselves, and grasp objectivity and actuality as mediated by the structure of the subject; and no, in so far as criticism insists on the finitude of human reason, its inability to access to the infinite and unconditioned to which, nevertheless, it necessarily aspires. In denying the unbridgeable gap between the finite and the infinite, Hegel denied a crucial Kantian insight, indeed a fundamental recognition, in which Kant, not Hegel, had anticipated the dominant tone of modernity. Kant regarded this hiatus as the lot of modern man, the price of critical enlightenment and freedom. A self-criticized rationality is all we have in Kant, our only valid source and authority: if it leaves the unconditioned beyond our reach, then *this* is the genuine "know thyself" that philosophy provides, the true, if painful, insight into ourselves and where we stand in being. Hegel refused to accept this conclusion. He aimed his heaviest artillery at the "philosophy of finitude," and, equipped with a dialectical teleology, claimed to have overcome it by "absolute Knowing." Personally, I think that on this issue, Kant had the more sober, profound, secular, and disillusioned view of the human (and the modern) condition than Hegel (although on other issues Hegel was more attuned to the inevitable realities of life and the world.). Moreover, I think Kant did not go far enough, that his immutable a priori principles barred him from recognizing the greater scope of human finitude and contingency, on which Nietzsche, and most existentialist and antiessentialist thinkers, including the pragmatists, later insisted. But Hegel is neither Kant nor Nietzsche, and a fair historian of philosophy must recognize that the metaphysics of absolute spirit was essential to *Hegel's* own project, even if it is incongruent with the aims of many who are otherwise deeply indebted to him.

Who Is the "Old Hegel"?

Every period has its "old Hegel." And in every period there are people who claim Hegel *did not* say what they think he *had better not*
say. My own "old Hegel" does not consist of actual Hegelian views
I consider untenable or embarrassing, but of views I think had been
falsely attributed to Hegel, which he did not, or could not (given his
texts and the logic of his other important positions) own. Thus, one
need not be apologetic, only careful, in order to deny that Hegel
proposed any of the following: (1) a return to pre-Kantian metaphysics; (2) an understanding of "spirit" as a Platonic world-soul, or the
personification of the universe; (3) a *transcendent* absolute God, conceived as a separate superperson, whose rational intentions precede
nature and history; (4) a *preestablished* essence of man (and of his
culture and ethics) which history only unveils, but does not constitute or remake; (5) a closed, rigidly knit, semideductive system of
truth, allowing of no contingency; (6) a calculus-like dialectical
method, separable from its content and driven by a formula (as in
Fichte), which can, in itself, attain to ultimate reality; (7) a semitotal-
itarian understanding of "totality"; (8) a social rationality in which
the universal suppresses the individual, rather than being mutually
dependent on the individual's consent and recognition.

At the same time, I think it equally untrue to suggest, as some
do today, that the historical Hegel (1) was antimetaphysical *throughout*; (2) that he viewed the climax of his philosophy in a stand-alone
social ethics and practice; (3) that philosophy for him was only a
historicist, relativistic vindication of contingent cultural forms (this
is more Rorty than Hegel); (4) that he had no interest in ontology
and the question of being; or (5) that he minimized the import of
religion, or postulated its superiority to reason. In other words, it
would be incorrect to play down the teleological, transhistorical,
and heterodox-theological import of his absolute spirit.

Hegel, Dead and Alive

Benedetto Croce, the Hegel-inspired Italian philosopher, wrote almost a century ago a famous essay entitled "What is Alive and

What is Dead in Hegel's Philosophy?" Croce's blunt and somewhat naïve title makes a worthwhile point. A philosophical interpretation of past philosophers must not deny or play down the flaws of an important philosopher, who can still greatly inspire us even if we do not make him suit contemporary tastes and fashion, or use him as tacit authority to promote our own ideas. Such practices, I might add, are often necessary in religion and in law, but not in philosophy. Religion uses authoritative, charismatic texts as its justifying vehicle, and therefore needs to read them selectively, by a flexible hermeneutics. The same holds for law, whether written or precedent-based. But philosophy has no authoritative texts or figures, only rational discourse by which to justify its claims, and a secular, strictly rational history of philosophy cannot adopt those practices without compromising its own project.

There is no textually fair way of making Hegel's overall system and ambitions withstand the test of our time: the result will either not be Hegel, or not stand. Even so, Hegel is an immense intellectual power, and still a vital philosopher in much of what he had to say. I see three important respects that make him indispensable. First, if one believes that ideas do not exist in a pure Platonic space, but rather are embodied in actual, historical men and women using shared language and concepts, then Hegel is absorbed into many ways in which we speak, think, and act today, and is a major factor for both the understanding and the critique of high modernity. As such, Hegel has become a kind of modern Aristotle, to Kant's Plato. (The extent to which he stands at the background, and crossroads, of much European cultural history is partially illustrated in the "Works on Hegel in English" section at the end of this book.)[45] Secondly, Hegel is a source of philosophical stimulation and insights large and small, and a path-setter in the modes, issues, attitudes, and goals of philosophizing. As such he can be an outstanding philosophical educator—in the sense that Nietzsche called Schopenhauer an educator—provided one is careful to avoid the pitfalls that his texts also contain, including his often esoteric style and his system's claims to totality and infinity, that is, its closure.

---

[45] Only partially, not only because of the brief survey, but because his influence was not only on philosophy, but also on history, sociology, law, art and politics.

But Hegel is relevant not only as educator, or in providing context to much of what we are, think, and debate. He is also, in the third place, alive and important in matters of philosophical substance—many actual positions in which he points in the right general direction. I cannot spell out all the relevant examples here (many will recur in some form in the following text and commentary); I can only summarily list their headings.

For example, Hegel conceives of human beings as basically creatures of desire, a desire for something that transcends mere survival and is considered more worthwhile than sensual happiness and instrumental utility—call it freedom, recognition, selfhood, existential meaning, coping with alienation, or self-actualization through a universalized principle. This approach, immanent and this-worldly, offers, I think, a more convincing alternative to the sensualist-utilitarian image of human life and desire, and also to the lofty, religious, spiritualist (and Platonic) striving towards an imagined world of the Beyond.

Other examples: the view that rationality—the *logos*—is *substantive* rather than merely formal; that it is a driving *power* and not just a calculus; that it operates through the "lower" and the "noncognitive" mental structures—imagination, recollection, emotion, desire, love, and so forth; that reason is always *embodied* in empirical situations and entities; and (as an implied consequence of all the above) that reason is impure rather than pure, and contains unreason, contingency, and negativity as integral ingredients. Further important Hegelian views: the *historical situatedness* of all human affairs; the essential role of *negativity* in all important matters, including the constitution of the self and of the real; the view that the human subject is *constituted* by its involvement in the world rather than given beforehand in a Cartesian way; the view that the *human will* (rather than a natural law, or the divine will) underlies the entire normative world (i.e., civilization itself); and, on a metalevel, understanding identity as involving difference in its very constitution, and accepting other elements of the Hegelian dialectic that make sense even without casting them into an overall systematic panacea.

Finally (to conclude these personal reflections), Hegel's concern with the meaning of existence, which, as he suggested, is not lying ready-made somewhere, but involves human input and action, indicates an existential interest that remains relevant independently of the social concerns with which it is linked in part. Of course, Hegel's messianic expectation that the modern world would make this meaning manifest, a redeeming power in people's lives and culture, had turned sour, as all messianism must. But the drive behind it— to reconcile modern individuals not only to their growingly complex and alienated societies, but to the being of the universe which has become estranged by modernity's disillusions, the price of intellectual emancipation and *désenchantement*—expresses a genuine philosophical problem that does not go away, and cannot be truly submerged in political and social activism.

Each of the above issues contains a world of philosophical potential. The problem is to release this potential from the grip of the "absolute idea," and from Hegel's dream of a final synthesis or reconciliation, that gives definite priority to unity and identity over their opposites. Some people have tried to amend the flaws they found in Hegel in a local, case-by-case approach. Yet much in Hegel cannot be moved or removed until the top is shattered—namely, until the claims of totality and final synthesis are gone, which close and lock the Hegelian system. The key to a fruitful Hegel critique does not lie in piecemeal counterarguments—if necessary, they can come later—but in renouncing in one critical sway the claims to infinity and absolute knowledge.

This move will open up an abundance of Hegelian ideas by which one can philosophize in a free, semidialectical, and historical way, unburdened by the grand illusions of Hegel and his opponents: on the one hand, the illusions of positivism (as if reality lies in the immediately given), and of analytic philosophy (as if we have a direct access to a univocal, ahistorical truth, governed by pure logic or some other formal canon); and, on the other hand, the illusion of the religious absolute translated into conceptual philosophy.[46] The result will be a free, historicized, and semidialectical

---

[46] These lines paraphrase the conclusion of the Hegel portion of my *Dark Riddle: Hegel, Nietzsche, and the Jews.*

philosophizing that would depart from Hegel in accepting human finitude and contingency, the lack of a final synthesis, the role of inreconcilable difference in producing our never-integral human identities, and more generally, in accepting immanence and finitude without giving up on the *logos*, while deflating its pure image as an overriding deity.

That would no longer be Hegel, but would not have been possible without him.

Text and Running Commentary

➤✦

IN A PREFACE it is customary to explain the goal which the author has set for himself, the circumstances of his writing, and the way he thinks his work relates to other, earlier or contemporary efforts at treating the same object. But in a philosophical text this custom seems to be not only superfluous, but, by the nature of things, inadequate and contrary to its purpose. For what would be appropriate to say about philosophy in a preface, and in what manner? Roughly, one would give a historical account° of the work's standpoint and tendency, its general content and results—a conjunction of assertions and assurances° made here and there° about what is true; but this cannot be the valid way of exhibiting° philosophical

Historical account: Meaning a narrative, a storytelling statement, or simply an empirical one. In a preface, all one can do is narrate the author's position "as in a story." Therefore, the general principles themselves appear within a preface as particular claims, lacking justification and severed from their systematic context. Such statements are in fact empirical (another sense of "historical" in Hegel's use) even when their content is philosophical.

Assurances (*Behauptungen*): Verbal warrants merely, as when saying, "Take it from me, I assure you this is so."

Made here and there: In a preface, one can express only dogmatic statements which, even when true as sentences, are only mere talk and, strictly speaking, because they lack their grounding context, are false (see below).

Exhibiting: The German *darstellen* (and *Darstellung*) acquired a special systematic meaning in Kant, retained by Hegel. The terms indicate the outer expression, indeed translation and transformation, of a rational essence or meaning into a sensual or empirical medium. This idea is best translated as "exhibition"; although "presentation" makes more readable English. (I make this remark once, and may later interchange between these terms as context advises.)

truth. Also, philosophy resides essentially in the element of universality which contains the particular; therefore philosophy, more than other sciences, gives rise to the illusion° that the matter itself—even in its accomplished essence—is expressed in the goal or final result, in relation to which the development is inessential. Yet, [even] in the common image° one has of, say, anatomy—roughly, that anatomy consists in knowledge of the body, considered in its nonliving existence—one is convinced that the matter itself, the content of this science, is not thereby possessed, but, in addition, one must take the trouble of dealing with the particular. Further, in such an aggregate of cognitions which has no right to the name of science, there is no difference between a conversation about the goal and similar generalities, and the historical and Conceptless

Gives rise to the illusion: It might create the illusion that what is essential resides only in the final end taken in isolation, while the detailed development is inessential, a mere vehicle which can be disposed of at the end of the road. This is the view of ordinary common sense and also of the formal (and mathematical) Understanding (*Verstand*), as opposed to philosophical Reason (*Vernunft*). In philosophy, the conclusion has neither meaning nor truth-value without the whole context within which it has evolved.

The common image: Literally, "the general image" (*Die allgemeine Vorstellung*). Hegel refers to what the formal understanding calls definition. By using the term *Vorstellung* (representation, image) he indicates that definitions are not genuine *Concepts*; they rather belong to a lower, more external level analogous to an image. Anatomy, for example, is a rationally inferior science, because it grasps a living body as if it were dead, and ignores its organic, dialectical structure. Yet even in anatomy, everyone will admit that a merely general definition of that science is inadequate and teaches us nothing, unless we consider the relevant particulars, namely, the diverse bodily organs. This is even more so in philosophy, which is organic and dialectical at a higher level, because it deals with reason. Nothing actual can be understood in philosophy by mere generalizations. We must observe how the generalization works within the body of the system, and how the particulars which realize it are integrated within the evolving context of the whole.

manner° in which the content itself—the nerves, the muscles, et cetera—are discussed. In philosophy, however, this would give rise to an incongruity° that consists in using a way of discourse which philosophy itself shows to be incapable of attaining the truth.

Similarly, to state how a philosophical work sees its relation to other treatments° of the same object introduces a foreign interest, obscuring that which is important in the knowledge of truth. The more the current opinion° views the opposition between the true and the false as rigid, the more it expects that every given philosophical system should be either endorsed or contradicted, and takes every explanation of such a system to be only the one or the other. It does not conceive the diversity of philosophical systems

The historical and Conceptless manner: "Historical" indicates here merely empirical, a simple enumeration of particulars lacking a Concept (*Begriff*), in the sense of an organic dialectical structure. Hegel is using the term "Concept" in his own, systematic sense (which is why I capitalize it). The universality of a genuine Concept is neither formed inductively, by abstracting from particulars, nor is it a priori in the sense of being independent of particulars. Rather, the universal Concept is an organic totality in which every particular makes its own contribution to the whole and is constituted by the dialectical movement of all the others. This is Reason's characteristic structure, as distinguished from the analytical Understanding, which expresses a lower level of rationality.

Incongruity: Anatomy, though its object is organic, is rather an inorganic body of knowledge, and thereby external to its object. This makes it mere talk *about* this object. However, in philosophy, the organic Science of reason, mere talk involves an incongruity, indeed a contradiction, between philosophy's *own* form of discourse and the form of discourse *about* philosophy.

Other treatments: Other philosophical treatises. In a preface it is customary to compare the author's views with other writers. In philosophy, that convention may be misleading because it presupposes that every philosophical opinion is either absolutely true or absolutely false. Hegel will criticize this view.

The current opinion (Meinung): "Opinion" here takes the sense of the Platonic *doxa* as distinguished from actual Knowing. Hegel frequently conflates the connotations of "opinion" and "image" (*Vorstellung*). Any sub-Conceptual view of things is an "image" in terms of its cognitive *medium*, and an "opinion" in terms of *epistemic status*.

as the progressive development of truth; it only sees contradic-
tion° in that diversity. The bud disappears in the eruption of the
flower,° so one could say that the flower contradicts the bud. In a
similar way, the fruit declares the flower to be the plant's false
existence,° and steps forward in its place as the plant's truth. These
forms are not only distinct; they reject one another as mutually
exclusive. At the same time, their fluid nature° makes them into

It only sees contradiction: The ordinary view of the understanding assumes
that any two contradictory claims, or philosophical doctrines, are mutually
exclusive. Only one of them can be true, whereas the other is absolutely
false. Hegel proposes a different view according to which conflicting philosophical doctrines are all dynamic ingredients or "moments" of a single
system of truth, which evolves out of their contradictions. In the fulfilled
system, every moment emphasizes a single, one-sided aspect of the overall
truth. As such, it is both true and false: false in its one-sided claim to
exhaust the whole truth of the subject matter; and true in so far as, liberated from that one-sided pretense, every philosophical doctrine contributes
some nuclear, positive content to the evolution of overall truth. Taken as
a "moment" of truth rather than its totality, each of the clashing philosophical doctrines has its inner necessity and is dialectically compatible with the
others. This Hegelian view of the history of philosophy was in some respects prefigured by Kant (see Yirmiyahu Yovel, *Kant and the Philosophy of
History* [Princeton: Princeton University Press, 1989], chapter 7).

The bud disappears in the eruption of the flower: Hegel frequently uses images of organic life to illustrate what he means by "dialectical evolution"
and the logical relations within it.

Existence: In Hegel's ontology, the term *Dasein* indicates the state of *speci-
fied being*, a being which has received some primary characterization, but
is still grasped as standing in merely external relations with everything
else, and as lacking a rational essence at its ground. Higher than *Dasein*
is the stage of *Existenz*, where we grasp the particular empirical existent
as expressing a rational essence latent in it. That stage corresponds to the
dualistic "Understanding," not yet to the level of "Reason," which rises
from existence to actuality (*Wirklichkeit*).

Their fluid nature: By "fluid" (and later "plastic") Hegel does not mean
shapelessness, but structured flexibility. It is a nonrigid grid in which every
ingredient refers us to all the others in a process of development and self-
shaping. Hegel wishes to expose the same kind of structure within

moments° of an organic unity, in which they not only do not struggle with each other, but one is as necessary as the other; and only
this equal necessity constitutes the life of the whole. However, the
contradiction° of a philosophical system does not usually conceive
of itself in that way, and the consciousness grasping the contradic-

---

philosophical thinking. Because it is the structure of true being, thinking
too must be characterized by it. The process of thinking which leads to
philosophical self-consciousness will be, for Hegel, the climax of being's
own development and self-realization. Both ought to have the same structure, since they are two moments of one and the same unity.

Moments: This term, borrowed from mechanics, is given new meaning in
Hegel's dialectics. It points to a dynamic factor or ingredient, which
works together with other contradictory ingredients to produce a common positive result. According to Hegel, the formalistic understanding
tends to isolate any such moment and turn it into an independent entity
or a rigid notion, losing the dialectical "plasticity" which characterizes
true being. In a system developing through time—like an organic body,
a society, or human history—the dialectical moments appear diachroni-
cally, one after the other; yet within the fully actualized system they
operate synchronically. This means that a dialectical movement persists
even at the stage when a system is fully realized: now it operates as the
principle which structures that system and repeatedly maintains it. In
other words, the dialectical movement is *interiorized* into the system and
becomes the constant, reciprocal transition in which each of the system's
ingredients passes into the others and is recurrently rebuilt by them.
Therefore, in an actualized dialectical system, every moment has an "ecstatic" existence transcending its limits. Even in the final stage no single
ingredient is self-sufficient; each is negated, and passes into the others to
be recurrently constituted through them as what it specifically is. Hence,
actuality in Hegel, as in Aristotle, is not static, but an activity (*dynamis,
Wirklichkeit*; the German word derived from *wirken*, to act). Hegel sometimes calls this process *"the inner movement of the Concept"* and uses the
metaphors of "drunkenness" and "Bacchanalian whirl" to describe it.

The contradiction: A second philosophical system which contradicts the
first (as in Locke vs. Descartes). By "the consciousness which grasps a
contradiction" Hegel means the historian, or observer, who grasps the
contradiction while reflecting on both systems. (Hegel frequently uses

tion does not know how to free it of one-sidedness, or to maintain
it as free; it fails to recognize mutually necessary moments° in
the shape of that which appears to be in conflict and opposition
with itself.

The demand for such explanations° and the satisfaction of this
demand easily count as the essential thing. Where could the inner
side of a philosophical text be better expressed than in its goals and
results? And how would these be known more precisely,° if not
through their difference from whatever else the period has produced in the same domain? But when such activity is taken to be
more than the beginning of knowledge,° when it is considered as
actual knowledge, then we must count it among the devices which
bypass the matter itself, and combine its actual neglect with the
semblance of serious exertion. For the matter is not exhausted in

---

this unusual style, which refers to real people and actual events by abstract nouns, or converts adjectives into substantives.)

Mutually necessary moments: The two opposing moments (like empiricism
and rationalism) are equally necessary for the complete truth—the totality—and for each other. Ordinary consciousness is driven by the law of
noncontradiction (which suits the empirical and formal sciences, but not
philosophy) to exclude one moment because of the other. This leads
to a "rigid" view of the role of contradiction. A dialectically educated
consciousness will identify the opposing systems as equally necessary
moments of the truth.

Such explanations: Statements about the author's goal, her difference from
other authors, and so forth.

Precisely: The German word *bestimmt* (determined), or *Bestimmung* (determination), is a key term in Hegel. It means being "specific," being
determined at some level of precision, having this and that particular
content.

The beginning of knowledge: At this point, Hegel starts to modify his critique
of "mere conversation" and prepares the ground for writing a preface.
A philosophical preface, he now claims, can be useful if we regard its
generalizations as a mere beginning calling for development and particularization. We must not take its statements as adequately conveying the
information to which they allude.

its goal,° but in its development; and the actual whole is not the result, but the result together with its becoming. The goal for itself is the nonliving universal, just as the tendency is the mere drive which lacks actuality, and the naked result is the corpse which the tendency has left behind. Just as much, diversity is the matter's boundary;° it exists where the matter ceases to be, or is what the matter is not. Such labor concerning goals and results, the distinction between one system and another, and their respective judgments is therefore much easier work than it seems. For this activity, instead of concerning itself with the matter itself, is always hovering outside it; instead of residing in the matter and forgetting itself in it,° such knowing always resorts to [*greift nach*] another, and re-

The matter is not exhausted in its goal: The term *Sache* means the real issue, that which is seen as essential, the actual subject matter of our talk or action. In Hegel's use the word *Sache* (or *die Sache selbst*, as distinguished from *Ding*, "thing", which recalls the Kantian *Ding-an-sich*) also signifies actuality as a unity of being and thought. In this more systematic sense, the issue referred to is the *philosophical subject matter in its actuality*; and this cannot be exhausted by generalized results. It can only exist through the full dialectical process in which it is particularized and realized. Thus the philosophical result cannot be cut off from the process of its becoming. The genesis of truth is an inseparable part of the philosopher's essential subject matter; so he must either understand the result *out* of this process, or be left with a dead corpse instead of truth.

Diversity is the matter's boundary: A philosopher explaining what distinguishes her work from others'—thus engaging in comparisons—conducts her discourse outside the actual subject matter. Hegel calls this "external reflection": talking about something from the outside, or thinking about something without participating in its constitution. This echoes Spinoza's critique of comparative thinking as external to being, though Hegel adds an idealist frame to it.

Residing in the matter and forgetting itself in it: This is the necessary condition for avoiding external reflection and performing an "inner" philosophical thinking. Philosophy is not *about* something; its thinking evolves and is actualized together with its object. Therefore, philosophical thinking must first "tarry" or "reside" within its content and even "lose itself" in it. This also indicates that in philosophy there is no a priori method or schema by which thinking must proceed. Rather, the material itself should guide

mains with itself rather than being with the matter and giving itself to it. To pass judgment on what has substance and content is easiest; grasping it is more difficult; and the hardest is to unite these two by performing its exhibition.°

---

philosophical reflection and shape the structure emerging from it. The dialectical method, we shall see, is not a schema imposed on the subject matter from the start, but a structure emerging from it retrospectively. The philosopher lets the subject matter itself be her guide and, following its inner dynamics and constraints, also discovers its deficiencies—that which turns out to be lacking and called for by it—and traces the structure arising from the subject matter's evolution. Some might see here a phenomenological approach in a quasi-Husserlian sense (which Hegel partly accepts); but seen in terms of Hegel's contemporary debate, this is a special kind of "intellectual intuition," though not a mystical experience but obedience to the *Sache's* inner *logic* and development. Hegel rejects intellectual intuition as a special *mental* experience, romantic or super-rational. He demands to interpret it rationally, in terms of a *logical* structure and conceptual constraints. These structural elements can manifest themselves to us only if we follow the lead of the subject matter and refrain from imposing a priori abstractions upon it (including the law of noncontradiction). When, on the contrary, our thinking neglects the *Sache* and starts by concentrating on *itself*—for example, by investigating its own methodology (Descartes) or its own power and limits (Locke, Kant), or when it starts from laws that are said to govern every thought a priori—then it puts itself on the line rather than centering on reality. That viewpoint, says Hegel, is "merely subjective" because it always remains enclosed within its own domain. And it is ontologically empty, because the object—actual being—remains outside it. Adequate philosophy does not apply ready-made formal laws of thought to an external object; it is rather the inner explication of the rational structure of the object itself (of being), as it evolves and alters its shapes in the process of its actualization, and as it eventually attains self-consciousness through human knowledge and culture. Thought fulfills a constitutive role in this evolution, not as an object-like *logos* governing outer nature, but as embodied in *human* thoughts, acts, and artifacts; and thereby the object discloses itself also as subject.

Performing its exhibition: *Darstellung*, as we mentioned above, is a key concept in Hegel as in Kant, though in a different sense. In Kant it means the exhibition or embodiment of a conceptual content within a medium of

The beginning of cultural education [*Bildung*], of working one's way out of the immediacy of substantial life, must always first consist in acquiring knowledge of universal principles and standpoints, and raising oneself to the thought of the matter in general. No less, one must learn to support or refute that thought with reasons, to capture the rich and concrete fullness with specific determinations, and to provide an orderly answer and serious judgment about it. This beginning of *Bildung* will then have to give place, first, to the earnestness of life in its fullness, which leads to experiencing the matter itself; and second, if, in addition, the Concept's earnestness will descend to the depths [of the subject matter], then this kind of knowledge and judgment will retain an appropriate position in conversation.

The true shape in which truth exists can only be its scientific system. The goal I set myself is to contribute to bringing philosophy nearer to the form of science—to help it renounce its name as love of Knowing,° and become actual Know-

---

intuition. Thus schematism is the *Darstellung* of the categories of the understanding. For Hegel, it means the full exposition of the philosophical system in the context of its evolution, whereby the ideas emerging in it are justified and refuted. It is impossible to exhibit philosophy by directly jumping to its final stage or "consequences." To present a philosophical truth, one must follow the stages of its becoming, exhibiting all parts of the system according to their mutual relations and evolution. This is also the only way to *justify* or ground the system. In a formal system, the doctrine and each of its parts possess an independent meaning and a separate truth-value; it is therefore possible to grasp the doctrine's meaning by a different procedure than that used to justify it. In philosophy, however, the consequences have neither meaning nor a truth-value except as part of a totality which includes the process of their genesis; therefore, the same movement by which the system of philosophy evolves and is justified is also the procedure by which we can properly understand its meaning and exhibit it to others. A single process controls the system's *evolution*, its *justification*, its *understanding*, and its adequate *exposition*.

Love of Knowing: Love indicates that we lack its object and are still searching for it. In wishing to put an end to "the love of Knowing," Hegel proclaims his far-reaching pretension to bring the philosophical quest to an end. This is the idea of the "end of philosophy" in its historical version, already

ing.° The inner necessity that knowing should become science lies
in its nature: and the only satisfactory explanation° of that necessity
is the exhibition of philosophy itself. However, the external necessity, so far as it is grasped in general, regardless of a person's contingency and individual dispositions, is the same as the inner neces-

---

found in Kant. On the one hand, the true system of philosophy depends
on its historical development; it cannot emerge atemporally from the
head of some genius, be he a Plato or a Spinoza. Yet on the other hand,
philosophical progress is not open-ended; it has an end, which Hegel
believes has finally matured and—following Kant's philosophy, the French
Revolution, and the Napoleonic code—can already be seen on the horizon. When the final stage is realized, philosophy will overcome its historical character, transcend time, and become supratemporal. This means
that it will continue to exist *in* time, but will no longer *depend* on it.
This will realize eternity within time. The supratemporal character which
Plato and other philosophers ascribe to philosophy from the start is attained in Hegel through history and is the result of a process in time.
(Moreover, in at least a metaphorical sense, time itself is said to come to
an end when absolute Knowing emerges. By that Hegel cannot mean
that time ceases as a sequential, continuous quantity, but as the bearer of
qualitative *novelty*; since, in principle, nothing new can emerge, time's
progressive direction becomes the eternal recurrence of the same.)

Actual Knowing: The Platonic ideal of *sophia*—wisdom—based on unconditioned knowledge (*epistēmē*). In Hegel this ideal awaits philosophy, at the
end of a long and complex process of education. *Philo-sophia* is to become
sophia: the Knowing mind will overcome *eros*, the element of love which
implies lack and remoteness from its object, and will become actual
knowledge and wisdom. While in Plato this process can be consummated
in a single individual's life, in Hegel it presupposes the history of the
whole human race. The *Phenomenology* thus historicizes Plato's theory of
education. A single individual, however talented, cannot jump beyond his
or her period and attain absolute truth in one ahistorical leap. All great
philosophers express the immanent potential which their periods entail,
and also its limitations, experienced as their own personal limitation,
which drives them to seek new solutions. This process can end only with
"absolute Knowing," into which all the major previous stages with their
mutual contradictions are interiorized as partial "moments."

The only satisfactory explanation: The complete justification of the system
of philosophy is immanent and can be grasped only from within it. Being

sity—shaped, that is, in the way in which time represents the existence of its moments. To demonstrate that the time has come° for philosophy to be raised to Science is, therefore, the only true justification of the efforts pursuing this goal; for that would manifest the goal's necessity even while realizing it.

I know that in placing the true shape of truth in its scientific character°—or, which is the same, in asserting that the Concept

---

circular and comprehensive, the system of truth includes its justification within itself as a kind of *causa sui* (cause of itself). In other words, its grounding does not depend on some singular, privileged item (evidence or axiom), but on the mutual dialectical relation linking its parts. The necessity of philosophy becoming an apodictic system thus follows from its own nature. This inner necessity can be grasped and justified only by someone who *already* knows the final system, having worked internally through all the parts of the *Logic*, and, eventually, of the whole Hegelian system. Still, the *external* necessity that philosophy should become systematic is exhibited by the *Phenomenology*. The *Phenomenology* expounds that necessity under a different configuration—temporal sequence. It follows the same logic that governs the system's formation as it manifests itself in the evolution of human consciousness in historical time. This is made possible because, in Hegel, the inner, supratemporal necessity of absolute Knowing must externalize itself as a *historical need*. Every philosophical standpoint and every historical configuration needs to reconcile its contradictions by evolving into a new form and—when the time is ripe—by passing into the complete system. Hegel offers here the nucleus of his well-known doctrine that the *system* of philosophy and the *history* of philosophy are two facets of the same organic whole, one existing within time and empirical history, the other transcending time and existing in a purely conceptual manner, which however, presupposes history and derives from it.

The time has come: In view of the previous note, the expression "now is the time" is not an exhortation, but a systematic claim: historical time has already ripened for that purpose. Yet this is only the *threshold* of the New Era. Before philosophical knowledge is fully actualized, we can justify the passage towards it only genetically, by historical need. The genetic justification of philosophy comes first in the order of time, although the system will justify itself also internally and become self-grounded.

In its scientific character: The word "scientific" indicates here a systematic character, which endows a body of knowledge with unshakable (apodictic) certainty. In philosophy, this occurs in a different mode than in the

alone is the element in which truth has existence—I seem to contradict a certain opinion° [*Vorstellung*] and its consequences, which are
as pretentious as they are widespread in the conviction of our age. It
does not seem superfluous, therefore, to explain this contradiction,
although my explanation cannot be anything here but a mere assurance, just like the assurance it opposes. Now, if the true exists only
in that—or rather, only as that—which sometimes is called intuition, sometimes immediate Knowing of the absolute, religion, or
being°—not being in the center of divine love, but the being of that

---

empirical sciences—mainly, in the "organic" mode discussed above (and
further below).

A certain opinion: By grounding the absolute (truth) of philosophy in its
comprehensive system, Hegel opposes the conventional view that philosophical knowledge is made absolute by some special mental experience.
Hegel thinks, among others, of his former friend and current opponent, Schelling, and also of the doctrine of irrational "faith" promoted by
F. H. Jacobi. These philosophers made absolute Knowing depend upon
a direct grasp unmediated by conceptual reason—either through immediate faith, or by an experience of intellectual intuition. Hegel fights the
Concept's war on two fronts: against romantic irrationalism he demands
that philosophy be grounded on reason; and against shallow rationalism
he denies that reason can be reduced to mere "Understanding." The
absolute, Hegel holds, must be attained through rational thinking: irrational experiences only provide emptiness and illusion. Yet for reason to
reach the absolute, it must be construed as *dialectical* rationality, which
recognizes the positive role of negation, and is linked to life, feeling,
and being, all while retaining conceptual constraints and the capacity to
universalize (= the basic conditions of rationality).

Intuition, . . . immediate Knowing . . ., religion or being: the joint critique is
of Schelling, Hölderlin, Jacobi, and romantic metaphysics (see the introduction above). A special target here is "intellectual intuition," which is supposed to grasp absolute truth by an original (and for Hegel, mysterious)
experience of the intellect. Kant had used the concept of "intellectual intuition" to define the *limits* of human reason, and gave it a precise cognitive
structure: it is a mode of knowledge which, by knowing the particular,
allows us to directly know the universal principle governing it, and vice
versa: if we know the universal principle, we can directly know all the
particulars belonging to its range. Kant's *Critique of Pure Reason* is based

love itself—then philosophy, too, will have to be exhibited in a form opposing the Concept's. The absolute should not then be conceived, but felt and intuited; not its Concept but its feeling and intuition should guide the word and be expressed in speech.

In order to grasp the appearance of this demand in its general context,° we must view it within the phase in which self-conscious spirit stands at present. Here we see that spirit has gone beyond the substantive life° it had previously led in the element of thought°—beyond the immediacy of its faith, beyond the satis-

---

upon the denial that humans can have such a privileged mode of cognition. By contrast, some of Kant's followers wished to restore an element of intellectual intuition to philosophy, but each construed it differently. For Schelling it is a privileged mental and experiential faculty (the inscrutable origin of all the other faculties); whereas Hegel accepts Kant's *structural* definition of intellectual intuition, but claims, against Kant, that it *can* be realized in human cognition through a dialectical logic of philosophy. Of course, it then is no longer intuition, but (a special kind of) conception.

In its general context: Following his rather sarcastic description of Schelling and the romantics, Hegel proceeds to explain why the philosophical culture of the time must produce such positions. At the present historical juncture, the "self-conscious spirit" (the subject matter of the *Phenomenology*) occupies the following position. On the one hand, it has broken away from the immediate, unexamined life in which it had previously felt complaisance and plenitude. From that doubtful paradise, spirit was expelled by the power of reflection and universal thought (Enlightenment) which, however, drove it to the other extreme—a world of mere abstractions. Cut off from concrete life, it now suffers from the acute sense of loss of reality and nostalgia for it. That nostalgia drives spirit to seek solid reality through irrational means—renouncing the intellect's achievements by blurring all distinctions and submerging itself in a chaos of opaque experiences.

Substantive life: This is life marked by conformism and unreflective confidence in one's existence and environment. In itself, this life is already transfused with thought, because it contains conceptions and world-images, norms, and traditions. Yet, thought itself is still immediate at this state, enclosed within life's plenitude without performing a critical reflection about it.

In the element of thought: Hegel here has in mind a high level of substantial life, structured by a rich culture and tradition. Yet people are submerged

faction and certainty which consciousness possessed of its reconciliation with the essence° [*Wesen*°] and its general, inner and
outer, present. Spirit has not only gone over to the other extreme—to a non-substantive reflection of itself in itself—but has
gone beyond that, too. Not only did it lose its essential life, it is
also conscious of its loss,° and of the finitude which [now] is its

---

in that tradition in a "substantial" manner without critical reflection.
Hegel may be thinking of medieval culture and more generally, of any
tradition-oriented culture like that of the *ancien régime*. Life in that conservative way gives a sense of concreteness and solidity, as if it were an inert
thing. Culture, knowledge, society is experienced as a substance. Yet in
its essence, this culture is not an inert substance but "the self-conscious
spirit," though only in a potential and alienated mode.

Its reconciliation with the essence: Here, consciousness is not cut off from the
real substance of life but is reconciled with it. The person feels at one with
this world; but this takes place dogmatically, without reflection, as if the
spirit were an inert substance. Hegel's philosophy makes conscious rational reflection a necessary condition for all spirituality and truth, but goes
beyond them to a third stage in which rational thought—the very same
power that has undermined the dogmatic universe—is reconfigured in
such a way as to restore the sense of plenitude and reconciliation with the
absolute, which was lost to human life when thought had first become
conscious and critical. While this project puts Hegel at odds with romantic
irrationalism, it also explains why, at the same time, Hegel speaks favorably
of the romantics' "nostalgia" towards the plenitude of life, which he considers a legitimate and necessary goal. Hegel thus transforms the romantics' nostalgia from a past-oriented into a future-oriented desire.

Wesen in German means both essence (principal meaning) and a being or
an entity. Hegel mostly uses the first, but sometimes connotes both by
the same word. (Miller chose to translate it "essential being." I prefer the
more classic translation "essence," which context will make us read with
or without the other connotation).

Conscious of its loss: Herein lies the driving force of the *Phenomenology*: it
is not simply the *fact* of being torn from the lost unity, but the *consciousness* of this rupture which generates the drive to overcome it. Hegel's
doctrine is not nostalgic; there is nothing attractive in the primordial
state: compact, dogmatic, immediate life is contrary to man's spiritual
essence and not worth living. As rational creatures, humans can elevate

content. Turning away from the pig's leftover food,° confessing how badly it is doing and cursing its state, spirit demands of philosophy not so much to provide it with knowledge of what it is, as to make it regain that [lost] substantiality and dependability of being. Hence, philosophy should satisfy this need not by opening up° the tightly closed substance and raising it to consciousness—not by bringing chaotic consciousness back to a thought-based order and to the simplicity of the Concept—but rather by dumping the distinctions of thought, suppressing the differentiating Concept, and putting forth the feeling of being, which confers not so much insight, as edification.° The beautiful, the sacred, the

---

their life only if intellectual reflection awakens in them—with all the sorrow, alienation, destruction, self-criticism, and the sense of rupture between a person and his world which this awakening will cause. Awareness of this rupture produces an acute sense of deprivation and the desire to restore the lost unity. Yet this cannot be satisfied by an impossible regression to the past, either in the form of nostalgia (abandoning oneself to the pure experience of yearning), or by a romantic attempt to retrieve the plenitude of the past through artificial and possibly violent means; it can be satisfied only by going *forward* within the element of reason and developing it further. The rational principle which, as "understanding," has produced the rupture, must now overcome it as "reason." It ought to evolve further, until it produces a *re*-conciliation, which must be attained not at the expense of reason and self-consciousness but *through* them—and on the basis also of the social and practical life which reason structures and expresses in concepts. From here, too, Hegel derives the need for a new philosophical logic expressing the power of onward-going life and not only formal thinking.

Turning away from the pig's leftover food: This comes from the New Testament story of the Prodigal Son (Luke 15:16 and passim), who was so hungry he was ready to eat the husks the pig was fed.

Not by opening up: Although that would have been the adequate way—breaking up the compactness of substance and raising it to rational self-consciousness. The romantics reject this answer; preferring vague feeling to the Concept, they confuse all distinctions.

Edification (Erbauung): A sort of arousal and uplifting produced, for example, by a lofty sermon or a vague yet deep experience which one cannot quite clarify to oneself. Hegel sees edification as unphilosophical and op-

eternal, religion and love are the bait needed to arouse the desire to bite. Not the Concept but ecstasy, not the cool progressing necessity of the subject matter, but effervescent enthusiasm, are to sustain and extend the richness of substance.

To this demand corresponds a strenuous effort, which looks irritated and almost zealous, to tear people away from their immersion in the sensual, the vulgar, and the singular,° and direct their gaze toward the stars; as if, forgetful of the divine, they were about to satisfy themselves with dust and water, like worms. In earlier times they had a heaven richly studded with ideas and images. Everything that is had its meaning in the thread of light linking it to heaven; and instead of abiding in this [-worldly] presence, the gaze of people followed the thread of light outside this world to a divine essence— to a transcendent presence (if such a phrase is possible). It took coercive power to redirect the spirit's eye back to the terrestrial domain and attach it to it;° it took a long time until that clarity,

---

posed to the "Concept." Philosophy must be "scientific," not edifying; it has to do with knowledge and understanding, not with preaching and creating sublime, yet opaque feelings. (Not accidentally, philosophers opposing the goal of philosophy as science—like Rorty today—argue that philosophy *ought* to be edifying.)

The sensual, the vulgar, and the singular: The new era, of which Hegel thinks himself the philosopher, restores to this-worldly existence the value it lost in the Middle Ages. Hegel objects to the philosophical preaching which negates this world in the name of a hidden transcendent world. Although he, too, seeks to rise from vulgar sensuality to reason, Hegel is not ready on that account to abandon the terrestrial, sensual element in reality: his goal is to provide the sensual and terrestrial with a new significance derived from the rational essence they embody. Hegel is therefore a philosopher of immanence. Philosophy is to give a new meaning and a higher, even divine, value to this world in all its concreteness. This goes against the transcendent tendency which despises the world and makes it depend upon the "thread of light linking it with heaven."

To redirect the spirit's eye back to the terrestrial domain and attach it to it: The return from the supernatural to the immanent world was expressed, among other ways, in the high value which Bacon, Galilei, Locke, and others restored to empirical experience, following the long medieval pe-

which only otherworldly things used to possess, could be reintroduced into the muddle and blur in which the sense of this world was lying; and a long time was necessary before the attention to the present as such, which we call experience, could be made valid and interesting. But now the opposite need seems to be felt: sensibility has become so strongly rooted in the worldly domain, that the same violent force is needed today to raise it above it. Spirit shows itself to be so impoverished, that like a wanderer in the desert who longs for a simple gulp of water, spirit seems to be craving to refresh itself with the meager feeling of the divine in general. From this little which satisfies spirit, one can tell how great its loss is.

But this humble satisfaction in receiving or parsimony in giving are unfit for Science. He who seeks edification only, who demands to shroud the diversity of his earthly existence and of thought in a foggy mist, and to bask in the indefinite enjoyment of that indistinct divinity, will see for himself where he can find it; he will easily find a way to stir himself into enthusiasm and thus pump himself up. But philosophy must beware of the will to be edifying.

Even less should this humble sufficiency, which has renounced Science, pretend that its enthusiasm and opacity° are higher than

---

riod (and scholastic metaphysics) in which sense experience had been despised. Hegel views this restoration as a major turn toward, and condition for, the rise of modernity. Contrary to what is sometimes believed of him, Hegel does not deprecate experience; on the contrary, as testified by our text, he sees great historical progress in restoring value and validity to what "we call experience." However, attachment to sensual experience is today overpowering and conceived as the essential thing rather than a necessary moment of truth. This one-sidedness manifests itself in philosophical empiricism, in the metaphysics of vague feeling, and in the theology that goes with it.

Enthusiasm and opacity: Hegel now criticizes the call for "enthusiasm" in religion and mysticism, which rejects the power of the intellect in favor of an ecstatic rapture considered more spiritual. This haziness sacrifices the conceptual distinctions in order to create an empty feeling of depth. (Hegel's sarcasm against "enthusiasm" recalls Kant's disdain for its parent-concept, *Schwärmerei*; yet Kant would so qualify Hegel's own presumptions to attain the absolute.)

Science. Believing itself to be residing in the center and in the very depth, such prophetic talk looks down with disdain on specific determinateness (*horos*), and intentionally distances itself from the Concept and from necessity, as belonging to a reflection which resides in the finite alone. However, just as there is an empty breadth, so there is empty depth; just as the extension of substance can pour itself in a finite diversity without a unifying force holding it together, so there is an intensity without content, holding itself as pure force without extension,° which is the same as superficiality. Spirit's force is only as great as its externalization;° its depth is only as deep as it dares expand and lose itself in its expansion. When this substantive and Conceptless knowing° pretends that it has sunk

Pure force without extension: In Hegel's dialectics, a force lacking outward manifestation signifies that the force *does not actually exist*. What these philosophers consider as their greatest discovery is an unreal thing, analogous to an occult quality.

Spirit's force is only as great as its externalization: Inwardness is meaningless unless it expresses itself outwardly: this is a major element of Hegel's dialectic. Every inward essence, every hidden potentiality will receive its meaning *as inwardness* only in so far as it has been manifested in the external world. This does not mean that Hegel dismissed the concept of interiority in the manner of positivists or behaviorists. On the contrary, the various forms of interiority ("essence," "principle," "force," "talent," "potentiality," and so forth) play a fundamental role in Hegel's system. Yet they receive their status *qua* interiority from being exteriorized, that is, embodied in a series of empirical manifestations (actions, events, particulars, and the like). On the other hand, no empirical series is actual if it exists as a discrete aggregate of particulars with no inner essence or power expressing itself in them. An empirical entity, or set, is actual only insofar as it embodies an inner principle of essence. Thus each of the two opposites (inner and outer, essence and empirical existence) receives its meaning and distinct status from their mutual constitution.

Substantive and Conceptless knowing: A vague inner feeling which cannot be articulated or expressed as a Concept.

the self's ownness [*Eigenheit*]° in the essence and is philosophizing in truth and sanctity, it conceals from itself that [in fact], because it disdains measure and determinateness, it does not give itself to God, but, at times, gives itself [rather] to the contingency of the content, and at other times submits the content to its own arbitrariness. In abandoning themselves to the unrestrained ferment of substance, [these people] believe that by shrouding self-consciousness and renouncing the understanding, they become God's own [God's elect], to whom he imparts wisdom in their sleep. And, to be sure, what they thus receive and engender in their sleep are dreams.

The self's ownness [Eigenheit]: The "ownness" meant here is that which distinguishes one individual self from others (not a personal trait but the self's ontic uniqueness, its being a separate entity). The mystics claim to have unified the self with the essence of the whole universe, and thereby with the deity; but because they follow a nonconceptual way, they inevitably miss their goal. The self is neither preserved in the mystical experience, nor built by it, but is rather sunk and lost. Worse, the mystical self is not even sunk and dispersed *in God*—the true essence of being—but in a shapeless mass of subjective feelings and arbitrary images. Because the mystics despise reason's lucidity, necessity, and conceptual distinctions, they miss the actual character of the deity and lose themselves within an empty illusion of God. Note that Hegel's criticism is partly immanent; his own philosophy also leads in the end to the self's dialectical unity with the absolute (i.e., the deity); but this involves neither a mystical leap nor the dissolution of the Self. In Hegel, the self's individuality is *built* (or constituted) rather than destroyed through its relation with the absolute; and this relation, moreover, presupposes the complex mediation of rational concepts, social practice, and a long historical evolution. In the final analysis, Hegel, like Plato and Spinoza, shares the *ultimate* goals of mysticism, but rejects the imaginary ways that the mystic suggests for attaining them. Those goals can be achieved only in a rational way, which calls for a different view of rationality—one based upon dialectic and mediated by history.

It is further not hard to see that our time is a time of birth°
and transition into a new era. Spirit° has broken away from its
former world of existence and imaging [*vorstellen*]; it is about
to sink all that into the past, and is busy shaping itself anew.

Our time is a time of birth: When writing the Preface Hegel had a deep sense
of a new historical era standing at the gate. The text vividly describes the
dynamics of historical transformation—how, from the decadence of the
old world, a new world emerges as both a continuation and a new qualitative leap, as in childbirth. The metaphor of the Nativity hovers over this
text. In 1807, when Hegel and the new world announced by Napoleon
were still young, Hegel seemed to believe that the approaching era was
to conclude the whole historical process: henceforth everything would
be an extension or repetition of a realized principle. Beside the negative
symptoms announcing the new world—the sense of decadence, the boredom, the irony and frivolity with which sensitive people regarded their
present culture—Hegel identifies positive signals, especially Kant's philosophy and the French Revolution. In Kant's philosophy, the human subject
recognized its autonomy and constitutive role in shaping knowledge, ethics, and objective reality; and the French Revolution gave that idea a political expression and propagated the principle of freedom. Yet, these two
revolutionary innovations took a one-sided form. Kant remained a subjective idealist and a philosopher of finitude; to overcome its flaws, his philosophy needed a synthesis with Spinoza (and Aristotle), a task which Hegel
set himself to perform. And the French Revolution needed to overcome
its abstract and ahistorical principle of Enlightenment, which severed it
from reality and led to terror. The first part of the *Phenomenology* offers
a theoretical *Aufhebung* of the Enlightenment, just as Napoleon (who at
the time was crushing the Prussian army near Hegel's city of Jena) was
performing a similar *Aufhebung* in the social and practical world. Unlike
Fichte, Hegel was not a German nationalist; he saw Napoleon as a dialectical agent of freedom, expressing the "cunning of reason" which operates
in history. Although motivated by ambition and egoistic desires, Napoleon was propagating and *institutionalizing* the principles of the French
Revolution in Europe. By embodying these principles in a code of law
and various political institutions, Napoleon, in Hegelian terms, was making an even greater contribution to the new era than the original revolution. Hegel's sense of an imminent new era in world history was later
diminished and sobered by the Restoration. His other major works al-

Of course, spirit is never at rest, but is in ever-progressive movement.° But this resembles the birth of a child where, after a long quiet nourishing, the gradual, merely additive progress is broken by the first breath and—in a qualitative leap—a child is born.° Similarly, self-shaping spirit matures slowly and silently

---

ready point to more realistic and sober expectations. Yet even then he seems not to have abandoned the vision of a last historical phase looming on the horizon, although the horizon now receded to greater distance and the road to it became far more marred by obstacles.

Spirit: Here the concept of spirit appears in its full significance. For Hegel, Spirit writ large is not simply identical with human history (as Kojève famously interpreted it), but is the *essential principle* of history—it is history together with the inner meaning and significance it reveals. As such spirit is both historical and transhistorical, and each of these aspects of spirit mediates the other. Spirit in the global sense exists through actual human beings, evolves with their changing culture, endows them with essential meaning, and attains its absolute state through them. In that respect, spirit is an autonomous principle assuming the form of otherness and self-alienation on its way to self-actualization. From a theologico-historical standpoint, spirit in the global sense is the divine principle which dialectically realizes itself through the secular, worldly spirit of particular human beings, including their practical lives, actions, laws, and institutions, and also their art, religion, and philosophy. When Hegel says that spirit stands at the threshold of a new era—presumably the last—he alludes to a kind of messianism whose attributes are secular, though its significance remains religious.

Ever-progressive movement: Spirit is a permanent activity transcending any given particular state. In history, this movement progresses in a semilinear way modified by detours and regressions. When the end is attained, spirit remains an activity, but its essential movement is interiorized and becomes circular. Within the final system, spirit still transcends every partial element which it professes to capture or express the whole of (notice the image of "Bacchic whirl," below). This maintains spirit's active character even at the stage of its actuality; but now its transcending takes place *within* the system rather than pointing beyond it.

A child is born: The vivid text before us undoubtedly alludes to the myth of the Nativity (perhaps even to the phrase *et homo factus est*, as recited in the Mass). If so, Hegel is saying that the imminent historical change is

toward a new shape, while shedding the edifice of its former world piece by piece. The tottering of the old world is indicated by few symptoms only. The frivolity and boredom which cut into that which [still] subsists, and a vague premonition of something un- known, are harbingers of a change that is about to come. This gradual crumbling, which does not change the physiognomy of the whole, is broken by the rising day which, in a flash, outlines the features of the new world.

However, it is essential to bear in mind that the new [world] has no more perfect actuality then the newborn child. Its first emerging is its immediacy or Concept.° Just as a building is not finished when its foundations are laid, so the attained Concept of the whole is not the whole itself. If we wish to see an oak in the strength of its trunk, the spread of its top, and the abundance of its foliage, we shall not be satisfied if an acorn is shown to us instead. So also Science, the crown of a world of spirit,° is not fulfilled in its beginning. The begin- ning of the new spirit is the product of a far-reaching upheaval in multiform cultural shapes; it is the prize given to a tortuous and diverse way, which requires an equally diverse effort and exertion. This beginning is the whole which returned to itself from succession

---

comparable in magnitude to the birth of Christ. Another allusion to the Nativity (with vivid descriptions of the mother's birth-pangs and push- ing), appears at the end of the *Phenomenology*, precisely where the birth of Christianity from the pagan world is discussed.

Its immediacy or Concept: By "immediacy," Hegel means the principle's existence in a preliminary and undeveloped way. By "Concept," he means here an abstract generality still lacking development and realization (see "simple Concept," below). Yet this abstraction is already a Hegelian Con- cept (Begriff) in embryo. Popular use opposes the sense in which the term *Begriff* is used in Hegel's systematic work, where it indicates *concrete universality*—that is, a universality that is spelled out in relevant particu- lars and has attained detailed embodiment in empirical reality. The two senses of "Concept" might mislead the reader, but can be distinguished according to context.

The crown of a world of spirit: In Hegel's system, philosophy, when accom- plished, is the conceptualization of "absolute spirit."

and its own extension,° and became a simple Concept.° But the actuality of this simple Concept consists in letting those configurations that have become moments develop again and reshape themselves—now within their new element and the meaning that has arisen.

While the first appearance of the new world is still only the whole shrouded by its simplicity—or is that whole's universal ground—consciousness, on the other hand, still retains the richness of the former world° present in its inner recollec-

Succession and its own extension: Time and space are essential to spirit, because it attains actuality only by being deployed in the empirical world and returning to itself through its temporal evolution. As we said above, the modern era is the beginning of spirit's self-reinstatement, its return-to-self from its dispersal and alienation in the external world; yet spirit's return-to-self starts in merely abstract form. The revolutionary new concept arises at first as a "mere" concept. In order for it to take concrete shape, all the previous cultural forms which have made the final stage possible (and are latently preserved in it) must evolve and and make it actual.

A simple Concept: Again, the term indicates an abstract, unrealized Concept. Whatever is "simple" is empty, impoverished, or a potential beginning without actuality. Hegel therefore opposes the philosophers who believe (like Descartes, the empiricists, and the positivists) that the building blocks of knowledge are simple units. Hegel argues that no simple entities exist at all, because everything depends on the negation and mediation of something else, especially of some universal factor. True, some things are simpler than others; but the simpler is also the less actual, the more impoverished and abstract. And mere undistinguished "being" is the dullest and emptiest concept of all. (In contradistinction to those, from Plato to Heidegger, who made being the most important philosophical concept.)

Still retains the richness of the former world: The diverse, empirical existence which spirit had in the past. *Dasein* in Hegel's vocabulary means "Being-there" (or existence), and should not be confused with actuality (*Wirklichkeit*). Not everything which exists or is there (*ist da*) is actual. Thus, spirit's past modes of existence, though part of objective reality, were never actual, because existence had not attained in them the ontological level of "actuality." A finer distinction is drawn between *Dasein* and *Existenz*. The latter is the external empirical manifestation of an inner rational essence or principles; yet *Dasein* has no such essence manifested in it, but is a merely particular and contingent mode of being. (The English language

tion.° In the newly appearing shape, consciousness misses the
breadth and specificity of the content;° even more, it misses the
cultivation of form,° by which distinctions are set with certainty
and ordered according to their solid relations. Without this cultivation science lacks Understandability [*Verständigkeit*], and looks

---

has no special words to distinguish between these two categories, so both
are rendered as "existence.")

Its inner recollection: This German term (*Erinnerung*) has a systematic function in Hegel's work, meaning both memory or recollection (the conventional sense) and interiorization. Memory, the mental preservation of past
experiences and cognitions is a form of interiorization; as such it is essential
to the dialectic. Every dialectical *Aufhebung* involves some content whose
deficient form is negated and abolished, but whose essential nature is preserved at a higher level of articulation. Preservation is made possible by
interiorization, which is a kind of memory, either conscious (as in mental
or cultural systems) or merely organic memory. Interiorization in one of
these forms is a necessary condition for a dialectical process, in which the
negation of negation does not revert the process to its point of departure,
but creates a more complex new quality. Thus the first original negation
is not annihilated by the second. They are both preserved in the subject
or Self which undergoes the process and, together with the consequences
which result from them, become an organic part of that subject's history.

This analysis makes clear that *dialectical logic is only suited to subject-like
entities, mental or at least organic*—that is, living, conscious, or cultural
systems, whose new states are capable of incorporating the negations of
earlier states, and to preserve them as an ingredient (or "moment"). On
the other hand, dialectical logic is unsuitable to inert or self-same entities—atoms, numbers, simple "facts," univocal terms in a logical calculus,
fixed propositions (p, q, r's), statements in daily discourse, in legal dis-
putes, and so forth, as well as any other "positivistic" item lacking interiorization and presumed to be simply what it is; for these are subject to
formal logic. It follows that the genuine domain of dialectic is spirit.
Dialectic requires a capacity for memory, that is, interiorization, be it even
an unconscious or merely organic interiorization. A so-called materialistic
dialectic is therefore an incoherent concept for Hegel; and so is any attempt to capture the dialectic by a formal schema. (It is true that Hegel
has a dialectical "philosophy of nature," but this, to be coherent, must be
understood as applying to the *philosophy* of nature, to the changing *Con-*

as if it were the esoteric possession of a few singular individuals: an esoteric possession—because it is present at first only in its Concept of inwardness; and of a few singular individuals—because its unextended appearance makes its existence singular. Only that which is fully determined is also exoteric,° capable of conceptualization [*begreiflich*],° and of being learnt and made everyone's possession. The understandable [*verständige*]° form is the road to Science which is open to all and equal to all; and the demand to access reason's [mode of] Knowing° through the understanding

---

cepts of natural phenomena (like physicalism, magnetism, life, et cetera) but *not* to particular, inert items. The latter's only possible dialectic is negative—they turn out *not* to be the real entities they purport to be, but to have their reality in something higher, like an organism or a cultural entity. Even the fact that nature is considered a moment of spirit does not exempt self-same inert natural entities from being nondialectical in all but this basic negative sense.

The breadth and specificity of the content: The principle has not yet been worked out and deployed in relevant particulars—the various cultural forms which will be discussed in the *Phenomenology*.

The cultivation of form: Shaping the new principle rationally, as a system of conceptual distinctions, is necessary in order to make absolute Knowing intelligible to every rational person, instead of its being the esoteric property of the few. For Hegel, this condition does not concern the system's presentation merely, but its very essence. If the system is to express actual reality, which is the active *logos*, then it must be rational in itself: this is a condition for its truth (or actuality) and not only for its accessibility. That the system should be open to everyone follows from its essence. Correspondingly, the inherent form of the philosophical Science and the form in which it must be presented are the same.

Exoteric: This term refers to being open to the many; the opposite of esoteric.

Capable of conceptualization [*begreiflich*]: The context indicates this translation, rather than the use of *begriff* in its technical sense.

The understandable [*verständige*]: Discursively intelligible: from *Verstand*, discursive reasoning.

Reason's [mode of] Knowing: The English adjective "rational" does not render the specific meaning of *vernünftig* in this sentence, which discusses the understanding (*Verstand*) as a bridge to reason (*Vernunft*).

is a justified demand which consciousness makes in approaching
Science.° For the understanding is thinking, the pure I° in general;
and the understandable is that which is already known [*das Bekannte*],° which is common to Science and to the unscientific consciousness, by which the latter can accede to Science.

The science which only begins, and has not yet gained complete-
ness of detail or perfection of form, is thereby exposed to reproach.
But if the reproach is aimed at the essence of Science,° it is as

Justified demand which consciousness makes in approaching Science: Philosophical Science must satisfy the need of the individual consciousness,
   which refuses to accept truth on the force of external authority or convention, but demands being able to testify to this truth and recognize it as
   its own truth. This requires philosophy to involve itself from the start
   with the individual consciousness, to adopt its standpoint, and evolve
   dialectically along with it. The flaws and contradictions which arise in
   every stage of philosophy's evolution are then experienced by the individual consciousness as *its own*; so it is driven to overcome them and move
   onwards, to new tentative solutions and to broader, more coherent standpoints, until, in the end, universal truth arises as the *self*-development of
   the individual consciousness itself. In this way the genesis of the system
   of philosophy and the evolution of individual consciousnesses mediate
   one another within a common process.
The pure I: According to Kant, understanding is the principle which con-
   nects different concepts or representations; and the ground of the understanding is the "pure" I, that is, the self-conscious subject which ascribes
   the diverse representations to itself in the unity of a single consciousness.
   Hegel further develops this idea. Thinking is the activity of the subject
   who, as I, is already at work in the nonscientific consciousness, and by
   whom the latter can rise to the level of philosophical Science.
That which is already known [*das Bekannte*]: When nonscientific consciousness—the ordinary unformed mind—attempts to know, it relies on that
   which seems familiar or reasonable to it, based on its previous experience.
   Although this cannot provide truth, it starts a process in which the I and
   the understanding are already latently at work, thus providing a lever
   for further dialectical progress, the beginning of a long movement towards truth.
Aimed at the essence of Science: If the claim tends to negate the very possibility of absolute Knowing (as both the empiricists and the rationalists of

unjustified as the refusal to recognize the demand for the well-formed development we discussed above. This conflict seems to be the foremost knot which contemporary scientific culture is struggling to undo, but does not quite fully understand. One side flaunts the richness of the material, and the [virtue of] understandability, while the other side disdains the latter (to say the least) and flaunts immediate rationality [*Vernünftigkeit*] and divinity. Even if the first side is reduced to silence, either by the force of truth alone or because of the other side's fervor, and even if it feels beaten in what concerns the fundamental issue, it is still unsatisfied in its just demands, which remain unfulfilled. Only half its silence is due to its opponent's victory; the other half derives from the boredom and indifference which follow from a constantly aroused expectation, when promises are not fulfilled.

Concerning content, others make it easy for themselves to have a broad extension. They draw a great deal of material into their territory, namely, that which has already been known and arranged;° and in busying themselves mostly with curiosities and

---

finite understanding, including Kant, maintain), then it cannot be accepted, just as one must reject the romantic demand that absolute Knowing be realized without the understanding. Hegel's targets here are not sufficiently clear. On the one hand, he seems to allude to the philosophy of the Enlightenment, in its three major trends of rationalism, empiricism, and Kantian criticism. Empiricism flaunts the richness and variety of its contents, and rationalism flaunts its intellectual rigor. Both are justified in their boasting, yet neither offers a comprehensive system which joins conceptual rigor and richness of content in producing absolute Knowing. Hegel believes this dilemma confronts his time and philosophical culture, and is resolved in the *Phenomenology*: in this sense we may say that Hegel, like Kant, seeks a synthesis of rationalism and empiricism, while transcending the finitude of reason on which Kant insisted. On the other side, Hegel confronts another contemporary trend—a romantic philosophy of the absolute, which despises the authority of the understanding and of systematized experience.

That which has already been known and arranged: Fichte and Schelling did not derive the particular contents of their respective systems from other contents in the system, or from underlying principles, but assembled

peculiarities, they look as if the rest—namely, everything with which knowledge has finished in its own way—is already in their possession, in addition to that which has not yet been regulated. In this way they appear to be subordinating everything to the absolute Idea, which looks as if it is known in everything and has extended itself to a comprehensive Science.° A closer observation, however, will discover that this extension has not been generated by one and the same [principle] differentiating itself into a variety of shapes, but is rather the shapeless recurrence of the same, which is applied externally to diverse materials and thereby acquires a tedious semblance of variety. As long as the development consists merely in such recurrence of the same formula, then the Idea, which is true for itself, remains always stuck at the beginning. To have the knowing subject° merely dis-

---

them empirically, by merely observing the various phenomena of life and knowledge. This was a frequent complaint in German Idealism. Kant had accused Aristotle of having merely picked the categories up as they came his way instead of deriving them "from a single principle." Fichte in turn accused Kant of only declaring the need for a deduction, but again assembling the categories of the understanding in an empirical manner; and Hegel wielded a similar accusation against Fichte.

As if it . . . has extended itself to a comprehensive Science: For Fichte and Kant's followers, a philosophical system had to unify the whole inventory of human knowledge under a single absolute idea, as that idea's own manifestation and adequate mode of existence. Hegel shares this general goal (which he attributes to Spinoza, as did all German Idealists), but claims that it must be carried out by an *immanent* evolution of the absolute Idea—the totality—and of every specific content which spells it out. The components of the system are not empirical details about the world but basic *categories*, such as "matter," "quantity," "movement," "gravity," "family," "state," and also "enlightenment" or "skepticism." The crucial question is (a) how do these categories particularize themselves from the absolute principle (the totality)? and (b) what happens to the absolute Idea itself as a consequence of their particularization?

The knowing subject: The absolute principle which Fichte "monotonously" applies to the material is *the unity of self-consciousness*, that is, the knowing subject's pattern of existence. From this, Fichte derives the

tribute° this one inert form to whatever comes its way, and to plunge the material into that immovable element from without, is to frustrate the requirement [of Science], just as it would be frustrated by using merely arbitrary flashes of ideas concerning the content. What is required is a richness which flows out of itself, and a self-determining differentiation of shapes. But this is a monotonous formalism to gets at only the material's differences, and only because these differences are already known and prepared in advance.

---

law of noncontradiction as the highest standard of thought and reality. Only that which is compatible with the unity of consciousness can be true or real; whatever is affected by contradiction can be neither true nor real, because self-contradiction destroys the unity of consciousness. Hegel rejects this consequence. The subject's identity, which indeed is the measure of philosophy, must not be understood as simple equality with itself (A = A), but as a unity of equality and difference, and therefore as necessarily entailing self-contradiction. This is a major difference between Hegel's dialectic and Fichte's triads. Fichte separates the domains of the I and the not-I so as to let each of them coexist; thus their alleged synthesis runs away from contradiction into compromise. Hegel's dialectic accepts contradiction as a productive principle and is built upon it. Both philosophers model the logic of being upon the structure of the knowing subject: this is what makes them Idealists and followers of Kant. But Hegel understands the subject's structure as a unity of oppositions, a self-identity realized through otherness. For Fichte, on the other hand, the subject is simple, primary self-identity from beginning to end. An important consequence is that Fichte's knowing subject remains a fixed, indifferent, and external accompaniment to the process of its Knowing, whereas for Hegel, the subject itself evolves (is *gebildet*) through the process of its Knowing, and together with its object.

Merely distribute: The dominant relation in Fichte's system is subsumption, applying a unifying form from the outside. Hegel demands an *immanent* development. A uniform formula applied to material foreign to it provides a false and artificial systematization which, therefore, cannot properly ground the philosophical doctrine. Philosophical claims made within an artificially devised system are as arbitrary as claims made outside of any system.

Yet he [the holder of this view] asserts° with assurance that this monotony and abstract universality are the absolute; and that whoever is not satisfied with them indicates that he is incapable of mastering the absolute point of view and holding fast to it. In the past it used to be sufficient to indicate the empty possibility of representing something in a different way° in order to refute it; and this

Yet he . . . asserts: By "he" Hegel means Fichte's method, which reiterates a single formula in a nondialectical manner. Fichte started from the I as a Spinozistic absolute from which he proposes to deduce all the domains of being and knowledge. In a second step, the I posits its opposite, the not-I (being, the world, the object), against itself; and in order to avoid contradiction, both the I and the not-I limit themselves to their respective domains, so as to allow for coexistence between them. Fichte calls the third act a "synthesis," but Hegel argues it is an external juxtaposition of two foreign elements which remain unaffected by each other. A true synthesis requires the opposites to reside *within* and not just *alongside* one another. Fichte's three primary acts generate his supreme methodological formula, "thesis-antithesis-synthesis," which is repeated in all subsequent deductions. The synthesis becomes a new thesis, which in turn generates a new opposition, and so on. Hegel calls this method formalistic rather than dialectical, because the opposite terms do not penetrate one another, and because each is relegated to a different domain, instead of applying to the same domain. Thus, contradiction does not actually obtain in them, but is the "boundary between them." For Hegel, as we have seen, the architecture of philosophy must arise from the evolution of its content. And because the philosophical material *demands* contradiction as a positive and constructive principle, one cannot impose a preordained formula upon philosophy, certainly not a formula which obeys the law of noncontradiction.

Representing something in a different way: In formal logic and metaphysics— for example, in Leibniz—it is enough to conceive without contradiction that something, Y, can be different from what it is, in order to deny it necessity. Hegel oddly calls this a "refutation" (perhaps because philosophy demands necessity, so an opinion that cannot claim necessity loses its philosophical support). This formal approach to metaphysics is abstract and, therefore, inferior in Hegel's eyes, because it presupposes that contradiction is sufficient for something to be annulled, and that, more broadly, a merely formal test can dismiss the reality of something, without having to consider its nature and specific content.

sheer possibility, the general thought, even had the full positive value of actual knowledge. In the same way° we see that all value is attributed here to the general idea in its form of nonactuality, and the dissolution of what is differentiated and determined°—or rather, its casting away into the abyss of emptiness, with no further development or self-justification—is regarded as a *speculative mode of thinking.*° To consider some entity [*irgendein Dasein*]° as it is in the absolute means nothing else here than saying: "Although just now we have referred to it as something, yet in the absolute, in the A = A,° there is no such thing, but everything there is one." To set this single

In the same way: Similarly, there are contemporaries of Hegel holding that the mere idea of the absolute, without further distinctions and development, can provide actual and even supreme knowledge. Hegel's critique now returns to focus on Schelling and the romantics.

The dissolution of what is differentiated and determined: The dissolution of rational distinctions within the mystical experience of a shapeless absolute.

Speculative mode of thinking: This was a laudatory adjective in Hegel and his milieu. It did not indicate wild and baseless conjectures, as in ordinary speech today, but a higher kind of rationality which grasps actual reality (see the introduction). Derived from Latin *speculare*, "to see," "speculative" alludes to the Platonic *vision of ideas*, which stands above scientific understanding and attains true being. Indirectly and also polemically, this alludes to the notion of *intellectual intuition*. Kant construed intellectual intuition (which he denied man) as a methodological *structure*, by which one grasps the particular by thinking it is universal and vice versa; whereas Schelling understood intellectual intuition as a kind of spiritual vision, a privileged mental experience (which he did attribute to humans). Hegel agrees with Schelling that philosophy is capable of transcending the finite understanding and grasp the absolute, yet not through intellectual intuition understood as a mental experience, but rather through a science which, following Kant, translates the vague notion of intellectual intuition into *precise logical terms*. This is the sense in which Hegel takes his own philosophy to be truly "speculative" and Schelling's to be falsely speculative, in the bad sense of enthusiasm and *Schwärmerei*.

Irgendein Dasein: This phrase seems to be used here in ordinary German, not in its systematic Hegelian sense, so I translate it as "entity."

A = A: The famous Fichtean formula (adopted by Schelling) which indicated the directly identical nature of the I as absolute principle.

knowledge, that in the absolute everything is equal,° against a knowledge that is differentiated and fulfilled, or that seeks and requires fulfillment, or to construe one's absolute as the night in which, as the saying goes, all cows are black°—this is the naïveté of the void in knowledge. The formalism which modern philosophy condemns and despises is nevertheless reborn in its midst;° and although its insufficiency is well known and felt, it will not disappear from Science until the knowledge of absolute actuality makes its nature fully clear to itself.

Taking into account° that when a general notion precedes the attempt to work it out it makes that attempt easier to comprehend,

Equal: Lefebvre (Hegel, *Phénoménologie de l'Esprit*, translated by Jean-Pierre Lefebvre [Paris: Aubier; 1991], 37n3) notes that Hegel wished to avoid the word "identity" too closely associated with Schelling, so he used *gleich* and *Gleichheit*, which anyway are ineptly rendered as "identical."

All cows are black: The irony here is directed mainly at Schelling. The romantic experience claims to attain the absolute while obliterating all distinct particular existents and, therefore, fails to grasp anything actual: everything dissolves into a shapeless homogenous whirl. This kind of mysticism misses its own goals and provides empty exultation instead, an experience in which (a) nothing can be distinguished, criticized, or assessed, and which (b) has no actual being at its core. Schelling was deeply hurt by Hegel's sarcastic remarks and the breach between the two former friends was never healed.

Reborn in its midst: Hegel does not say that Fichte or Schelling are intentional formalists. Yet contrary to their stated intention, they fall back into formalism because they failed to coherently clarify to themselves the implications of their project—namely, to create an overall system based on an absolute principle. (This illustrates to Hegel the irony—and dialectic—of cultural history.)

Taking into account: In these seemingly innocent sentences, Hegel sets out to write his own philosophical preface after having explained why such a preface must be inadequate. A closer look at the text will show that Hegel considers the forthcoming preface to be "mere conversation" whose goal is didactic and *pre*philosophical. Although it lacks the value of genuine philosophical discourse, it may prepare the reader to philosophize by externally challenging some basic prejudices in her mind.

According to my way of seeing: *Einsicht* is often translated as "insight," but here it more plausibly means "way of seeing." This famous statement is so

it will be useful to give a rough outline of it here. Another intention is to remove on this occasion certain forms [of thinking] whose habitual use stands in the way of philosophical knowledge.

According to my way of seeing,° which must justify itself only through the exhibition of the system itself, everything depends on comprehending and expressing the true not as substance, but equally also as subject.° It should be also remarked that substantiality includes° the universality° or immediacy of knowing, no less

---

rich in systematic implications that we can only discuss some of them here; for fuller elaboration see the introduction ("The Absolute as Subject").

But equally . . . as subject: Viewing the true (the absolute) as subject does not abolish its being substance but adds a vital dimension to it. The addition has the structure of *Aufhebung*, in which the new form negates its predecessor's inadequate form but incorporates its essence within itself. Grasping the absolute as substance (as did Spinoza) and grasping it as subject (as did Fichte and Hegel himself—both following Kant and, theologically, following Christianity) are dialectically compatible moves. Still, the concept of subject is the higher one; it is constituted by the dialectical negation of the concept of substance while preserving its ground. Of course, this will change the meaning of the concept of subject. The synthesis of subject and substance generates a *new* concept of subject, a subject that has being, that has a substantive aspect (the subject/object); it is therefore distinguished from Kant's or Fichte's pure ego, which Hegel calls *"merely* subject."

Substantiality includes: To view substance (the ground of reality) also as subject implies that we have from the outset recognized the element of thought or knowledge as present in being. Earlier philosophers have recognized this in dim form: thought has appeared in the ground of being in a rudimentary, still undeveloped form, a latent potentiality which cannot be discovered before it starts actualizing itself. That is why premodern philosophy has been dominated by a one-sided view which takes substance to be a kind of "thing," a merely external object that only *faces* knowledge but contains no subjective ingredient in itself. To make progress in philosophy, Hegel says, one must—and in his own time, already can—grasp substance *itself* as entailing subjectivity, namely, as capable of development and eventually of self-consciousness. Note that in demanding that substance be recognized also as subject, Hegel does not impose an external meaning on the object but claims to discover the roots of the new meaning immanently within the object itself.

The universality: *Das Allgemeine*, here in the sense of generality, a "simple" or "immediate" universal.

than the immediacy which is being,° that is, which is immediacy
for knowing. If conceiving God as the single substance aroused
the indignation of the age° in which this definition was pronounced, this indignation was, on the one hand, due to the in-
stinctive [feeling] that self-consciousness was thereby not preserved,° but only submerged.° Yet on the other hand, the opposite

The immediacy which is being: This is the ordinary view. Substance is usually
taken to indicate the element of being, to which knowledge refers as
object. Hegel accepts this element as only a partial and one-sided moment
of substance. The Concept of substance includes the "immediacy"
(roughly, the being) of *both* domains, of knowledge as well as of the object.
Incidentally, Hegel uses the term "immediacy" to denote the element of
simplicity in general; as such, "immediacy" is more fundamental than
"being." Yet this fine distinction is often overlooked and Hegel uses
"being" and "immediacy" as equivalent.

The indignation of the age: An allusion to Spinoza's doctrine that God and
nature are one and the same substance. Hegel explains the furious reac-
tions to Spinoza's doctrine by the fact that it negated God's subjectivity,
his character as spirit. (Actually I think it was the *immanent* nature of
Spinoza's God—the denial of God's transcendent role as Creator—that
generated most of the hostility.) Accepting Spinoza's immanent view of
the absolute, Hegel demands that the absolute be interpreted also as
subject and spirit, and not only as substance or thing. Hegel's critique of
Spinoza is indeed helpful for understanding the famous statement in our
text; see Hegel's chapter on Spinoza in *Lectures on the History of Philosophy*
(translated by E. S. Haldane and Frances U. Simon [London: Routledge
and Kegan Paul, 1898], vol. 3, 253, et passim) and Hegel's remark on
Spinoza in *The Science of Logic* (ed. G. Lasson, vol. 2, 218); for an analysis
of these texts see my *Spinoza and Other Heretics*, vol. 2, chapter 2, "Spinoza
and Hegel: The Immanent God—Nature or Spirit?"

Not preserved: Spinoza rightly abolished the crude image of the absolute-
as-subject—namely, the image of an external God who created the world
by a special act of his will. Yet Spinoza was unable to provide the higher,
more valid philosophical interpretation of the absolute as self-consciousness. This required the work of German Idealism following Kant.

Submerged: In Spinoza, Hegel suggests, the element of self-consciousness
inherent in substance is being submerged and made to disappear. It only
persists as latent, abstract generality, hidden from Spinoza's eyes.

position,° which clings to thinking as thinking—to universality as such—is the same immediate, immovable, and undifferentiated substantiality. And when, in the third place,° thinking unites the being of substance with itself and conceives of immediacy, or intuition, as thinking—the important thing is still to know whether this intellectual intuition does not fall back into immovable simplicity, and does not present actuality itself in a nonactual manner.

Further, the living substance° is being which is truly subject, or—to say the same°—which is truly actual only in so far as it is a movement of self-positing,° or the mediation of itself with its

The opposite position: Fichte's construal of the pure subject as a substance-less "I think," which faces substance (the "not-I") externally. The Fichtean subject, like the Cartesian, is identical with itself through the pure and immediate act of thinking, independently of its relations to the "not-I."

In the third place: Hegel alludes to Schelling who tried to unify the I with substance by the power of intellectual intuition. This solution returned him to "inert simplicity," namely, to a subjectless substance. A subject entails a process whose unity is constituted by the various differences it generates, whereas in Schelling's intellectual intuition everything falls back and concentrates into the compact point of a semimystical experience.

The living substance: Life—the organic world—is the first manifestation of substance having "subjective" features. Even before substance attains self-consciousness, it manifests an organic movement of self-realization as described in the text. It is a dialectical movement in which substance exists through its own mediation, namely, becomes the "other" of itself and returns to itself as actual in and through this otherness.

To say the same: Saying that being is really a subject means it is actual only as a process of *self-actualization*. Hegel's idea is far-reaching: not only the *accidents* of substance, its particular states and modes, but *substantiality* itself undergoes development and actualization. Thereby, substantiality is a subject, a process of self-constitution which proceeds through negating itself and again negating the first negation.

Self-positing: The word "positing" (or setting, *Setzung*) originates in Kant, who used it to denote *an existential statement*, as distinguished from predication or the ascription of properties. In German Idealism, the term "to posit" means to set something as existing. In Fichte, the I posits itself, which implies that it is uncreated but is a kind of Spinozistic "cause of itself"; and it also posits the "not-I," or the world of objects

becoming-other. As subject, substance is pure simple negativity,° and precisely thereby it is the splitting of the simple in two, or an opposition-setting duplication which again is the negation of that indifferent difference and of its opposite: only this self-reconstituting identity° [*Gleichheit*], this self-reflection° in being-other°—

facing it. Though Hegel uses the same language, he argues that the subject—or I—does not exist as *direct* self-positing. A subject posits itself in a way that immediately undermines its simple identity and drives it to transcend itself toward a series of figures and modes of being distinguished from itself, which eventually it negates again and thereby returns to itself as concrete, actualized identity.

Negativity: A fundamental Hegelian idea that construes subjectivity as primarily a negative power: to be a subject is to transcend every partial, immediate identity, and to go beyond any given state. The subject is primarily this power of negation both with respect to itself and to its other. In Existentialist philosophy (Sartre), this negation adds up to a frustrating pursuit of stability which cannot attain its goal; in Hegel, on the contrary, it is capable of producing a stable positive result—not as inactive rest but as a *recurrent* activity, a constant cycle of negation and re-affirmation which follows a rational pattern. Negation and the negation-of-the-negation repeat themselves on higher levels of expression, and realize the latent conceptual structure at their base. Thus, the "subjective" process is teleological in Hegel as in Aristotle: the movement of transcendence and negation is guided by a latent final end, and eventually leads to its realization.

Self-reconstituting identity: This is the kind of identity characteristic of the subject. A subject reconstitutes its identity at the end of a process which is marked by otherness and contradiction. This pattern is the origin of dialectical logic, as the logic of actual being (see the introduction).

Self-reflection: A key term in Hegel's dialectical vocabulary, used according to need in one of two main senses: (a) something mirrored in something else, (b) something mirrored (or expressed) in *thought*. Hegel also distinguishes between external and internal reflection. In external reflection— a house reflected in a lake—the relation is accidental from the standpoint of both related terms. Internal reflection, however, is not simply mirroring but also mutual *mediation*, namely, a reciprocal relation which constitutes the being and the specific nature of each of the opposite terms. In addition, each term is reflected not in some straight double which mechanically reproduced its features, but in its opposite or *specific other*, whom it needs in order to become what it is. (Thus, correlates like "essence" and "appearance," "inner" and "outer" are "reflection Concepts.") According to Hegel, reflection can also exist in a substantive way without

and not some original unity as such, or an immediate thing° as such°—is the true. The true is the becoming of its own self,° the circle whose end is presupposed as its goal and constitutes its beginning, and which is actual only through its development and end.

---

consciousness. This is how a ground relates to its consequence, a cause to an effect, substance to accident, or internalization to externalization. Although they seem to be dualistic relations, actually each of the terms constitutes the other even if none is conscious of it. Another example: most individuals are unaware of the fundamental unity between themselves and their other—like the natural object or the social and political environment; however, the relation of reflection, as mutual mediation, exists between them *in itself*, that is, in a substantive or ontic manner, even though it does not exist *for* consciousness, which continues to view its other as alien to its essence and merely facing it. Thereby it has a flawed self-awareness, because its reflection as *consciousness* fails to adequately express the *ontic* reflection at its base. In order to overcome that flaw, the ontic mediation must be reflected also in consciousness, and thereby actualized. This occurs in concrete philosophical knowledge which enables me to grasp my self within the other, and grasp the other as a constitutive moment of my self. At that point, reflection as ontic mediation and reflection as consciousness are united. As for external reflection, it persists even at the top stage, as long as we merely "converse" or think about the world from the outside, and also when investigating the abstract aspects of the world, as in the formal and the empirical sciences.

In being-other: "Self-reflection in being-other" is perhaps Hegel's most succinct formulation of a dialectical relation. It includes everything we mentioned about the subject's pattern of existence and how dialectical logic—the logic of being—derives from that pattern. Although the dialectic cannot be squeezed into an a priori formula, when a short characterization is needed, we might prefer to speak of "self-reflection within otherness" instead of the problematic formula "thesis-antithesis-synthesis."

An immediate thing: Hegel usually avoids the word "thing" (*Ding*), which recalls Kant's "thing-in-itself"; but sometimes, as here, we may add it with no harm to the sense. On the other hand, Hegel likes turning adjective into nominative, which makes his style peculiar and requires some training in order to read it properly.

As such: Against philosophical realism, but also against the view that something can be immediately true or absolute. (Here Fichte, Jacobi, and of course Hölderlin are specifically meant.)

The true is the becoming of its own self: "It" in this phrase refers to "the true" (or absolute). Hegel stresses the teleological nature of the absolute

The life of God and divine knowledge may therefore be expressed as the play of love with itself.° [But] this idea descends to the level of edification° and even triteness when lacking the earnestness, the pain, the patience, and the work of the negative.° In itself, this life is the undisturbed identity and unity with itself, which fails

---

as subject. The system's purpose is immanent. It serves nothing but itself; the goal of its movement is the system itself as *actualized*. Therefore we can view the system as a circular process whose goal resides in its beginning, as an abstract essence which predefines its direction. The concrete subject is generated from that process as its result. Mediated by negation and otherness, it becomes actual only at the end of the road. (Strictly speaking, this is not a regular circle but a *spiral*, whose closing elevates it to a higher level.)

The play of love with itself: Dialectical logic—the absolute subject's form of being—is here metaphorically compared to love. This idea recurs in Hegel's thought from early on and is expressed more clearly at the end of the *Logic*. Love is the relation in which I rediscover myself within the other—*my own other*—and thereby actualize my existence. To love is to alienate or lose yourself in another, but thereby to regain and actualize your own life and selfhood. And this, as we have seen (here and in the introduction), is what a dialectical relation consists in. Love serves Hegel as an image of the fundamental relation governing the absolute subject, God, and reality at large. It is God's love for the world, his love for humans, and his love for himself through them, just as it is the human's love for God and love of himself through God. Hegel's dialectic thus translates an idea—cosmic love—which has come down in philosophy and mysticism since Plato (or at least since Plotinus), and can be found in Jewish Kabbala, Renaissance thinkers like Pico, Leone Ebreo, and Meister Eckhart, recurred in Spinoza, and was revived by Schelling and the young Hölderlin. Yet Hegel refuses to use the notion of love as a mental state or vague cosmic experience; he translates it into a *conceptual* pattern which becomes the basis of his dialectical logic. He also objects to interpreting love as the absolute's *direct* relation to itself, a kind of narcissistic play by God which is unrelated to the struggle and suffering of human history.

Descends to the level of edification: Compared with conceptual thinking, edification is a lower mental form. Instead of understanding, it offers a kind of enthusiastic sermonizing about the absolute which repeats one single idea or hazy feeling. Reason, however, must follow and laboriously decipher all the stages of the absolute subject's evolution.

to take seriously either being-other and self-alienation, or the over-coming of self-alienation.° This in-itself, however, is an abstract universality which overlooks the essential nature of this [God's] life° to be for itself°—and thus loses sight of the self-movement of the form in general [as pertaining to life]. When the form is pronounced to be identical to the essence, it would be misleading to conclude that, therefore, knowledge can be satisfied with the in-itself or essence, and spare itself the need to deal with the form—as if the absolute principle can dispense with being spelled out, and

The earnestness . . . of the negative: The term "the negative" indicates two ideas here: (a) God is identified with himself not immediately but through the negation of the negation, and (b) God is identified with himself through the mediation of human life and following a "laborious and patient" historical process, with all its human pain and suffering; therefore it is not a playful "disporting" but "earnestness." (Moreover, it makes of human history a kind of secularized "passion-tale"—of God becoming God through his becoming human and undergoing suffering.)

Self-alienation (*Entfremdung*): This key Hegelian concept makes its first appearance here. Alienation is a radical form of becoming other; it occurs when existence takes a form which not only opposes its essence (as a particular opposes the universal) but *impedes* and *falsifies* that essence (as in self-servitude, masked as freedom). It is sometimes difficult to distinguish alienation from ordinary otherness by their content, but ontologically they are distinct. Also, alienation is a temporary state which can in principle be overcome and abolished; whereas otherness is present at all stages, including the last, as a necessary moment mediating the self.

This [God's] life: The life of the absolute subject. From the narrow theological standpoint, Hegel alludes to God's dialectical necessity to exist as other than Himself, that is, as the world and as human history, with all the negativity and suffering they entail. (This also sketches a Hegelian solution of the problem of theodicy.) The pattern of alienation and its overcoming has, however, a much wider scope and is manifest in many other domains of Hegel's system (an organic creature, an individual person, a society, a historical era, and so forth).

To be for itself: To exist for self-reflection and have a distinct singularity as subject. And that also means to move oneself by negating and transcending one's primary essence, to undergo alienation, overcome it, and return to oneself as actual.

absolute intuition makes its development superfluous. Precisely because the form is as essential to the essence as the essence is to itself, the latter must be grasped and expressed not merely as essence—that is, as immediate substance—but equally as form, with all the richness of the developed form. Only thereby is the essence grasped and expressed as actual.

The true is the whole.° Yet the whole is but the essence which brings itself to fulfillment° through its development. Of the absolute it must be said that it is essentially a result, that only at the end is the absolute what it is in truth; and herein consists its nature—to be actual, subject, or becoming-its-own-self° [*sichselbstwerden*]. However contradictory it may appear to conceive the absolute as essentially a result, a slight consideration will suffice to redress this apparent contradiction. The beginning, the principle, or the absolute, however it is called immediately and at first, is only the universal.° When I say "all animals," the word does not count as zoology; and just as little can words such as "divine," "absolute," "eternal," and the like express what they contain;° yet only in such words is [intellectual]

The true is the whole: A major dictum in our text. Together with the epigram "the absolute . . . is essentially a result," it complements the idea of the absolute as subject. (For a fuller explication, see the introduction.)

Fulfillment (*Sichvollendende*): Driving itself both to perfection and to plenitude.

Subject, or becoming-its-own-self: Viewing the absolute as subject entails that it is a becoming-itself (*Sichselbstwerden*; see the introduction). The absolute has brought itself into perfection through its evolution, and so is a result.

Only the universal: In the sense of merely universal—undeveloped universality.

Express what they contain: The ideas that "the true is the whole" and that it is a subject are here applied to the theory of language. Linguistic expressions that do nothing more than denote an object actually miss it. Therefore one cannot construct an adequate philosophical discourse by aggregating singular indicative expressions. In philosophy, every expression points beyond itself towards a whole context which the reader must first actually traverse in order to grasp the meaning of the original expression. Putting it somewhat more loosely: behind any such expression, there is a whole story without which it cannot be understood. The unit of discourse which is adequate for philosophy must therefore transcend indica-

intuition expressed as the immediate. Anything that contains more than such a word, be it even the transition to a sentence, entails a becoming-other that must be taken back, and is [thereby] mediation.° And this is what provokes indignation° [in those believing the divine is immediate], as if we forsake absolute Knowing when we

---

tive expressions and convey the whole story behind them in a holistic and evolutionary manner; and it must weave these expressions into the story so that each is formed and becomes significant in its proper place. This explains (a) the narrative background of the *Phenomenology* (and on a more abstract level, also that of the *Logic*), and (b) Hegel's tendency, which gives his readers so much trouble, to use as his basic unit of discourse not the single sentence but larger blocks of text—the paragraph, or even a whole chapter—which he also often forces into loops, so as to provide more context and dialectical reversals.

And is [thereby] mediation (*Vermittlung*): Even when trying to express a philosophical truth in the inadequate form of a single subject/predicate sentence, we must go beyond the subject and say something else about it in order to start explicating that subject. Thereby, Hegel believes, the subject "becomes other" within the predicative form of discourse. As predication gets richer, the subject is further transformed into new states of "otherness"; yet throughout all these "others" (the predicates), the same subject is implicitly referred to, and in the end, we return to it explicitly as something developed and more complex. To take an abbreviated example: in a sentence or definition like "man is a thinking animal," the first predication says that man is an animal—that is, "makes him into another." The second predication then says he is an animal of a special kind, to which only the human race corresponds, and thereby returns the subject to itself, now in a more developed and concrete manner than in the original expression, "man." One may wonder if Hegel is not confusing two functions of the copula ("is"), ascribing a property and affirming existence. In any case, by invoking the predicative sentence which he usually dismisses as inadequate for philosophy, Hegel makes an a fortiori ("even more so") argument: the relation of "mediation and becoming-other" is so fundamental that even the lower form of discourse cannot rid itself of it.

Indignation: The "indignation" was shared by romantics and those who regard the law of noncontradiction as supreme. The former reject *any* rational reflection, any mediation whatsoever by thought, because they attribute something positive to mediation, rather than merely [saying] that it has nothing absolute and is not in the absolute.

Actually, the indignation derives from lack of familiarity with the nature of mediation and of absolute Knowing itself. Mediation is nothing but the self-identity which moves itself; in other words, it is reflection into itself [*in sich selbst*], the moment of the I° as being-for-itself, pure negativity, or—when reduced to its pure abstraction—it is simple becoming.° The I or becoming in general, this activity of mediation, is, on account of its simplicity, precisely the immediacy-that-becomes° [*die werdende Unmittelbarkeit*] and the im-

---

consider logical thinking extraneous to the absolute and as alienating its nature; whereas the latter do require mediation by thought, but only of an analytic and not a dialectical style.

The reflection into itself, the moment of the I: This sentence demonstrates the inner link Hegel establishes between the concepts self-reflection, being-for-itself, I, and negativity. They are all different aspects of the subject, as a system moved by self-negation and marked by an inner split.

Simple becoming: The most abstract model of self-mediation or becoming. Unlike Plato, Hegel does not consider the category of becoming as excluding being. Becoming entails being and is necessarily derived from it. An attempt to think being makes clear it is not as simple and immediate as it seems at first. Being entails self-mediation, and therefore splitting and self-motion, and appears at first as a merely general and abstract category, namely, as "immediate."

The immediacy-that-becomes: Insofar as becoming (or the I which stands for it) is at first only simple and immediate, there is no difference between it and being. Initially, therefore, becoming and being have the same character. This may seem a forced or scholastic quibbling, but it should be noted: (a) Hegel has no other concept by which to designate the element of being or existence (as opposed to knowledge or spirit) except "immediacy." Words like "matter," "fact," "datum," or "spatiotemporal perception" will not do, because they indicate items in whose constitution some categories of the knowing mind are *already* at work; (b) at the same time, there is no *absolute* immediacy in Hegel—everything in the world has a certain degree of mediacy; and (c) immediacy in the minimal (or crudest) sense exists in the domain of spirit itself: Hegel calls it "the pure I," or "simple becoming." This will help Hegel argue later that spirit has a dimension of being, just as substance has a dimension of subject or spirit.

mediate itself.° One therefore misconstrues reason by excluding reflection from the [domain] of the true and not grasping it as a positive moment of the absolute.° It is reflection which makes the true into a result, but it also sublates the opposition° between the true and its becoming. For this becoming is equally simple,° and hence is undistinguished from the form of the true, which consists in presenting itself in the result as something simple; indeed, the becoming is precisely this being returned to simplicity. Although the embryo is in-itself a man, it is not so for-itself; for-itself, it is a man only as a formed reason which has made itself into what it is in-itself. This alone is its actuality. Yet the result is itself simple immediacy, for it is a self-conscious freedom at rest within itself, which did not push the opposition to the side and let it lie there, but is reconciled with it.° We can also express the above by saying

And the immediate itself: Simple becoming is, in that respect, being itself.

A positive moment of the absolute: This again directly opposes Hölderlin (and Jacobi, among others).

Sublates the opposition: Hegel rarely uses the term "antithesis" which is more central in Kant and Fichte.

This becoming is equally simple: Despite its complexity, the result of the process is compressed in a person's consciousness into a quasi-simple state, which a new person, generation, or era can experience *as if* it were immediate. In other words, they will experience it in the mode of plenitude and primary identification, free of the alienation and splits of identity which occurred while the process was going on. Hegel's use of the word "simple" should be taken with caution. Actually he means an elaborate process which, for the person who has undergone it, has crystallized into something *seemingly* simple. This should not be confused with the undialectical concept of "second naïveté," which is far from Hegel's mind.

Is reconciled with it: The reconciliation overcomes the contradictions and alienations that had characterized the former stages. (This is what "simple" in the previous note means.) The individual can now experience the result of the historical process in direct, simple, and harmonious identification with it. For instance, feeling herself free within society and the world, she can enjoy this sense directly, almost as self-evident, without needing to live again through the pains and contradictions of the historical past which led to this result and are embodied in it. But that direct experience lacks self-knowledge. The reconciliation cannot be under-

that reason is a purposive activity.° Those who elevated pseudo-nature° over and above misconceived thinking, and, in particular, those who banned external teleology, have brought the form of purpose in general to disrepute.° Yet, even as Aristotle says in defining nature as teleological activity, the purpose is the immediate, the resting, the immovable which is itself a mover; and so it is subject.° Its power to engender movement, taken in the abstract, is being-for-itself or pure negativity. The result is the same as the beginning only because the beginning is purpose,° or [in other words], the actual and its Concept are the same only because the immediate, as purpose, holds in itself the self or pure actuality. The

---

stood without deciphering the former dialectical conflicts and bringing them to light.

A purposive activity: Hegel means internal purposiveness, the movement he called "becoming-oneself," or the "circle that presupposes its end, as its goal."

Pseudo-nature: *Vermeint*; I follow Lefebvre's suggestion here.

Have brought . . . to disrepute: Following Leibniz (and Kant in his way), Hegel wants to rehabilitate the concept of teleology which modern mechanistic science has rejected. As precondition, he must first reject the superstitious kind of teleology (the idea that an entity or event A exists in order to serve an entity or event B), and allow only internal or immanent purposiveness. The latter is the subject's mode of being; it is realized in the organic world, in history, in culture and society, and in the pattern of absolute spirit.

And so it is subject: Though Hegel claims Aristotle as his source, in fact they differ. In Aristotle, the purpose as unmoved mover is fixed and motionless; it moves all other things by being the focus of their aspiration (*orexis*). Not so in Hegel: the subject is not a motionless purpose but a whole teleological system, including its movement. One cannot therefore agree with Hegel that Aristotle's unmoved mover had already been a kind of subject. It certainly had been an intellectual activity (as *nous* and *noein*) but not a subject in the Hegelian sense.

The beginning is purpose: In a subject-like teleological system, the purpose is given at the beginning as abstract and recurs at the end as actualized. It is therefore a circular-spiral system, "having its end also as its beginning," because the purpose is given both at the outset (abstractly) and at the end-result (as actualized).

realized purpose, or the existing actual [*das daseiende Wirkliche*], is movement and unfolded becoming; but this unrest is precisely the Self. And the reason why the Self is the same as that simplicity and immediacy of the beginning is that it is the result, that which returned into itself; and that which returned into itself° is precisely the Self, and the Self is self-relating identity and immediacy.

The need to represent the absolute as subject uses propositions° like: God is the eternal, or [God is] the moral world-order, or [God is] love, and so forth. In such propositions° the true is posited as subject in a merely direct way,° but is not presented as the move-

That which returned into itself: Selfhood is attained as "return-to-self." Yet this is a return to one's *own* self. What has been actualized at the end is not something new or foreign but the system's own latent identity and purpose.

Uses propositions: At this point, Hegel launches a critical discussion of philo-sophical language and its limitations. He is about to criticize the predica-tive sentence ("S is P" or "S is PQR") which links diverse predicates to a fixed subject in a unilateral way, making the predicates depend upon the subject but not vice versa. This common grammatical subject does not suit the *philosophical* Concept of subject as explicated above. Ordinary grammar is incongruent with the needs of philosophy.

In such propositions: When philosophers say, "God is the eternal Being," or "God is the moral world-order," or, in general, "God is P," they are trying to capture and express the ontological subject, being-as-subject, by a grammatical subject which is incongruent with it. For in ordinary lan-guage, the subject-term is taken to be immediately identical with itself regardless of its predicates and not depending on them; it therefore lacks "reflection within itself" and cannot count as subject in the philosophical sense. In order to express the philosophical subject, the grammatical sub-ject must be a complex construct, derived from the mutual relation—and dialectical movement—between all its predicates. Yet ordinary predicative language is incapable of performing this move, which goes against (a) ordinary syntax, (b) the law of contradiction, and (c) the unidirectional nature of speech and writing. It is therefore a form of discourse unfit for philosophical truth.

A merely direct way: In such discourse, only the predicates have some infor-mative value, whereas the expression of the grammatical subject seems superfluous.

ment of that which reflects itself in itself. In this kind of proposition
one starts with the word "God." In itself, this is a senseless sound,
a mere name. Only the predicate says what it is, and is its filling
and meaning;° only in this end does the empty beginning become
actual knowing. In this respect one may wonder why people should
not speak of the meaning only (of the eternal, the moral world
order, etc.) or, in the manner of the ancients, of pure Concepts (like
Being, the One, etc.) without adding the senseless sound. This
word [God] serves indeed to indicate that what is posited is not a
being or an essence or something merely general, but is something
reflected in itself°—a subject.

Yet this is only anticipated.° The subject is taken here as a rigid
point, to which the predicates, as to their support, are attached by
a movement which belongs to the one who knows° about the subject, but which cannot count° as belonging to the point itself; yet

---

Its filling and meaning: I use "meaning" for *Bedeutung*, since Hegel did not
mean "reference" in its Fregean sense here.

Something reflected in itself: Retracting his fast dismissal of "the senseless
sound," Hegel now admits that the word "God" does have some informa-
tive value, for it alludes to an entity with self-reflection rather than to
mere being.

Yet this is only anticipated: It is only as an embryonic hint that the absolute
is here understood as subject. Also, the idea takes a form that contradicts
its content and impedes its execution. This is because the subject is still
understood as a finished unit rather than as a movement which constitutes the subject by its particularization into predicates and by their mutual relations.

The one who knows: In ordinary philosophical discourse, the predicates are
linked to their subject by an external agent—namely, the knowing subject,
the mind of the person who studies and investigates the matter; it is she
who, as in Kant's Metaphysical Deduction, ascribes the predicates to the
subject from the outside. Therefore the movement of thought is here external to the matter itself; in Hegel's idiom, it is "an external reflection."

But which cannot count: Ordinary language forces us to use predicative
propositions in philosophy, and thereby veils the subject-like nature of
reality from us. This produces a problem for Hegel which elsewhere I
have called "the antinomy of language" (that is, of philosophical language;

only through this movement would the content be presented as subject. The way in which the movement is here obtained° prevents its belonging to the fixed subject of the content; yet having presupposed that point, the movement cannot be obtained differently, and can only be external. This anticipation—that the absolute is subject—is therefore not only not the actuality of that Concept, but

---

see Yirmiyahu Yovel, "Reason, Actuality, and Philosophical Discourse in Hegel" [Heb.], *Iyyun* 26 [1975]: 59–115; see also Menahem Rosen, *Problems of Hegelian Dialectic* [Dordrecht: Kluwer, 1992], part 5.) On the one hand, ordinary, historical language is predicative by nature and therefore unfit for philosophy; on the other hand, philosophy is the conceptualization of real life, practice, and culture, and must arise from the historical modes of our discourse. Hegel is barred from turning to the language of poetry in the manner of Heidegger or Hölderlin, since philosophy is concerned with the Concept; and he ought not invent a separate, artificial language for philosophy because philosophy must arise from its own history and that of our social, cultural, and linguistic practices. Result: what is necessary from one standpoint of the Hegelian system (his logic of discourse) is impossible and impermissible from another Hegelian standpoint. Furthermore, this contradiction seems to be irreconcilable. Evidently recognizing the problem, Hegel alludes later in the text to a "speculative proposition" which is supposed to replace the predicative proposition, but he sheds little light on that enigmatic idea. In the end, the only effective way Hegel copes with the problem is pragmatic: he uses a mode of writing whose basic unit is not the single sentence but the whole paragraph, the section, even whole chapters, and which include many "loops" and special expositions. These broader units of discourse allow Hegel to partly overcome the predicative nature of the sentence, to maintain a back-and-forth movement between the various ingredients, go from one issue to its opposite aspects and return to it from a new angle, and so forth. This can explain the notorious difficulties of Hegel's style, and the often awkward, back-and-forth movement characteristic of the *Phenomenology* and the *Logic*. (It should be clear, however, that the antinomy affects only the language of strict philosophy. There is no antinomy regarding the natural social discourse, which, as a basic practico-theoretical activity, is an ingredient in the constitution of the self—or regarding the language of the formal and empirical sciences.)

Obtained (*Beschafft*): Here meaning "figured out," "constituted."

even makes it impossible. For it posits the subject as a point at rest, when the subject's actuality is self-movement.

Among the many consequences which follow from what we have said, let me emphasize the following in particular: [first], that knowing is actual and can be presented only as Science, or as system.° Further, that in philosophy, a so-called principle or basic proposition, if it is true, is on that account also already false,° so far as it is only a principle or basic proposition. Therefore it can be easily refuted. The refutation consists in showing its deficiency, which lies in its being only general or a principle, in its being a beginning. When the refutation is fundamental, it is drawn and developed from the principle itself,° and is not contrived externally, through

As science, or as system: In the idiom of German idealism "Science" does not denote any special discipline (like physics) but a certain epistemic level—that of complete, accomplished truth (*epistēmē*). For Kant, Fichte, and Hegel, Science and system are equivalent. A necessary and sufficient condition for philosophy to rise to the level of Science is that it should be formed as a complete system—that is, as the original totality of its ingredients. Yet the three philosophers differ on the shape and order of that system: Kant and Fichte start from a fundamental principle which they take to be true without qualification from the outset, and see the rest as deriving unilaterally from it. But this, in Hegel's eyes, commits his two predecessors to the same philosophical fallacy he analyzed in the predicative proposition.

Is . . . already false: If truth exists only as a complete system, then as long as the system's grounding principle stays undeveloped, it is also false. It is thus vulnerable to criticism and refutation, because it has not been grounded in all its opposing aspects. To actually ground the principle, we have to refute every partial aspect of it which pretends to be exclusive. In the end, only the fully developed system will maintain the claim of truth, whereas its partial developments will find their place within it as "moments."

It is drawn and developed from the principle itself: A dialectical refutation of philosophical doctrines does not destroy what it criticizes, but develops and complements it; its act of negation becomes a positive layer in building the system of truth. As a first condition, such refutation must be immanent, that is, performed in terms of the criticized principle itself rather than thrust against it as an external assertion ("mere assurance").

opposite assertions and flashes of ideas. The refutation is in fact the principle's development and the fulfillment of its deficiency, provided that it does not misconceive itself by paying attention to its negative activity only, but takes notice of the positive side of its progress and result.°

On the other hand, the beginning's positive development is at the same time a negative relation toward it, that is, toward its one-sided form, [which consists in] being only immediate or in being a purpose. Hence it can also be taken as the refutation of the first principle which constitutes the system's foundation; but it is more appropriate to see it as indicating that the system's foundation or principle is, in fact, only its beginning.

That the true is actual only as system, or that substance is essentially subject, is expressed in the notion which pronounces the absolute to be spirit:° this is the most sublime Concept, a Concept

---

A dialectical refutation actually completes the criticized principle, because it solves a specific problem, or fulfills some definite lack that it has identified in it; thus it enriches and further develops the principle it refutes. That process will continue as long as the principle has not been fully developed, that is, until the series of its possible immanent refutations is exhausted.

Takes notice . . . of its progress and result: Hegel's description fits the *history* of philosophy and the construction of the pure *system* of philosophy; but the relevant state of consciousness is different in each case. A philosopher refuting his predecessor (like Aristotle vs. Plato, a Stoic against an Epicurean, or Locke vs. Descartes) is unaware of the dialectical complementarity which exists between them. All he sees is an irreconcilable opposition between himself and his opponent. In retrospect, however, when constructing the pure system of knowledge, the philosopher's mind (like Hegel's in writing the *Phenomenology*) must already be aware that every negation is immanent determination, and every position which he negates and transcends is preserved in the system's positive texture and adds further to it.

Pronounces the absolute to be spirit: This further explicates the idea that the absolute is subject and expresses the historical (and not the merely evolutional) nature of the absolute. Hegel's concept of spirit comprises both "objective spirit," the world of social and political institutions, and

which belongs to the modern era and its religion.° The spiritual alone is the actual: it is [1] the essence, or that which is-in-itself; [2] that which relates itself and becomes determined—a being-other and being-for-itself; [3] that which, in its determinateness, remains within itself: in other words, the spiritual is in-and-for-itself.°

At first, however, its being in-and-for-itself is so only for us, or in itself;° it is the spiritual substance.° The spiritual must yet be

---

the higher "absolute spirit" which includes art, religion, and philosophy, in which a given culture or period expresses (and justifies) itself in its reflective mental products.

The modern era and its religion: The idea that true actuality ("the absolute") is spirit rather than substance entails the principle of idealism, which Hegel sees as defining the modern era. In this respect, Spinoza was only a premodern philosopher. Genuine Modernity, according to Hegel, did not arise with the Renaissance or the seventeenth century, but with the appearance of German Idealism, first in Kant's limited form marked by finitude, and then in Hegel's more comprehensive form of Idealism, which sets the ground for reconciling modern philosophy with religion, and, thereby, for creating a theory of the absolute.

In-and-for-itself (an und für sich): This expression usually indicates in Hegel the mode of being in which a system or an individual has realized its essence through its other and returned to itself as actual. Thereby it has become fully autonomous, or free. It now possesses both a dimension of being ("in-itself") and a dimension of reflection ("for-itself") which mutually mediate one another. Because nothing external limits that system or that individual anymore, it has been fully realized as free or self-sufficient. From a metaphysical standpoint, this freedom entails idealism. At our present point it the text, Hegel, again criticizing Spinoza, identifies the in-and-for-itself with spirit or spirituality in general. Spinoza was wrong in believing substance to be free or self-sufficient ("cause of itself"); only a spiritual principle can be that. At first, however, the spiritual principle itself appears as a kind of "spiritual substance"—namely, in abstract or self-alienated form and therefore as not-yet-free. (See "spiritual substance," on the next page.)

For us, or in itself: A common expression in the *Phenomenology*. The experiences and adventures of consciousness—the protagonist of the story—are described in this book from the standpoint of the *experiencing* consciousness as it is involved with and immersed within the process. But

spiritual for itself too, it must be knowledge of the spiritual and knowledge of itself as spirit. This means that spirit must be an object to itself, but at once a sublated object, which is reflected in itself. Spirit is for-itself only for us, in so far as its spiritual content is generated by itself; but insofar as it is for-itself also for itself, then this self-generation,° the pure Concept,° is also the

---

the *Phenomenology* also takes a second standpoint—that of *our* consciousness, of the philosophers who observe and study the experiencing consciousness and its evolution from the vantage-point of the final result, of which "we" are already aware. That which for the experiencing consciousness is only latent or potential ("in-itself") is already manifest to the investigating consciousness ("for-us"). Hence, the equivalence in Hegel's usage between the two expressions: "in-itself" and "for-us." What something is in itself, it is also for us, though not for itself: we know something about it that it does not.

Spiritual substance: The essence of spirit is to be free and self-sufficient in the sense described above; yet at the outset, the principle of spirit still appears as a kind of substance. The substantive form of spirituality shows itself in the immediate ways in which people live, act, and relate to each other and to nature; it is embodied in their forms of work, discourse, intercourse, and conflict, in their social customs and political institutions. Yet it lacks self-reflection: people *live it*, but are not aware of its actual nature. Therefore its subjective dimension is not yet realized: it is *spirit in the form of a substance*. This dialectical opposition between content and form creates a flaw which helps drive the process further. Spirit has existed in that substantive form in most historical periods, though to different degrees; whereas the modern era signifies for Hegel that true being has become spiritual "for-itself"; namely, it is aware of its spirituality through an explicit philosophical system. This is a true revolution which started with Kant's Idealist philosophy and the historical situation from which it matured.

Self-generation: Idealism provides a more adequate interpretation of Spinoza's notion of "cause of itself": overall reality derives from its own resource. It is self-generated both as object (or being) and as subject (or reflection). These two aspects—reflection and being, concept and existence—belong to each other in the context of one whole.

The pure Concept: This refers to the subjective aspect of the absolute which includes self-motion and self-generation. In the *Logic* (the part called "The

object-element [*das gegenständliche*] in which spirit has its existence; and in this way, in its existence, spirit is for-itself a self-reflecting object. The spirit which, thus developed, knows itself° as spirit is Science.° Science is its actuality, and the realm it builds itself in its own element.

Pure self-knowledge in absolute being-other, this ether° as such, is the foundation and territory of Science, or is knowing in general. The beginning of philosophy presupposes or demands that consciousness reside in this element. But this element acquires its completion and transparency only through the movement of its becoming. It is pure spirituality, as a universal in the mode of simple immediacy.° This simple, which, as simple, has existence, is the soil

---

Subjective Logic") Hegel draws a parallel between the structure of the "Concept" and the structure of the "I think." Both exist as self-particularizing universals, that is, as a dialectical self-engendering unity of universality and particularity. Hence the subjective interpretation that should be given to expressions like "the Concept in general" or "the pure Concept."

Knows itself (from *Selbsterkennen, in the sense of self-recognition): I recognize myself in the way one recognizes someone known in the past.*

Science: The final system of philosophy. Spirit, in the course of its evolution, undergoes several degrees of *partial* self-consciousness—either because it becomes aware of itself through the less-than-adequate medium of religious and artistic images, or because its adequate medium—philosophy, the Concept—has not yet evolved into a fully coherent and explicit state. When the final system of philosophy arises, spirit becomes conscious of itself as it is in truth, a reflection that has also an objective side, a side of being. This is the moment of idealism in philosophy. It then resides in its own element, its genuine environment, as when one says that the element of fish is water.

Ether: Hegel picks the metaphor of ether to characterize the "element" of knowledge, because ether had traditionally been considered the purest, most transparent and "minimally corporeal" body, yet a real being, one of the elements of the universe.

Simple immediacy: As mentioned, the only way Hegel believes he can explicate being is by such notions as "immediacy." What characterized being is its being posited immediately, barring reduction to anything else. Since this is how spirit, too, appears at first, spirit, too, has being; it is a real form of existence and not a lofty abstraction.

[*Boden*]: it is the thinking which has its being only in spirit. Since this element, this immediacy of spirit, is spirit's substantiality in general, it is the transfigured essentiality; the reflection which is itself simple;° the immediacy which, as such, is for itself; it is being which is, in itself, reflection. Science requires that self-consciousness, by its own agency, be already elevated to this ether, so it can live—and will live—with and within it. But from the opposite side,° the individual has a right to demand of Science that it give him at least the ladder° by which to access that standpoint—and that it point out [that ladder] within the individual himself. The individual's right is grounded in his absolute independence, which he knows he possesses in every shape which his knowledge assumes.°

The reflection which is itself simple: This and the following two phrases are further attempts to say that reflection has an aspect of being, and that being is of itself reflection.

From the opposite side: At this point, Hegel starts a discussion explaining another major role of the *Phenomenology*. The individual person cannot be expected to get out of himself and embrace an absolute truth which to him is foreign and in which he cannot recognize his own self. Rather, philosophy must start with the individual as s/he is, responding to the particular individual's demands and state of consciousness *as* individual. This is Kierkegaard's objection to Hegel which Hegel here recognizes as valid (see the introduction). Hegel also accepts Descartes' demand that philosophy start with the individual's subjective state of certainty. Yet, unlike Descartes (and following Kant), Hegel shows that the "I think" is neither primary nor simple. There are different levels of consciousness and self-consciousness making one another possible, which the experiencing consciousness—the protagonist of the *Phenomenology*—will traverse as its *own* states of consciousness. This is why the *Phenomenology* must not be written as abstract theory but as a kind of existential experiment, as if describing the adventures and experiences of some real (though universal) mind capable of using the first person.

The ladder: This ladder is the *Phenomenology.*

In every shape which his knowledge assumes: The process we are going to reconstruct will therefore be the individual's own process of evolution: At every stage, his knowledge and self-knowledge will take a different form; but he, as individual, will persist in all of them and attain subjective satisfaction according to the conditions of every given stage. And just as

For in each of these shapes, whatever its content, and whether or not it is recognized by Science, the individual is the absolute form, namely, the immediate certainty of himself,° and thereby (if someone prefers this phrase) he is unconditioned being.

The standpoint of consciousness° is to know the object-like [*gegenständlich*] things as standing opposite it, and to know itself as

---

the higher standpoint implicit in the new stage will become the individual's own standpoint, so the lack or flaw affecting that stage will also be experienced by the individual as his own deficiency. This will drive him to continue searching for the specific standpoint that would respond to the particular successive flaws he experiences. In that way, reliance on the individual's mind is a necessary condition for the overall spirit's evolution.

The immediate certainty of himself: Unlike Descartes, the experience of certainty (*Gewissheit*) has only subjective value for Hegel. "Certainty" stands in opposition to "truth." Certainty is the illusion of complete simplicity and lack of mediation, whereas truth requires that everything be mediated by everything else. Certainty therefore stands at the starting point of the *Phenomenology* whereas truth emerges at its end. The individual subject begins by knowing herself in the primitive form of "certainty" and ends as the consciousness of herself in the developed universalized state of "truth." This entails that the subject knows and recognizes his self through the complete system of philosophy, and through those natural and social configurations which embody—and partly also alienate—his essential selfhood, and from which the subject reconstitutes itself as actualized spirit. In every case, the subject, the self, remains at the center while its content and modalities change as it reaches toward more complex and universal levels of self-consciousness.

The standpoint of consciousness: This phrase, in the strict (and narrow) sense of "consciousness," which is distinct from "self-consciousness" and "reason," is a recurring systematic term in Hegel. It means the standpoint of dualism, the severance between man and world, subject and object. Dualism is inherent in the way the ordinary person ("natural consciousness") experiences the world as self-evident; on a higher level, dualism characterizes the scientific and philosophical consciousness at the stage of the "understanding." All of these standpoints accept the severance of consciousness from its objects as self-evident. But for a philosophically formed mind taking the standpoint of "reason," dualism is false. It is the other of spirit in which spirit is lost. Each side thus experiences the other's

standing opposite them. For Science, however, this standpoint is the other; and the state in which consciousness knows itself to be by itself is to Science the loss of spirit. To consciousness, on the other hand, the element of Science is something remote and lying beyond, in which it no longer possesses itself. Each of these sides appears to the other as the reversal of truth. In entrusting itself directly to Science, natural consciousness, drawn by something it does not know, attempts for once to walk on its head.° And the compulsion to take this unfamiliar posture and move in it is a needless and unprepared for violence° which natural consciousness is expected to do to itself. Science can be what it may in itself; in relation to immediate self-consciousness it presents itself as being upside down.° In other words, since immediate self-consciousness has its principle of actuality° in self-certainty, Science has the form of nonactuality as long as

---

standpoint as utterly alien, distant, and impossible, a position which it cannot adopt without self-betrayal and self-deception. The role of the *Phenomenology,* as said before, is to offer the "ladder" by which one can pass from the standpoint of natural consciousness to that of speculative philosophy by way of self-*realization* rather than self-*betrayal.*

To walk on its head: This is what the ordinary person feels when agreeing to philosophize, and what the philosopher of the "understanding" (or "consciousness") feels when experiencing the philosophy of dialectical reason. Hegel in this passage shows comprehension for the gap and strangeness separating philosophy from ordinary life, and from ordinary discursive science, too. (The image of "walking on the head" has served Marx's polemics against Hegel's.)

Unprepared for violence: A rational standpoint might land on a person as a violent imposition from the outside if she has not evolved toward it gradually out of herself. Hegel seems to aim this criticism against the Enlightenment, whose radical rationalism led to violence—not only mental and intellectual, but physical violence—in the name of reason.

Being upside down (verkehrt): The idea here is stronger than a mere "reversal": it is a world which looks completely out of order.

Self-consciousness has its principle of actuality: The actuality of self-consciousness lies in the certainty it has of itself, without which it would lose itself and disperse. One cannot therefore reach the standpoint of philosophical Science by provoking a violent rupture between consciousness and itself, namely, by losing self-certainty. Without the subjective

this principle stands for itself outside Science. Hence, Science must unite this element with itself, or rather, it must show that—and how—this element belongs to it. In lacking that actuality, Science is but the content as in-itself,° the purpose which is still only in-wardness—not spirit, but a spiritual substance. This in-itself must exteriorize itself and become for-itself; which means it must posit self-consciousness as one with itself.°

This becoming of Science in general, or the becoming of Know-ing [*Wissen*],° is what this phenomenology of spirit presents. Know-ing as it is at the outset, immediate spirit, is the spiritless: sensible consciousness. In order to become actual Knowing, or to generate the element of Science which is its pure Concept, that conscious-ness must work its way through a long road. That process of be-coming, as it will constitute itself [*aufstellen*] in the shapes and con-

---

experience of conviction, philosophical Science will lack actuality and be abstract, empty talk. One must therefore combine Science and self-certainty; and since at first they contradict each other, we need a gradual bridging between them in the form of the *Phenomenology.*

The content as in-itself: This refers to the content of truth given dogmati-cally, as dead philosophical doctrine, in which the subjective mind cannot recognize itself. Such doctrine, even when it has an inherent ground, is a mere in-itself, an end that has not been realized by existing consciousness. Therefore, we may regard it neither as spiritual, nor as actually rational, but only as a spiritual *substance* in the sense described above. (Ironically, this is how some of Hegel's later writings, like the *Encyclopaedia*, might look from the viewpoint of the *Phenomenology.*)

One with itself: What is required is not only that self-consciousness recog-nize truth as the content of philosophical science, but that it identify and recognize *itself* within it; so that philosophical science will be formed as a form of self-consciousness (and self recognition). In its attempt to grasp being, philosophy thus discovers that it has actually understood con-sciousness itself. This discovery leads to philosophical self-conscious-ness—Hegel's brand of idealism—which, in comprehending being, also comprehends the constitutive role of knowledge within being.

Knowing [*Wissen*]: A cognitive attitude distinguished both from sheer faith (*glauben*) and from active behavior (*praxis, handeln*). Actually, however, by *Wissen* Hegel understands not only rational science proper, but also opinions, myths, and practical attitudes.

tents which are to show themselves in it, will be different from one's image° of an introduction by which a nonscientific conscious-ness enters into Science; and, in particular, will differ from that enthusiasm° which, as in a gunshot, starts immediately with the absolute and is finished with other points of view by simply declar-ing that it will take no notice of them.

The task of guiding the individual from his uncultured stand-point to Knowing had to be taken in its universal sense;° that is, we had to consider the universal individual—self-conscious spirit°—in its cultural education [*Bildung*].° The relation between these two is

That process . . . will be different from one's image: The *Phenomenology* is neither an introduction to the philosophical Science nor its grounding, although it contains elements of both. It resembles an introduction in that it introduces the unphilosophical mind into philosophy, yet not externally, not by summarizing a set of rules and results, but rather through an inner existential thought-experience which the mind under-goes in the first person. At the same time the *Phenomenology* also provides an external grounding for philosophical Science in that it demonstrates its historical necessity.

That enthusiasm: Abstract rationalists leap directly into their truth and, with patronizing disdain, dismiss all the preceding false opinions, myths, and unphilosophical standpoints as useless. By contrast, the *Phenomenol-ogy* works hard to understand those inferior forms, both from within themselves and from their role in the overall process of the spirit.

In its universal sense: The subject of the *Phenomenology* must be an individ-ual, but one whose scope transcends the limits of the single person and encompasses the whole history of humanity. The true subject of the pro-cess is therefore the human race taken as a universal individual. Hegel follows up on Kant and Herder, but modifies their ideas with a principle of totalization derived from his own metaphysics.

The universal individual—self-conscious spirit: The ground for viewing the human race as a singular subject derives from spirit's need to be actual-ized through human history. The human race creates history as the sub-ject of the process in which it both manifests and constitutes itself.

Cultural education [Bildung]: The link Hegel sets between *Bildung* (culture or formative education) and humanity at large indicates that the *Phenome-nology* can be read as the story of the human race's self-education, a process in which it creates culture (by spiritualizing nature) and creates

the following: in the universal individual, every moment displays itself in the same way that it assumes a concrete form and gains its own configuration, whereas the particular individual is an incomplete spirit, a concrete shape whose whole existence is dominated by one single determination, while all the others are present in him in blurred outline only. In a spirit that stands higher than another, the lower concrete existence has been reduced to an indistinct moment.° What formerly was the matter itself is now but a trace; its shape is shrouded and become a simple shadow. An individual whose substance° is the higher-standing spirit traverses this past in the same way that someone undertaking an advanced science would go over the preparatory cognitions he already possesses, in order to make their content freshly present to his mind; he calls

---

itself through culture. We have here a parallel with the Platonic process of education which is also supposed to lead eventually to absolute Knowing. Yet in Hegel the disciple is not a single person, a Glaucon or a Theaetetus, but the "universal subject" underlying the whole human race; and the educator (or "midwife") is not a separate individual (Socrates) but the *same* overall subject, the human race itself. For this reason, the process of *Bildung* is not merely biographical, but historical; it is the self-*Bildung* of spirit through human history. This process entails a special relationship between the single and the universal individual. On the one hand, there can be no universal individual separate from the particular individuals in whom alone it exists, thinks, and acts, and through whose sense of lack or insufficiency it changes and transforms itself. On the other hand, the single individual depends upon the universal individual, both as the source from which single persons derive much of their identity, and also as the framework limiting the ranges of the achievements they may expect.

An indistinct moment: The previous stages of spirit have sunk and been compressed into its past and are no longer at the center. They have been interiorized, and become a kind of "memory."

An individual whose substance: The single individual is nourished by the achievements which the universal spirit has accumulated up to her time. These are now the individual's "substance" or "inorganic nature" which she no longer has to reach and conquer, but only to reappropriate, in the same way that a learner reappropriates the mental acquisitions of former generations.

those cognitions back to memory without focusing his interest in them and dwelling on them. The singular individual must also°
go through the content of the stages in universal spirit's cultural education, but as configurations which spirit has already left behind, like stages in a road that has been worked out and leveled. What in former periods had occupied the mind of mature men we now see descending to mere [ready-made] cognitions, exercises, even games of a youthful age; and in the youth's pedagogical progress we shall recognize the history of the world's cultural education outlined as in silhouette. This past existence is the acquired possession° of universal spirit, which constitutes the individual's substance—or inorganic nature—and thus appears external to him. Seen from the individual's perspective, the process of cultural edu-

The singular individual must also: The single individual during his education must go again through the stages which the universal spirit has traversed, no longer as a new conquest but as something that has been passed and become past. In every boy's education, one can observe the major stages in the development of the world-Spirit drawn "as in a silhouette." For example, the Ten Commandments, Euclidean geometry, Aristotelian logic, popular religion, or Bach's chorales—the great spiritual conquests of the past—have become items in the curriculum of eighth- to twelfth-grade children, or are routinely learned within the family. (As we shall presently see, this is also Hegel's particular, historicized version of the Platonic idea of "recollection.")

The acquired possession: What has been transmitted by former generations—tradition in its broader sense—contains something which the individual finds foreign from the start, unfitting her own spirit, although in-itself (in a "substantial" and "inorganic" manner) it is a spiritual essence nevertheless, which even contains that individual's essence, albeit in an inert mode. The solution lies in that the individual appropriates tradition, and makes it her own property and thus assimilates the inorganic to her own organism. Against abstract rationalism, Hegel stresses the necessary weight of tradition; but he demands that tradition receive its import from the individual's *making* it her own; and this, as long as the process has not attained final reconciliation, must lead to the immanent critique of tradition and to transcending some of its vital features. Thus the individual remains the ultimate test and the "absolute form" of the process.

cation consists in that the individual appropriates that which is offered to him ready-made, nourishes himself with his inorganic nature, and takes possession of it for himself. Whereas from the side
of universal spirit taken as substance, the process consists in its
giving itself self-consciousness, and generating its becoming and its
reflection within itself.

Science in its design [*Gestaltung*] exhibits [*darstellt*] this formative
movement in all its developed detail and necessity, and exhibits also
that which has already sunk into a moment and possession of spirit.
The goal is for spirit to gain insight into what Knowing is. Impatient
minds° demand the impossible—to reach the goal without the
means. However, one must endure the length of this road, since
every moment is necessary; and one must [also] abide in each of
these forms,° since each is a whole individual shape, and is considered in an absolute way only so far as its specific determination is
considered as whole or as concrete, or [in other words]: when the
totality is considered within this form's own distinctive determination. Even the individual's substance, that is, world-spirit° itself,
has had the patience to go through these forms in time's long ex-
panse, and to undertake the prodigal work of world history, in
which it fashioned its whole content into each of these forms to

Impatient minds: This section again criticizes abstract rationalism which
    wants to erase history and advance to the pure rational system in one
    leap ("as in a gunshot," see p. 119).

And one must [also] abide in each of these forms: Every previous stage and
    passed moment deserve that their essence be contemplated in depth: first,
    because they are a necessary condition for the resulting totality,
    and second because this lingering contemplation will bring out the
    specific deficiencies in every stage and generate the immanent drive to
    pass onward.

World-spirit: This important term makes here its first appearance in the
    Phenomenology. The world-spirit is the subject of world history (*Welt-
    geschichte*); as such, it is a moment, or dimension, of the absolute subject,
    that is, the universal individual whom Hegel has discussed before. The
    self-expression of the world-spirit in a certain era is *Zeitgeist*, "the spirit
    of the time."

the extent of that form's capacity.° Now since world-spirit could not attain self-consciousness with less work, the individual, too, by the nature of things, cannot reach a Conceptual grasp of his substance with less. Yet the effort required of the individual is today smaller,° because the task is already accomplished in itself. The content is now an actuality suppressed into possibility;° it is a coerced immediacy,° a shape reduced to its abbreviation,° to simple thought-determinations. As something which is already thought, the content is not the possession of substance. It is no longer existence in the form of being-in-itself—neither an original in-itself, nor an in-itself that has sunk into existence—but an in-itself that was interiorized into memory [*erinnerte Ansich*]° and must now be con-

To the extent of that form's capacity: Every historical shape is capable of expressing the spirit's essence only in a partial and limited way. This applies also to the individual's belonging to that *Zeitgeist*.

The effort required . . . smaller: At every given period, the individual must reappropriate spirit's past achievements. Yet she needs much less effort because this is no longer a new acquisition.

Suppressed into possibility: In past periods, when spirit had attained cultural contents for the first time, it had turned them from abstract possibility to actuality. When, later, the individual reappropriates these contents, they devolve to a possibility for her, though from the standpoint of the world-spirit, they are already actual; therefore, acquiring them does not involve the same amount of innovation and labor.

Coerced immediacy: An immediacy which is forced on the particular individual, as his "substance."

A shape reduced to its abbreviation: Now we can remember it as a kind of code, no longer in its previous living actuality.

An in-itself that was interiorized into memory [erinnerte Ansich]: The immediacy of spiritual content retained from the past should not be confused with the immediacy of inert entities, or of being in general. It is rather the immediacy which is specific *to spirit*—that is, substantive memory. Memory is the inventory of past experiences and cultural forms which human spirit has accumulated, and which is not conscious of itself but needs to be brought to the form of self-consciousness (in Hegelian jargon, the interiorized and memorized "in-itself" must become "for-itself"). The term *Erinnerung* means both *interiorization* (creating substantive memory) and *recollection* (calling to memory). The process of interiorization creates

verted [from the form of being-*in*-itself] into the form of being-*for*-itself. Let us describe more closely how this is performed.

At the stage in which we take up this process, we are spared the sublation of existence. What remains, and calls for a higher transformation, are representation and the familiarity with the forms. The existence which, in a first negation, has been taken back° into the [spiritual] substance, was thereby transposed into the element of the self only immediately. Therefore, the newly acquired property of selfhood still retains the same character of unmoved indifference, of unconceived [*unbegriffner*] immediacy, as existence itself; existence has passed only into representation.° This

---

a mental inventory of images, language, knowledge, experiences, aspirations, conflicts, norms, and so forth, which serve as material for spirit's evolution (and, at the end of the day, enables the philosophical system to particularize itself into specific topics and categories). The thought-contents of the past, having fulfilled their role in the life of the spirit, are thereby interwoven into spirit's own texture, even though they have not attained self-consciousness. Furthermore, a thought-content belongs by nature to spirit itself rather than to something outside it; and because that content has never been absolutely external, we are actually "recalling it" when thinking it. This is why Hegel considers his system's particularization into specific concepts to be a *self*-particularization; for when spirit derives these concepts from its recollection of its own past, it can be said to be deriving from itself. (The concept of interiorization is, I think, Hegel's chief version of Plato's theory of recollection and is as central. It stands at the background of the concept of cultural education and is the substrate enabling the activity of dialectic.

Has been taken back: By being thought, existence was negated as something completely external; it became the property of spirit and entered into the general element of selfhood or reflection. However, it first entered that domain as something immediate, which is not yet comprehended and lacks a concept of itself—namely, as image or figurative representation (*Vorstellung*). This representation must be negated in the next stage in order for the Concept to arise.

Representation (*Vorstellung*; also, "mental image"): This is what the imagination, using sense perception, builds as a representation of reality. The real has thereby been made mental or spiritual—taken up the form of the

makes it something familiar,° in which the existing spirit no longer has its interest and activity, but is done with it. To be thus done with existence is the typical activity of a merely particular spirit [mind], which does not grasp itself conceptually. By contrast, Knowing is directed° against this being-familiar and against the representation that has so emerged; it is the activity of the universal self, and the interest of thinking. The familiar or well-known in general, because it is well-known [*bekannt*], is not known [*erkannt*]. The most common deception in matters of knowledge, a deception of oneself and of others, is to presuppose something as well-known and let it placate us.° Such knowing, with all its talking here and

---

self—but only in a rudimentary, inert way. The representational image is the passive, immediate mode in which existence—which appears as external—is internalized and becomes spirit's own property. (In philosophy, this moment corresponds to empiricist idealism, as in Berkeley.) The image shows a "motionless indifference" to reality, by relating to it as a passive and inert representation. By contrast, the Concept plays an active role in constituting true actuality. (This moment corresponds to Kant's and Hegel's own idealism.)

Familiar: At the stage of sense perception and figurative representation, consciousness is still enslaved in its direct experience. Familiarity becomes the supreme test of what it ought to accept or reject (and is given the dignified name of "philosophy of common sense"). Because the world as it appears in sense perception and image representation looks so familiar, one hardly bothers to investigate it any further and reach out for its truth. As a result, (a) the familiar thing remains the *least* known and understood; (b) it generates dogmatism; and (c) it expresses the standpoint of particular subjectivity, in which every person views things in his or her own way.

Knowing is directed: Philosophical knowledge requires that the dogmatism and tyranny of the familiar be overcome, and that the mind rise to the standpoint of universality. This, as we have seen, cannot be performed in one leap, but requires that the particular consciousness be satisfied in all subsequent stages. Yet that satisfaction will no longer consist of relating every new idea to something directly familiar.

Let it placate us: Hegel recognizes that every act of knowledge must refer the unknown to something known. But he opposes the arbitrary connections which simply link something distant and abstract to something famil-

there, and without knowing what is happening to it, does not move
an inch from its place.° The subject, the object, God, nature, the
intellect, sensibility, and so forth are laid down at the foundation
without examination, as well-known and valid elements, to serve
as rigid points for both the outgoing and ingoing movement [of
knowledge]. The movement° passes back and forth between these
immobile points—and thus only crosses their surface. Likewise, to
understand and verify something° consists [in such philosophy] in
checking whether what is being claimed is found in everybody
else's representation, whether this is how it appears to him and
looks familiar, or not.

Yet, even an ordinary analysis of a representation,° as it is usually
performed, is nothing but the sublation of the form of its being-

---

iar *as it is*, without transforming the latter in any way—neither breaking
it down into its constituent parts, nor relocating it into the proper context,
nor following its internal dialectic. And once the direct linkage to the familiar is made, one thinks it gives us an explanation, when all it does is silence
our curiosity or anxiety. This procedure is not an attempt to understand
but to cater to the popular mind, which is satisfied by what is considers
familiar, thereby overcoming its apprehension of the unknown.

Does not move an inch from its place: Without alerting the reader, Hegel
extends his attack to include Fichte. Not only the partisans of commonsense and the familiar, but also Fichte, their apparent opponent, who
claims to represent a rational science as against commonsense empiricism, actually commits the fallacy of basing himself on the familiar.
Fichte's *Theory of Science* contains a large number of categories—forms
of knowledge and existence—which it explains by simply weaving them
one after the other on the thread of a single principle, and often linking
the abstract to the familiar in the way just criticized.

The movement: The activity of discovery, proof, and the like, which in Fichte
is external to the subject matter and belongs to the I alone.

To understand and verify something: All the allusions here are to the procedure, or "movement," by which Fichte constructs and justifies his *Theory
of Science*. This movement affects the I alone, but not its object, actual
reality.

Analysis of a representation: Even analytic thinking dissects an image into
its constituents, thereby abolishing it as an image and passing over to the
meaning it has for the intellect. It also tries to penetrate the deep structure

familiar. To break down a representation° into its original elements is to go back to its moments which, at least, no longer have the form of the representation as initially found, but are the immediate possession of the self. True, the analysis gets only to thoughts° that are themselves familiar, that are rigid and static determinations. But this severed, nonactual° element is nevertheless essential as moment, because the concrete can move itself only by severing itself and becoming nonactual. The activity of dissolution is the force and work of the understanding, which is the greatest and most wondrous power°—indeed it is the absolute power. The circle, which rests enclosed in itself and holds its moments in the immediate relation of substance, provokes no sense of wonder. But that the accidental in detachment from its surrounding—the accidental as such, that connected [entity] which is actual only in mutual dependence with others—should gain its unique existence and

---

of its subject matter, its "inner" or "true" form as it exists for the understanding. Hegel implies that Fichte forgoes even the analytical stage: he not only lacks true dialectic, but fails to perform even a genuine analysis of the concepts which he simply threads together.

To break down a representation: Hegel does not mean breaking a complex image into its image-ingredients, but into its categorized elements; analysis is also categorization.

Thoughts: Even though analytic thinking reaches fixed or rigid thoughts only, the understanding's activity of division and analysis is the model of thinking in general.

Nonactual: Analysis and division do not belong to the actual thing itself; they express the external limit between its parts. Even so, they are an essential element of thought—the ground of the understanding, which is the preparatory condition for philosophical reason.

The greatest and most wondrous power: From Parmenides to Spinoza, philosophers of unity and totality had trouble explaining the origin of negation, and therefore the origin of movement, particularity, and difference. Hegel says that the origin of negation is the understanding (*intellectus, nous, Verstand*). Therefore, the understanding is the most wondrous power, for it explains and makes possible the "wonder" of there being a diversified universe with movement and distinctions—it makes creation itself possible.

a separate freedom, this is the colossal power of the negative;° it is
the energy of thinking, the pure I. Death° (if we wish to give that
name to nonactuality) is the most awesome thing of all; and up-
holding the dead requires the greatest force. A powerless beauty°
hates the understanding, because the understanding expects it to
do what it cannot.° But the life of the spirit is not a life that shuns
death° and bewares destruction, keeping clean of it; it is a life that

The colossal power of the negative: Understanding (the intellect) is the negative
  principle which constructs the world by undermining the compact monotony of being and generating distinctions, diversity, and movement. Understanding also penetrates beyond the immediate images into what is considered their underlying structure. Yet at the same time understanding
  generates severance, rupture—even terror—in life and the mind; it creates
  a break between the mind and itself, between man and world, finite and
  infinite, subject and object, and so forth. Therefore, in the next stage one
  must go beyond the understanding, though not before having exhausted
  the positive power which the understanding's "negative energy" holds.
Death: A metaphor for the power of negativity. Just as negativity is necessary for the constitution of positive reality, so death is needed for the
  constitution of life and of spirit's power.
A powerless beauty: Hegel says *kraftlose Schönheit*, "powerless beauty," as
  distinguished, I think, from a powerful beauty which admits negativity
  and death. Powerless beauty is shallow, pale, rosy, one-dimensional; it
  hates the understanding, not only because it cannot stand analysis, but
  also because it abhors negativity. (Abhorring all negativity is a possible
  characterization of kitsch.) Beauty, however, need not be powerless or
  kitschy—it can and should accept negativity with all its implications, including tragedy and death.
To do what it cannot: This concerns only powerless beauty, which is superficial; powerful beauty can sustain the negative.
Not a life that shuns death: Hegel now turns from logical and metaphysical
  negativity to the role of death and destruction in the life of the spirit. Just
  as reality entails negativity, so the spirit is built by coping with death,
  suffering, and destruction. Spirit does not build itself as pure positivity
  shunning or ignoring these factors. Spirit can grow only by "looking the
  negative in the face," coping or struggling with it and residing within it.
  Thereby, negativity becomes a positive, constructive force. This is a major
  implication of Hegel's dialectic: suffering, passion, war, destruction, false-

bears death and maintains itself in it. Spirit gains its truth only through finding itself within absolute rupture. Spirit is that power not as a positive which turns away from the negative, as when we say of something that it is nothing or false, and having thus finished with it we turn to something else; rather, spirit is that power only in so far as it looks the negative in the face and dwells in it. This dwelling is the magic force which converts the negative into being. That power is what we called above subject:° the power which, in giving the specific determination existence in its own element,° sublates the abstract immediacy, namely, that which merely *is* in general, and thereby is the true substance: it [the subject] is being or immediacy which does not have mediation outside itself, but is that very mediation.

The fact that what is represented becomes the possession of pure self-consciousness, this elevation to universality in general, is only one side of cultural education° and not yet its fulfillment. The

---

hood, violence, and the other modalities of negativity are organic constituents of truth and of spirit's growth and actuality. Even the end of the road will not abolish them completely. History does not lead toward utopia in the fairy-tale sense of pure positive freedom and happiness. (This, to the dialectic, is *historical* kitsch.) The negative elements, though no longer dominant, will still be there when reason is actualized, functioning dialectically within an overall positive and rational system.

Subject: Again identifying the subject with the power of negativity.

In its own element: The same specific content is believed to exist in two ways: as external being, and as a thought-content grasped by the mind. In the latter mode, it receives existence from the subject within the element of the spirit, albeit in a low level of spirituality—that of sense perception, imaging, or inarticulate thought. Even so, the content no longer merely exists but, in order to exist, enters mediation: and that which mediates it is the subject. Hegel thinks it follows from here that the subject does not face an external substance, but is itself the substance: it is mediated being, both being and its self-mediation. Therefore, the true element of being is the spirit, by which being is mediated and becomes what it is.

Cultural education: The process we have described in epistemic and ontological terms (the transformation of apparently external being into spiritual reality through perception and thinking) is for Hegel a privileged

mode of study in antiquity differed from modern times° in that the ancient mode of study was the genuine education of natural consciousness. Examining itself separately with regard to every aspect of its existence, and philosophizing about everything that came its way, it produced itself as a thoroughly active universality. In modern times, however, the individual finds the abstract form ready-made. The effort to grasp and make it one's own is more like directly pushing the inner toward the outside, and like an abbreviated birthgiving° [*abgeschnittne Erzeugung*] of the universal, rather than developing this universal out of the concrete and the manifold of existence. Therefore, our work today is not so much to purify the individual from the immediate mode of the senses and make him into a substance that thinks and is thought, but rather the opposite task—to sublate the rigidly determinate thoughts, and thereby to actualize and spiritualize the universal.° However, it is much harder° to give fluidity to the rigid thoughts than to sensible existence. The reason was given above: the determinations of thought have the I, the power of negativity or pure

---

example of *Bildung*. This may indicate that *Bildung* is not something we make *in addition to* other things, nor does it depend on specific institutions; rather it derives from our cognitive relation to being. Culture continues and develops the primordial mode of *Bildung* in which humans exist in the world.

Antiquity differed from modern times: In ancient times, cultural formation consisted in breaking away from the apparent concreteness of the senses and rising to the standpoint of understanding and universality in general. In modern times, the universal standpoint of the understanding has already been attained (or, rather, reappropriated on a higher level) by the philosophy of the Enlightenment. Now we should overcome the abstractions of the understanding with its gaps and dualisms and assume the standpoint of dialectical reason.

An abbreviated birthgiving: Sounds like a caesarian birth! . . .

Spiritualize the universal: The understanding's analytical and merely general mode of thinking is not yet true spirituality. One must (a) negate the rigid self-identity of the thoughts of the understanding and make them "fluid" and dialectical; and, even more difficult, one must (b) reunite the understanding with the senses, the interiority of thought with external empirical being. Both tasks call for dialectical reason.

actuality, for their substance and for the element of their existence, whereas the sensible determinations have only the powerless abstract immediacy,° or being as such. The thoughts become fluid when pure thinking, this inward immediacy,° recognizes itself as moment;° or when sheer self-certainty° abstracts from itself.° This does not mean° that it neglects itself or turns aside, but that it

It is much harder: In its modern position, the dualistic understanding entails two forms of dogmatism: (a) the analytic rationalist kind, which clutches its rigid laws as if they were the last word of thought; and (b) the empiricist kind, which takes sense data to be absolute and certain in their givenness. ("The myth of the given," as some later philosophers call it.) Hegel demands to abolish the dogmatic compactness of both these views and render them "fluid." The first task was made possible by Kant's discovery that the activity of the understanding derives from the I (which is, Hegel adds, essentially the process of self-negation). Yet the second dogmatism, that of sense data, is far harder to remove, because sense data refer to immediate being as their principle (cf. the beginning of both the *Phenomenology* and the *Logic*), and because people tend to grasp being as a rigid external "thing-in-itself" immune to the subject's intervention. Even Kant, Hegel charges, did not overcome this powerful fallacy.

Powerless abstract immediacy: The immediacy attributed to external being is abstract because it lacks distinctions; it is powerless because it is passive and inert. Whereas the immediacy of being which is attributed to the I is a distinction-creating activity and in this respect powerful.

Inward immediacy: The aspect of being or existence pertaining to the I, that which allowed Descartes to say: *cogito, sum*.

Moment: And not as the first and last stage, not as absolute.

Self-certainty: The primary self-certainty of the "I think" and of its immediate thought-contents: in both cases, the I is attached to them—and is attached to itself—with the same kind of certainty and dogmatic fixity.

Abstracts from itself: The ego's certainty of itself is the source of the certainty it has of other things. The latter, whether they are sense objects or objects of thought, derive their certainty from their unchallengeable presence within the certainty which the I has of itself. Yet this initial certainty is uncritical and must be overcome—must be "abstracted" from—as a prerequisite for moving toward truth.

This does not mean: We have seen that the individual's self-certainty is preserved throughout the process, though not as fixed in its primary form, or as attached to the seemingly immediate experience of being in which

gives up the fixity of its self-positing—both the fixity of the purely concrete, namely, the I° in opposition to the differentiated content, and the fixity of the differences° which are set in the element of pure thinking and participate in the same unconditionality° of the I. By this movement, the pure thoughts become Concepts,° and are for the first time what they are in truth—self-movements, circles,° or (that which is their substance) spiritual essentialities [*geistige Wesenheiten*].°

---

it had first appeared to itself. The process of *Bildung* transforms self-certainty to its true configuration: at the end of the road, the individual will be conscious of himself, no longer in a direct mental experience, but through a complete philosophical system in which the individual rediscovers his own self, and through the diverse natural and social forms which that system conceptualizes.

The fixity of the purely concrete, namely, the I: Perceiving the Cartesian I as a separate entity capable of existing in-itself even without there being a world, other persons, and intellectual truth—that view was "given up" (overcome) by Kant.

The fixity of the differences: What Kant was unable to "give up" was fixing the laws and categories of the understanding as a rigid set, subject to the law of noncontradiction which receives its fixity from a self-identical I. Kant could never overcome this second fixity because he refused to introduce self-contradiction into the I. Recognizing that the second overcoming is necessary leads to Hegel's philosophy.

Unconditionality: This is Kant's term for the absolute.

Concepts: As distinguished from images, representations, and also self-identical determinations of the intellect which common language calls "concepts." Hegel uses the term "Concepts" here in his special sense of dynamic structures of thought and reality alike, which have objective existence in nature and society and not merely in the thinking mind. In that respect, Hegel's Concepts broaden the scope of Kant's categories which are also said to simultaneously determine both the structure of subjective understanding and that of objective reality. (This is the essence of Kant's Copernican revolution, or principle of idealism, which Hegel accepts and reworks.)

Self-movements, circles: At this point we are peering into the heart of Hegel's speculative thought. The Concepts in the strict systematic sense are sub-

This movement° of the pure essentialities constitutes the nature of scientificity in general. Seen as the mutual connection of their content, the movement is the content's necessity and its extension° into an organic whole. Moreover, this movement also makes a complete and necessary Science of the way in which the Concept of Science is attained. The preparation of Science ceases to be a con-

---

ject-like principles moving in purposive motion—as was said earlier about the subject. These are the fundamental patterns of reality—the categories of the Hegelian philosophical Science.

Spiritual essentialities [geistige Wesenheiten]: This uncommon term stands as a synonym for the system of categories which constitute philosophical Science (and, to a certain extent, it is Hegel's substitute for Plato's "realm of ideas"). The categories or "spiritual essences" are not only notions but, at the same time, principles of objective reality, and thereby unite thinking and being. When philosophy rethinks those categories, it is therefore dealing not with itself only, but with actual being and its structure. The first Science in which Hegel worked out these "spiritual essences" is the *Logic*, which treats the basic categories of thought as the foundations of actual reality. Still, the *Logic* is only a "kingdom of shadows" (Hegel's idiom), for it lacks the rich variety of *natural* and *historical* forms, which Hegel worked out in other parts of his system. Eventually he tried to unify them in the *Encyclopaedia of Philosophical Sciences*.

This movement: The dialectical movement in which all basic concepts are negated and reconstituted through further negations, as described above. The movement of the categories within an organic whole is what, for Hegel, gives philosophy its own kind of scientific character (*Wissenschaftlichkeit*), which must be distinguished from that of the formal and the experimental disciplines.

The content's necessity and its extension: When we try to think a concept from all relevant angles and grasp its various and opposing implications, it leads us to further concepts, which again take us further. This expansion can cease only if it turns out to be a circular movement which produces an organic whole. As the thought-movement expands, it incorporates concepts which philosophers have used here and there, in a piecemeal or "rigid" manner, and liberates them of the accidental and dogmatic character they had before, endowing them with necessity within the complete system.

tingent philosophizing which hangs on to these or other objects, thoughts, or relations of the imperfect consciousness as they arise by accident, or which seeks to ground the true in arguments turning here and there, or drawing inferences and consequences from [pre]determined thoughts.° Rather, by the movement of the Concept, this road will encompass the complete worldliness of consciousness in its necessity.

This exhibition constitutes the first part of Science.° The reason is that, at first, spirit's existence is nothing but the immediate or the beginning, and the beginning is not yet its return to itself. What distinguishes this part of Science from its other part is therefore the element of immediate existence.° Pointing out this difference leads us to examine some rigid thoughts° which arise usually in this context.

Spirit's immediate existence, consciousness, has two moments:° Knowing and objectivity. The latter is the negative with respect to Knowing. Since spirit develops itself in the element [of consciousness]° and expounds its moments in it, they all assume this opposi-

---

[Pre]determined thoughts: Like axioms or first principles.

The first part of Science: Meaning the *Phenomenology*; see the introduction.

Immediate existence: In its concrete or immediate existence, spirit takes the form of consciousness: this is the medium in which the *Phenomenology* will move. Therefore, the *Phenomenology* is also called "the Science of consciousness' experience." In a different context, Hegel says the *Phenomenology* exhibits spirit according to its empirical appearance and development in time. The two descriptions are compatible. The subject of the *Phenomenology* is spirit, manifested as consciousness and embodied in time and in phenomenal reality.

Some rigid thoughts: Dogmatic ideas which Hegel intends to undermine and criticize through a dialectical process.

Two moments: Consciousness is by nature a consciousness of something; it has an intentional character. It therefore has two moments: the moment of knowledge, and the moment of the object (of objectness), which is negative with regard to knowledge. The two moments relate to one another as an opposition or mutual negation; both belong to consciousness' characteristic intentional relation, and therefore, to its essence.

In the element [of consciousness]: Presenting spirit within the element of consciousness means that all the ingredients of spirit appear as configurations of consciousness and are subject to the duality which characterize it.

tion and emerge as shapes of consciousness. The Science of this
road is the Science of the experience° which consciousness undergoes: substance together with its movement are here considered as
an object of consciousness. Consciousness knows and conceives
nothing but that which is in its experience; for what is in consciousness' experience is the spiritual substance, [which is there] as object
of its self° [*ihres Selbst*]. Spirit, however, becomes object because it
is this movement: becoming other to itself, that is, becoming an
object of its self,° and sublating this being-other. And experience is
indeed the name given to this movement, in which the immediate,
that which is not experienced, that is, the abstract°—be it the [ab-
stract] of sensible being, or the simple which is merely thought—
alienates itself, and then returns to itself from this alienation, in
which stage it is, for the first time, manifest in its actuality and
truth, while also being the property of consciousness.

The disparity [*Ungleichheit*] found in consciousness between the
"I" and substance, which is the I's object, is their difference, the

The Science of experience: The object of our study is consciousness-in-its-
experiencing, in which the world of substance appears as part of consciousness' own world, that is, as the object of experience rather than as
an object-in-itself.

As object of its self: The dualistic relation is not abolished but is interiorized
into consciousness' own world.

Becoming an object of its self: At a higher stage, when consciousness is expressed as self-consciousness, then, as its own object, consciousness has
its other within itself and is the overcoming of that otherness. This structure is analogous to the "subject" as we discussed it in the introduction.
(Yet Hegel seems here to have leaped from consciousness as a dualistic
principle to self-consciousness as the restoration of unity.)

That which is not experienced, that is, the abstract: Hegel means Kant's
"thing-in-itself," which takes two forms: (a) sensation presupposes some
indefinite ("abstract") element existing in itself beyond experience; and
(b) the understanding presupposes an "abstract" element both as a primary truth, and as a separate, noumenal world. In Hegel's concept of
experience—according to which consciousness experiences the world as
the experiencing of its self, and vice versa—no room is left for a "thing-
in-itself," which always remains alien. Rather, the ontological other is
now interpreted as the self-alienation of consciousness (or spirit), which

negative in general. One might view it as their deficiency, yet it is rather their soul, or their mover;° which is why some ancient thinkers conceived the void° as mover: they grasped the mover already as negative, but did not yet grasp the negative as the Self. If this negative appears at first as the disparity between the I and the object, then, to the same extent, it is a disparity between substance and itself. What seems to be going on outside substance and looks like an activity directed against it, is actually its own doing,° and substance shows itself to be essentially subject. When this has been made manifest in a complete way, then spirit has made its existence identical to its essence; now it is object to itself as it is, and the abstract element of immediacy,° and of the split between Knowing and truth, is overcome. Being is now absolutely mediated; it is a substantial content which is immediately the property of the I:° it is self-like [*selbstisch*], or the Concept.°

---

returns to it as its property. (See also "the abstract element of immediacy," below).

Their mover: Each of the sides is lacking something, and that lack moves it—it is its "soul." (As in Aristotle, soul is the principle of self-movement.)

The void: Even those ancients who understood that movement presupposes negativity still imagined negativity as a kind of thing or substance (the void), rather than as subject (selfhood).

Is actually its own doing: At a later stage (over which Hegel passes here), it will emerge that the negation between consciousness and its object is actually an inner negation within the object itself; therefore, the object manifests itself also as subject (as subject/object). This can take place only when spirit has so developed that its actual existence becomes equal to its latent essence.

The abstract element of immediacy: That again is the "thing-in-itself," the illusion of rigid unmediated being. Overcoming this phase of spirit's evolution implies that nothing in the world lacks mediation, that being itself has been mediated in all important respects, and no irreducibly alien residuum remains beyond spirit's synthesis of the subject/object.

The property of the I: In the state of universal mediation, reality (the substantive contents) has a subject-like property, and the subject has a substantive dimension: this is Hegel's so-called "objective idealism." Neither side overcomes or overwhelms the other; a unity of opposites is rather obtained within them, which endows each side with its distinct character and status.

This concludes the phenomenology of the spirit. What spirit prepares for itself° in this phenomenology is the element of Knowing. Within that element, the moments of spirit deploy themselves in the form of a simplicity which knows its object to be itself.° They no longer fall outside each other into the opposition of being and Knowing, but remain within the simplicity of Knowing; they are [now] the true in the form of the true,° and their being-different

The Concept: Hegel here describes the "Concept" as a substantial content which is self-like, meaning a unity of object (substance) and subject (selfhood). The Hegelian *Begriff* is a specific expression of the unity of these two.

What spirit prepares for itself: With the conclusion of the *Phenomenology*, the metaphysical illusion, which holds that beyond the spirit there is a separate being in itself, is finally abolished. Henceforth, being and thought are grasped as mutually mediating each other, and as moments of a single overall context: absolute Knowing. Within this context, the road is open to performing the complete philosophical Science.

Which knows its object to be itself: This is another characterization of objective idealism, or absolute Knowing. At this stage, external being has been sublated. The spirit's object, its other, is spirit itself as it becomes conscious of that fact through a detailed philosophical Science, and the dualistic opposition of being and knowledge has been abolished. Being manifests itself as an inner moment of knowledge, whereas knowledge turns out to be (as in Spinoza) a mode of reality itself rather than an external representation of it. Moreover, as we saw in the introduction, the emergence of absolute Knowing is even the self-*actualization* of reality. This is the high point of idealism. But it must be stressed that *it is an idealism of knowledge and not of consciousness*. It does not maintain that being is only "*for* someone's mind," but that being is actualized and acquires meaning only through the rational categories which human knowledge (and previous action) have actualized and made manifest.

The true in the form of the true: This is another way of describing the final stage. Until then, truth has appeared in untrue forms, inadequate for its content—like sense perceptions and images, or like the lower and contradictory degrees of conceptual understanding. Absolute Knowing requires that the true content assume also the genuine *form* and *medium* of absolute truth, and reside only within that form. Yet this occurs only in pure philosophical contemplation. In the historical arena, the inadequacy

is only a diversity of content. Their movement, which organizes itself in this element into a totality, is the Logic° or speculative philosophy.°

Since the system of spirit's experience deals only with the appearance [*Erscheinung*] of spirit, progressing from here to the Science of the true in the shape of the true may appear to be a merely negative move; and of the negative, as false, one might wish to get rid, demanding to be led without delay to the truth: why occupy ourselves with the false?°

The demand to start directly with Science was already discussed above; now we should respond to it by examining the character of the negative as something false in general. The current notions°

---

between truth and its form cannot be completely abolished. A certain degree of contingency, imagination, sense perception, violence, and other negative elements is inevitable in the real world, and will persist even when historical progress has attained its highest point. This means that the real world will remain the other of philosophical knowledge even when the latter is realized and recognizes itself within it. In this respect, there is no utopian end to history in Hegel.

The Logic: Hegel does not mean formal logic, but rather his own kind of transcendental logic—the logic of being and of actual objects. More specifically, he means the *logos* that structures reality in its self-development. This is the system of pure ontological categories in their mutual relations; and more broadly speaking, it is speculative philosophy.

Speculative philosophy: The term does not indicate "theoretical" as distinguished from "practical," nor does it mean "speculation" in the sense of wild, unfounded opinions (on its meaning see the end of the introduction and commentary on page 93).

Why occupy ourselves with the false?: One cannot enter truth without understanding its relation to falsity. Truth needs falsity and affirmation needs negation—both as a motive for its development and as part of its texture. The following discussion therefore comes close to explaining the foundations of the dialectic.

The current notions: (Literally, "representations," but here opinions are meant.) Most philosophers ("of the understanding") follow one of two ways: either they ignore the opinions of other thinkers and start immediately with what seems true to them, or else they deal with other

about this issue are a major barrier to the entry into truth. This will give us an opportunity to speak also of mathematical knowledge, which unphilosophical knowing sees as the ideal which philosophy should have attained, but has so far sought in vain.

The true and the false belong to the determinate thoughts which, being unmoved, are seen as separate essences, rigidly standing in isolation, one here and one there, without communion [*Gemeinschaft*] with each other. Against this view we must stress that truth is not a minted coin which can be pocketed as such, finished and ready.° Nor does the false have being, any more than evil has.° To be sure, the false and the evil are not as bad as the devil, for in

---

philosophers only in order to refute them and manifest their falsity. The Hegelian philosopher deals at length with other thinkers, including his immediate predecessors; and when refuting them, does so in order to draw the nucleus of truth latent in their thoughts, and makes their refutation a positive ingredient of his own system of truth. Thus in Hegel, rethinking the role of falsity is linked to a new understanding of philosophical refutation.

Finished and ready: Philosophical truth is not a static statement (like mathematical formulae) but a system whose ingredients are always in mutual movement. It therefore has no static final state. Within that system, negation and falsity fulfill a constitutive role. There is no treasure of pure gold (truth without falsity) waiting to be discovered in some hidden vault. Kaufmann notes that Hegel alludes here to Lessing's play *Nathan the Wise*, where Nathan is pressed by the Sultan to prove which of the three monotheistic religions is the true one, to which Nathan retorts ironically: "He wants the answer in cash so ready and shining as if truth were a coin" (Walter Kaufmann, *Hegel* [Garden City, NY: Doubleday, 1965], 414–15). I agree: the young Hegel was strongly influenced by *Nathan* and knew it thoroughly. See my *Dark Riddle: Hegel, Nietzsche, and the Jews*, (Cambridge: Polity Press, 1996), part 1, chapter 2, pp. 45–49.

Nor does the false have being, any more than evil has: Falsity and evil do not exist as independent entities. This can be said only of the devil, and he is a creature of legend. Falsity and evil are moments of a wider system in which they mutually share in constituting truth and the good; and within that system, each of these elements has a different meaning from that which is attributed to it in separation.

the devil they even become a particular subject, whereas as false and evil they are only universal, although each has its own essentiality in opposition to the other.

The false—for here we are speaking of it alone—is supposed to be the other, the negative of substance, which, in being the content of knowledge, is the true. But substance itself is essentially the negative, partly in being the differentiation and determination of the content, partly in being simple differentiation, that is, in being a self and knowing in general. One certainly can know falsely. To know something falsely means that knowing is in disparity with its substance.° Yet this disparity is differentiation in general,° which is

Knowing is in disparity with its substance (or, they have no equality, *Gleichheit.*): Hegel seems to be using the ordinary definition of truth and falsity: truth is the "equality" (agreement) of knowledge and its object, and falsity is their disagreement. Yet Hegel interprets that tired definition in his own way. Falsity resides not in the failure of some particular cognitive attempt, but in the way in which knowledge understands its relation to its object. As long as the subject—the world, reality—is conceived as utterly external to knowledge, we are subject to falsity in the sense of a fundamental "inequality" (disagreement) between knowledge and its object. The falsity in question does not arise because knowledge misses some separate object existing in itself, but because knowledge separates the object from itself and itself from the object. *It is therefore knowledge itself which (as in Spinoza) generates the realm of falsity*; yet it does so as a necessary condition for realizing truth. Hegel's underlying presupposition is that an original, though abstract and as-yet-unrealized unity exists between knowledge and its object (substance). To actualize that latent unity, knowledge must go through a long intermediary process in which it first separates itself from substance and regards the two of them as unequal— that is, generates the realm of falsity. The intermediary phase—dualism— is a precondition for knowledge and substance to become equal again (that is, identical), in an actualized and concrete mode, which produces truth. The gap characterizing that intermediary phase assumes many shapes and forms, all of which are therefore marked by some measure of falsity. So familiar is this dualistic situation to us that we tend to see it as primordial, a timeless ontological state, when in fact it is a lower phase in spirit's development.

Differentiation in general: The separation of substance from knowledge which introduces their "inequality" or severance, and thus generates falsity.

an essential moment.° From this differentiation their identity arises, and this having-become-identical is truth. But not in such a way that the disparity was thrown out of truth like dross from pure metal, or like a tool that is removed from the finished vase. Rather, the disparity, as the negative, as the Self, is still immediately present° in the true as such. Even so, one cannot say° that the false is a moment of truth, or that it is an ingredient of it. In the proverb which says that everything false contains something true, the two are linked externally, like oil and water which cannot mix. In order to give its full significance to the moment of perfect otherness, these expressions [true and false] should no longer be used where their otherness has been sublated. In a similar way, the talk about the unity of subject and object, the finite and the infinite, being and thought, is improper, because [the terms] object, subject, and so on refer to what they are outside their unity, whereas in their unity they no longer mean the same as their expressions enunciate. In the same way, the false as false° is no longer a moment of truth.

Essential moment: It is essential for knowledge to separate itself from the object and thus introduce falsity as a condition of the eventual reidentification.

Immediately present: The resulting system of truth entails the mutual negation between its moments. As such, it interiorizes the inequality into its own texture. While the outcome, the system as a whole, is equal to itself, this result does not occur directly, but through persisting inner negations and oppositions.

One cannot say: Although negation, refutation, and contradiction are moments of truth, Hegel avoids saying the same about falsity. The reason for his prudence seems to be verbal and tactical. I think Hegel is concerned that people might say that the system of absolute Knowing is, according to its author, "only partially true"—a conclusion that does not follow, yet might be drawn nevertheless. So Hegel warns that expressions drawn from the world of dualism must not be used where dualism has been sublated, and where these terms have thereby acquired a completely different meaning. For example, a subject/object is not a conjunction of subject plus object, but something new; and within their synthesis, the terms "subject" and "object" have a different meaning from the one they had beforehand.

The false as false: Hegel means to say, if "false" is understood in the absolute sense of dualism, as an absolute negative state which excludes truth, then

Dogmatism, as a way of thinking in knowledge and philosophy, is nothing but the belief that the true consists in a proposition which is obtained as a rigid result, or else is known immediately. To questions like, when was Caesar born? how many yards [*Toise*] are there in one stadium? and the like, one must give a straight and definite answer, just as it is definitely true that in a right-angled triangle, the square of the hypotenuse is equal to the sum of the squares of the other two sides. Yet the nature of this so-called truth is different from the nature of philosophical truths.

Regarding historical truths° (to mention them briefly), one will easily grant that, in their purely historical aspect, these truths concern a singular existence° and the contingent, arbitrary side of the content, namely, its non-necessary determinations. But even naked truths° like those we cited above are not devoid of the movement

---

of course one cannot say that falsity is a moment of truth. Yet falsity in the *non*absolute sense is indeed a dialectical moment of truth, even if Hegel was reluctant to say so openly.

Historical truths: In German philosophy from Kant to Heidegger the term *historisch* is usually distinguished from *geschichtlich*, though both are translated into English as "historical." *Historisch* means the empirical gathering of data, and *geschichtlich* refers to the latent pattern governing the events, or the history-dependent nature of something or someone. (See my *Kant and the Philosophy of History*, chapter 6, 240–51.) Though Hegel is one of the creators of the second sense, here he is mainly using the first, which approximately means, "particular empirical truth."

Singular existence: Empirical history refers to non-recurring particulars, not to general patterns and laws. It therefore deals only with the contingent side of reality. (This view became prevalent in German philosophy after Hegel, especially through Dilthey and his followers.)

But even naked truths: Hegel admits the aforementioned claim but refuses to give it a positive interpretation. There are no "naked truths." Even the empirical historian investigating non-recurring facts needs a broader context, an explanatory scheme, in which to place those facts and by which to understand them. At this point, Hegel brusquely stops the discussion; had he continued, he certainly would have argued that the schemes of historical explanation must derive from an overall philosophical structure—the one studied by the *Phenomenology*—rather than being fragmentary and arbitrary.

of self-consciousness. In order to know one of them, one must make many comparisons, consult books, do some research. Even in direct observation [*Anschauung*], a cognition is held to have true value only when accompanied by its justifying grounds, even if the naked result remains the thing which one is really looking for.

As for mathematical truths,° it is even clearer that a person will not be considered a geometer if he knows Euclid's theorems only by heart [*auswendig*], without knowing their proofs—without, so to speak (to invert the expression) knowing them from within [*inwendig*]. Similarly, if a person has measured° many right-angled tri-*

Mathematical truths: A philosophical convention in the eighteenth century distinguished between two kinds of true statements (or cognitions): "mathematical" and "historical." The distinction was not between mathematics and history, but between general rational cognitions and particular empirical ones. Kant recasts the above distinction as holding between knowledge "from principles" and knowledge "from data," and further divides the former into two kinds, philosophical and mathematical. The mathematical (actually geometrical) cognitions are constructed by a deductive method, which Descartes, Spinoza, and other early rationalists, like Kant's predecessor, Christian Wolff, wanted to impose on all branches of knowledge that claim certainty, regardless of their content. Kant rejected this method as unfit for philosophy, because it is unilateral, and because every partial step in it is absolute and conclusive; whereas philosophical cognitions consist in the *gradual self-explication* of reason, which always turns back to correct and complement its previous steps (see *Critique of Pure Reason*, II, "Transcendental Doctrine of Method," chapter 1, section 1.)

Hegel follows the Kantian approach, but complains that Kant subjects even philosophical reason to "rigid" principles which obey the law of non-contradiction. In this respect, Kant's rational cognitions are as dogmatic as cognitions "from data." This is in essence the backdrop of the next few polemical pages. Hegel's attack focuses at first on mathematical truth in the narrow sense, and on the geometrical method which he, too, bans from philosophy, though his reasons are different from Kant's. At the same time Hegel criticizes the kind of philosophical reason by which Kant proposes to replace the geometrical reason of Descartes and Spinoza.

If a person has measured: Geometrical propositions are not inductive. They are not learned "from data." Incidentally, Hegel's two demands, (a) that

angles and concluded that their hypotenuse and two other sides stand in the well-known relation to each other, his knowledge will be considered deficient. Still, the essential role which demonstration plays in mathematical knowledge does not have the significance and nature of a moment of the result itself;° on the contrary, the demonstration vanishes and disappears in the result. The theorem, as a result, is indeed something that appears true;° yet this adjunct circumstance does not concern its content, but only its relation to the subject. The movement of a mathematical demonstration does not belong to that which is the object; its activity is rather external to the matter. For example, the nature of the right-angled triangle itself does not disassemble in the same way as its construction° exhibits, the construction which is needed to demon-

---

knowledge derive from general principles, and (b) that knowledge arise through subjective understanding—are both included in Kant's definition of "rational cognitions." (See my *Kant and the Philosophy of History*, chapter 6.)

Of the result itself: Although geometrical demonstrations, to be rational, must be internal to the learner's mind, they are not considered internal also to the result, that is, to the conclusion they produce. The demonstration is viewed as external to its conclusion, a kind of vehicle that can be disposed of at the end of the road. (Cf., by contrast, Hegel's words earlier in our text that a bare result is a "corpse," and that in philosophy, the true is the whole which includes its genesis as an integral part.)

Something that appears true: That is, something accepted as true on grounds that are sufficient for our subjective conviction. Such grounds are provided by a formal deductive demonstration which, nevertheless, may not be the reason which constitutes the truth of the matter in itself. (At best, the demonstration makes us see *that* something is true, but not why.) In several places Hegel therefore reiterates that knowledge based on formal logic or mathematical inference is merely "subjective," or an "external reflection": the reasons why we arrive at that knowledge are not the reasons because of which the matter itself is what it is.

Construction: The activity, according to Kant, by which mathematical items are produced. Hegel follows Kant with a noteworthy difference: in Kant, construction sets up the matter itself—the mathematical entity as such—and deduction is external to it; for Hegel, both these activities seem to be equally external. (So "construction" in our text might perhaps be replaced with "deduction," and the sentence modified as follows:° "Thus

strate the proposition expressing that relation. The production of
the result is [here] a means and a procedure of knowledge alone.

In philosophical knowledge,° too, there is a difference between
the becoming of existence as existence, and the becoming of essence, that is, of the inner nature of the matter. But, first, philosophical knowledge includes them both,° whereas mathematical knowledge exhibits only the becoming of existence—namely, the
becoming of the being of the nature of the matter°—in knowledge

---

the nature of the right-angled triangle does not divide itself into parts in
just the way set forth in the *deduction* necessary for the proof of the
proposition expressing that ratio.") What Hegel is saying is that the mathematical subject matter's order-of-being [*ordo essendi*] is not the same as
its order-of-knowledge (*ordo cognoscendi*).

In philosophical knowledge, too: In philosophy, too, there is no identity between the pure system's inner order and the genetic order in which it
manifests itself in time and history (for example, between the order of
the *Phenomenology* and the order of the *Logic*).

Includes them both: Philosophical knowledge includes both the *Phenomenology* and the *Logic*, both the conceptualization of spirit's inner essence
and the conceptualization of its empirical appearance in historical time.
Furthermore, both these aspects (as Hegel will soon argue) belong to the
nature of the subject matter. That the essence should appear in time and
in external reality is an inner philosophical necessity—that is, it is essential
to the essence.

The being of the nature of the matter: Here Hegel contrasts the *being* of the
nature of the thing with the *essence* of the nature of the thing, using the
technical sense which "being" and "essence" have in the *Logic*. Mathematics, the science of quantity, is discussed in the division, or supercategory,
of "Being" rather than the division of "Essence," because, as quantity,
mathematics belongs to pure externality, to the surface dimension of reality (discussed under "Being") and ignores, or abstracts from, the depth-
dimension of reality, its interiority (discussed under "Essence"). While
empirical reality is always external, it makes a crucial difference whether
it is also grasped as the externalization of an inner essence, or not. Mathematical knowledge does not grasp it so, but as purely quantitative, explores the properties of being only in its inessential externality. In summary, the present text can be rephrased as follows: philosophical
knowledge presents its subject matter (reality) in its inner essence,

as such. In addition, philosophical knowledge unites° these two particular movements. The inner generation or becoming of substance is an unbroken passage to the outside or to existence, it is being-for-another; and vice versa: the becoming of existence is the taking-itself-back into essence. In this way, the movement is a duplicated process, a becoming of the whole in which each of them posits the other and therefore has them both as two aspects [of itself]. Together they constitute the whole, by dissolving and making themselves into its moments.

In mathematical knowledge, the act of insight is external to the matter;° in consequence, the true matter is changed by it. The instrument—construction and demonstration—does contain true propositions; but it must be said that the content is false. In the example above, the triangle is torn down, and its parts are conveyed to other figures which construction builds alongside it. Only at the end is the triangle restored—the one with which we are actually dealing, but which has disappeared from sight in the course [of the demonstration] and appeared only in segments belonging to other wholes. So here, too, we see the negativity of the content entering, a negativity which ought to be called its falsity, just as, in the movement of the Concept, this name applies to the disappearance of the rigidly construed thoughts.

---

whereas mathematical knowledge presents only its quality-indifferent surface properties.

Unites: In addition, philosophical knowledge grasps the external appearance from the standpoint of its essentiality, that is, of the necessity that essence has to appear outwardly.

The act of insight is external to the matter: A geometrical demonstration dismembers its object into other figures by which it demonstrates the relations governing that object. The object is altered and reduced to something else, and only at the end (at the stage of q.e.d.) do we return from that "other" to the original object of proof. Hegel sees this "becoming other" as a sign that, not only in philosophy but even in mathematics, negativity (or "falsity," as he called it before) has a role in the generation of truth. However, in geometry the process of becoming-other is not essential to the subject matter itself, but only to our subjective state of mind: it lacks dialectical import.

The genuine deficiency of this mode of knowledge affects both knowledge itself, and its material. Concerning knowledge, one cannot, in the first place, see the necessity of the construction. The construction is not drawn from the Concept of the theorem, but is put forth as a command.° We must blindly obey an instruction which bids us draw precisely these, rather than infinite other possible lines; meanwhile we know nothing further, but must only have faith that this would serve the purpose of the demonstration. True, the purposiveness becomes manifest later, but on that account it is only external,° since it manifests itself only after the fact, when the demonstration is done. [Initially] the demonstration follows a road which starts somewhere, while we ignore how it is related to the expected result. In its course it picks up these determinations and relations, and leaves others out, by what necessity we cannot see. An external purpose dominates this process.

The evidence that characterizes° this deficient knowledge, which is the pride of mathematics, and which it vaunts even against philosophy, relies only on the poverty of its purpose and the deficiency of its material; therefore it is of a kind which philosophy must find repugnant. The purpose or Concept of mathematical knowledge is

Put forth as a command: A person offering a geometrical demonstration usually starts with a move whose reasons initially look arbitrary ("let *AB* be parallel to *CD*"), and invites us to follow a series of further instructions. Only late in the process, or at its very end, can we understand where these moves were leading. In this sense, we are called to follow in blind obedience a procedure which is not essential to the matter itself, and its purpose is not clear even subjectively. (I think Hegel is unfairly attacking the element of *creative imagination* in geometry—a rather attractive and rewarding power, which Hegel sees as evidence that geometry is not "conceptual"—that is, does not follow the subject matter's own order and necessity.)

Purposiveness . . . is only external: Although the sequence of steps does have a rational form, it concerns only the way in which our subjective knowledge is to be satisfied, so it is external to the subject matter.

The evidence that characterizes: The intellectual experience of certainty which made Descartes and Spinoza set geometry as the model for all branches of knowledge, including philosophy.

the magnitude. This is precisely an inessential, Conceptless relation.° Hence, the movement of Knowing proceeds on the surface
and fails to touch the matter itself, the essence or the Concept; so
it is therefore no Conception [*begreifen*] at all. As for the material
about which mathematics offers such a delightful treasure of truths,
it is space and the unit. Space° is the existence into which the Concept inscribes its distinctions as to an empty, dead element, in which
they are likewise lifeless and unmoved. The actual is not something
spatial,° as it is thought to be in mathematics. Neither philosophy
nor concrete sense perception° is as interested in such nonactuality

An inessential, Conceptless relation: Magnitude belongs to quantity and thus
to the surface of being, the area lacking interiority and essentiality. As
such it is Conceptless. The division called "Concept" holds the third
super-category in the *Logic*, following "Being" and "Essence," and is considered their synthesis. Since mathematics has no relation to essence, it
is a fortiori irrelevant to the Concept. Also, as we have seen, a Concept
has the structure of an organic whole, yet in a quantitative science, where
diversity is merely aggregative, an organic structure is impossible.

Space: Hegel accepts most of the characteristics Kant gave to space, but
opposes viewing space as merely a "form of intuition." Space is a form
of *being*, though of a low, quantitative kind. (a) In *The Philosophy of Nature*
(part of the *Encyclopaedia*) Hegel defines space as the Concept's externalization into existence; more precisely: space is the merely quantitative
first stage of that externalization. (b) According to our more picturesque
text, the Concept inscribes its differences onto the inert, undifferentiated
matter of being, and this is the origin of space. (c) In any case, space is
not a pure form, but a homogenous continuum of being, which still lacks
motion and qualitative distinctions; the only differences it recognizes are
those of addition and subtraction: expansion and shrinking of one and
the same mathematical quality. As such—as pure quantity—space is the
substrate of reality, but is not itself fully actual. This view excludes Berkeley's kind of idealism, which allows space no reality whatever, and also
rejects Kant's view of space as an external form of intuition.

The actual is not something spatial: An imprudent sentence, which calls for
more precision. Hegel does not say that what is actual cannot have spatial
characteristics—it certainly can, and has; he says that what is actual is not
spatial "*it is thought to be in mathematics.*" In other words, its actuality
does not consist in its spatiality as inert quantifiable being. Space is only
a moment of actuality, the basis for its externality, and as such is necessary

as are the things of mathematics. In a nonactual element there is only nonactual truth, namely, fixed and static propositions. We may stop at any of these propositions; the next starts anew for itself,° without the former moving further into its other, and therefore without maintaining a necessary and mutual interconnection between them, as ought to arise from the nature of the matter itself.

Also—this is the root of the formal character of mathematical evidence—because of its principle and element, knowing proceeds here on the track of identity.° That which is dead, because it does not move, does not reach the differentiation of the essence, or the essential opposition or nonidentity, and therefore does not get to the passage of opposite into opposite, to the qualitative, immanent movement, and to self-movement. For it is only magnitude, an inessential difference° which mathematics considers. It abstracts from

---

for it. Yet actuality cannot be reduced to its spatial dimension alone (against materialism).

Sense perception: Even the one-sided, illusory appearance of the world as grasped by the senses is more real than space, because it contains a diversity of qualities.

Starts anew for itself: This echoes Kant's critique of the deductive ("mathematical") method, in which every proposition is considered fully significant and conclusively true at any stage of the development. There is no corrective backward movement, and no drive to go forward. Wherever we stop, the system shuts off. In philosophy, however, which is the gradual self-explication of reason, earlier cognitions depend on those which follow them. Therefore, the movement does not stop before one reaches the complete system.

The track of identity: Hegel here uses *Gleichheit* (equality) in the sense of identity. Because the matter of pure mathematics is homogeneous and lacks distinctions (except for quantitative distinctions, which are themselves uniform), mathematical knowledge is capable of being formal and thus attaining great clarity and convincing power. The price it pays is renouncing the actuality and content of material differences.

An inessential difference: Distinctions in magnitude are secondary or unessential. Things are distinguished from one another by their contents, their essence, the degree of their being, and these cannot be reduced to

the fact that it is the Concept which divides° space into its dimensions and determines the connections within and between them. For example, mathematics does not contemplate° the line's relation to the plane, and when comparing the circle's diameter to its circumference, it runs into incommensurability,° namely, into something infinite—a relation of the Concept which eludes its comprehension.°

Immanent mathematics (also called pure mathematics) also does not consider time as time° in juxtaposition to space as the second material of its consideration. Of course, applied mathematics° deals with time, and also with motion and other real

---

distinctions in magnitude. This goes against Descartes, and against taking mechanism to be the last word of philosophy.

It is the Concept which divides: As the Concept externalizes itself into space, (a) it endows itself with external being (albeit at the lowest level), and (b) geometry finds its foundations within the Concept.

Does not contemplate: Mathematics is unaware of its foundations. For example, the relations between basic elements of Euclidean space (point, line, plane, volume) are not discussed in mathematics, which accepts them as given, dogmatically.

Incommensurability: The phenomenon in mathematics of irrational numbers and of incommensurability in general testifies that quantity is not reality's last word. (This line of argument recalls Einstein's refusal to admit quantum physics as the last word about the universe.)

Something infinite . . . which eludes its comprehension: Hegel distinguishes between "a good infinity," which is a circular, subject-like system, and the "bad infinity" of open-ended quantitative sequence. The first is the symbol of reason, the second is a model of irrationality—of that which eludes reason's grasp. Strictly speaking, the "bad" kind should not be called "infinity" but only "indefiniteness."

Time as time: Time as pure duration or continuity (which Kant saw as the ground of arithmetic)—as distinguished from physical or applied time (time as the *t*-factor in scientific formulae). The latter is discussed in physics and other fields of "applied mathematics." Yet, Hegel complains, we have no proper discussion of time *as time*—its essence, properties, relation to space, and so forth. Whereas geometry is also an investigation of the properties of space, number theory is not in itself a study of the properties of time.

Applied mathematics: Mathematics as functioning in the natural sciences.

things.° But the synthetic propositions concerning the relations between those things—relations which [actually] the Concept determines—are drawn from experience; applied mathematics only applies its own formulae to these presuppositions. The fact that the so-called proofs which mathematics allegedly gives to these [physical] propositions—for example, concerning the lever, or the relation between space and time in a falling motion—are indeed given and accepted as proofs, only serves to prove how strongly knowledge needs proofs; for when it lacks them, it will revere even the empty appearance° of a proof and draw some satisfaction from it. A critique of such proofs will be as remarkable as it is instructive, first, in order to purify mathematics of these false ornaments,° and secondly, in order to indicate its boundaries,° and thereby show the need for a different kind of knowing.

Other real things: So it does not deal with it as time. For example, the *t* units in a physical formula use a notion of time as a variable in physics, but do not contemplate what time as time is, philosophically.

Empty appearance: The mathematical demonstrations working in physics are external to the content of their subject matter. They impose a certain type of order and procedure upon opaque cognitions, which we get from experience; but they cannot explain the physical phenomenon itself and why it is as it is. Mechanics, the basis of classical physics, is grounded on the phenomenon of motion; and motion entails a relation of time and space which can be expressed mathematically; but we do not thereby understand what the matter itself is, why a relation between time and space exists at all, and what binds them together. The sense of satisfaction which applied mathematics raises in us is therefore exaggerated, and tinged with illusion.

False ornaments: Vain expectations of those using mathematics.

Indicate its boundaries: This is Hegel's main purpose. His critique is not intended to abolish mathematics, or to restrain its development or that of physics and the other natural sciences in which mathematics is applied. These are all indispensable branches of knowledge. However, their *philosophical* value is poor, because they don't reach true actualities. Hegel's critique of pure and applied mathematics is only meant to point out the external character of mathematical measurements and proof-procedures, and thereby to indicate the limitations and relative failure of mathematics when it claims to explain and interpret reality.

Concerning time: One might think° that time, as counterpart to space, constitutes the material of the second part of pure mathematics [arithmetic]. Yet time is the existing Concept itself.° The principle of magnitude, the Conceptless difference, and the principle of identity, the abstract unit devoid of life, cannot come to terms with that pure unrest of life and of [time's] absolute differentiation. This negativity, therefore, becomes the second material of mathematical knowledge only in paralyzed form, namely, as the One. It is a knowledge which, as external activity, degrades the self-moving into material, in which it finds an indifferent, external, and lifeless content.

Philosophy, by contrast,° does not consider the inessential determination, but the determination insofar as it is an essential one; the element and content of philosophy is not the abstract and non-actual, but the actual, which posits itself in itself and lives in itself—existence in its Concept.° It is the process which engenders its mo-

---

One might think: It appears as if time stands on the same ontological level as space. Actually time is higher with respect to its status and structure.

The existing Concept itself: Unlike space, time is not a mere externalization of the Concept, but is the Concept itself as existing. In that respect, temporal duration is a mirror image of the Concept's own movement, and can likewise not be reduced to a series of simple units. Time, with the organic form of the Concept at its base, expresses "the pure unrest of life," and therefore the going-beyond, the ecstasies of every discrete unit which must transcend itself. This is why time, as a continuum produced by the self-transcendence of each of its alleged units, cannot be captured by a simple series of numbers. The attempt to do so results in an inadequate presentation, a paralyzed view of time's flow and negativity. The back-and-forth movement between the discrete and the continuous dimensions of time is frozen by the theory of numbers into an inert unit, a unit indicated by the expression "one." That unit is then added to itself in an external aggregative manner $(1 + 1 + 1 \ldots)$, and this is the foundation of the theory of numbers, and of numerical calculations in other sciences.

Philosophy, by contrast: As distinguished from mathematical knowledge, and from the empirical-historical knowledge which we have discussed.

Existence in its Concept: As distinguished from the two kinds of knowledge mentioned above. Mathematics and empirical knowledge of particulars, presents being (*Sein*) and existence (*Dasein*) respectively, neither as within

ments and goes through them; and the complete movement constitutes the positive and its truth. Truth, then, contains the negative—that which would have been called false, if it could have been viewed as something from which one must abstract.°

That which vanishes must be rather considered essential, though not in the mode of something rigid that should be cut away from the true and left outside, who knows where; just as the true must not be considered a lifeless positive [element] which lies inert on the other side. Appearance° [the phenomenon] is the generation and passing away which itself is neither generated nor passes away, but is in itself and constitutes the actuality of truth and the movement of its life. The true is thus the Bacchanalian whirl° in which

---

their Concepts, nor according to their essence. They therefore lack truth, which is the unity of existence and its Concept.

From which one must abstract: Which one must completely abolish. This is how people think of falsity—that it must be completely done away with. Hegel at this point accepts the ordinary manner of speaking, reiterates that falsity must not be seen as a moment of truth, even though truth contains negativity. As I mentioned earlier, Hegel's interest here is rhetorical rather than substantive. Because the nondialectical sense of "falsity" dominates public discourse, and there is little chance of changing this, Hegel decides to rephrase his position in terms of the current idiom. So instead of calling the essential element "false," he calls it "negative" or "evanescent," but—this is the main point—insists that as such it ought to be preserved within truth.

Appearance: According to Hegel's metaphysics, essence must appear externally. Appearance is therefore a constant moment of truth. Particular things appear and pass away, though appearance itself persists. It is as fixed and eternal as essence.

The Bacchanalian whirl: A famous image of the *Phenomenology.* An extended explanation is given in the introduction, and a parallel image is offered on the previous page: "the pure unrest of life." Basically, the "Bacchanalian whirl" indicates that the system of truth is a circle of mutual negations. Every ingredient in the system, when considered in itself, transcends its own particularity and passes over into the others. Their mutual negation and interconnection constitutes a stable system, which is pure and eternal but not frozen, rather existing as permanent motion. Hegel compares this movement to worshippers dancing in the cult of Bacchus

there is no link which is not drunk; but since each [link] dissolves immediately when disconnecting, the whirl is equally a simple and transparent rest. Before that movement's court of justice,° neither the singular shapes of spirit,° nor the determinate thoughts° can subsist; nevertheless, they are just as much positive and necessary moments as they are negative and vanishing. In the whole of the movement taken as rest, that which differentiates and gives itself particular existence is retained as something that interiorizes and remembers itself° [*sich erinnert*], whose existence is its knowing of itself, just as its knowing itself is immediately existence.

(that is, Dionysus), each of whom ecstatically transcends himself or herself, and passing into the other, thereby regains singularity from the general movement. Hegel cautiously exploits the mystical implications of this image, but insists that the final outcome is dominated by the Concept. The circle as a whole seems to exist in a state of purity and rational transparency, yet it comprehends the power of life and even the power of mystical experience, translated into rational terms. (Nietzsche used a similar image in *The Birth of Tragedy*—the drunken dance of the Dionysian cult, though without a rational outcome—to explain the power of life and tragedy underlying his philosophy.)

Court of justice: This passage alludes to the pre-Socratics, especially Anaximander, for whom the coming-to-be and passing away of particulars was dominated by the principle of "justice." Hegel may also be hinting that the movement of history is a kind of "divine justice," a theodicy, since previous forms of life and spirit which have passed away contribute to spirit's progress and the coming-to-be of truth. This is surely no consolation to an individual sunk in suffering or falsity, but Hegel does not wish to console such an individual, because he recognizes no individual providence, not even in a secular version.

Neither the singular shapes of spirit: Meaning the historical shapes of spirit as they arise in the *Phenomenology.*

Nor the determinate thoughts: [Any more than] the categories of philosophy as they arise in the *Logic.* Hegel speaks here, in a general way, of both parts of his intended system. Both are supposed to be shaped by the form of the Bacchanalian revel, that "whirl" which is the court of justice, condemning each particular form to perish as long as it stands only as particular.

Interiorizes and remembers itself: The Concept of memory, or interiorizing-into-memory (*Erinnerung*) receives a further meaning which, not accidentally, directly precedes Hegel's discussion of philosophical method. In a

It may seem that the method° of this movement, or of science, requires a long prefatory discussion. Yet its Concept is already contained in what we said above,° and its genuine exhibition belongs to logic,° or rather, is logic. For method is nothing but the structure of the whole as it is constructed [*aufgestellt*] in its pure

---

dialectical, subject-like system, whatever has gone before, and passed away, is retained in the inwardness of memory. That interiorization, as we have seen before, is the reason why a negation of negation does not result in a return to the dialectical starting point. A system's capacity to interiorize its previous experiences at some level of consciousness (or subconsciousness) is therefore a necessary condition for a dialectical form to exist. In an inert, nondialectical system, which lacks the capacity for interiorization, the negation of negation does lead back to the point of departure, and the order dominating the system is that of formal logic or mathematics. However, each entity that has an organic structure, and hence the capacity to interiorize a previous set of relations, even if it has already been negated and transcended, is a possible subject of a dialectical process and capable of demonstrating the characteristic Hegelian structure of *Aufhebung*. In addition, the very capacity to interiorize into memory demonstrates that at some level of consciousness the substrate of the process is *not* knowledge. The reality we are dealing with is not only an object, but also a subject, not merely an inert substance, but one having the capacity for awareness and self-consciousness.

The method: The following pages are devoted to discussing philosophical method.

What we said above: The general principle of philosophical method is implied in the principle we have discussed: the absolute is subject, the true is the whole which includes its own becoming, and philosophy must follow the progress of its own subject matter from within. Given these principles, it is easy to understand why no a priori method is possible in philosophy.

Its genuine exposition belongs to logic: One cannot present the method of philosophy without spelling out the philosophical system itself. The system's complete exhibition (which Hegel here calls "Logic") is the only adequate way of realizing the method. The *Logic* works out the basic categories of all there is. As such, the *Logic* does not *deal* with the method, but *is* in itself—in its full layout—also the method. There is no special theory of, or chapter on, method in the *Logic*, because philosophy has no theory of method distinct from its actual unfolding. Hegel is opposed

essentiality.° As to what has been going on until now in this do-main—the whole system of opinions about the nature of philo-sophical method—we must take notice that it belongs to a culture that is now obsolete. If this claim sounds boastful or revolutionary (although I know this tone is far from what I intend), let me point out that even current opinion views the scientific apparatus of-fered by mathematics—with its explanations, divisions, and rows of theorems, its demonstrations, principles, and the conclusions derived from them—at least as old-fashioned.° Even when its in-adequacy is not clearly seen, it is never or seldom used; and

---

to most modern philosophers, from Bacon and Descartes onward, who wanted philosophy to begin with the theory of method as a separate topic which must precede actual, substantive philosophizing, and provide a priori rules to guide it. Locke's *Essay*, and even Kant's *Critique*, can also be seen as "an essay on method" preceding substantive philosophy. Amongst all of Hegel's major philosophical predecessors, only Spinoza opposed this trend. He argued that a method is knowledge of knowledge, but we cannot know what knowledge is before we have actual knowledge. Therefore "method" must be studied retrospectively, after we have al-ready gained true knowledge (*Treatise on the Improvement of the Intellect*, paragraph 38). Hegel holds with Spinoza the minority position, as will be seen in the next sentence.

Method is nothing but the structure of the whole as it is constructed [aufgestellt] in its pure essentiality: This is Hegel's most succinct statement about method. There is no a priori method in philosophy. The word "method" does not refer to a set of procedural rules guiding philosophy, but to the structure of its result. When the complete system attains its form, and we view and reconstruct its pure structure from this retrospective standpoint, then we have its method. Of course, this is not the ordinary sense of method, as Hegel would agree. But he would add that philosophy does not have a method in the "ordinary sense." Its pure, logical structure arises out of its evolving subject matter, as a result of that process. The science of method is therefore a reflexive science which contemplates the unfolded result of the system, and extracts its distinctive features ex post facto.

Old-fashioned: The view that philosophy needs a quasi-mathematical method has become old-fashioned. Hegel interprets its decline as the decline of the demand for an a priori philosophical method, though they are not the same.

although not denied in itself, it is not loved. But we must have the prejudice that an excellent thing will put itself into use and make itself loved.

It is not hard to see that the manner which puts forth a proposition, adduces reasons in its favor, and refutes its opposite by other reasons, is not the form by which truth can emerge.° Truth is the movement of itself within itself; whereas that [reasoning] method° is knowledge which is external to the material. Therefore, it is proper to mathematics°—whose principle, as mentioned, is the

Is not the form by which truth can emerge: Having criticized and limited the power of mathematics per se, Hegel now attacks the desire to transpose mathematical method onto philosophy.

That [reasoning] method: The reasons why mathematical method does not fit philosophy are as follows: First, mathematics is a quantitative science, and therefore inappropriate for knowing anything qualitative; and actual being, the topic of philosophy, is qualitative. Second, the underlying topics of mathematics, space and unit, are inert; it is therefore inappropriate for systems possessing the capacity for organic, or semiorganic, subject-like self-movement. There is a further objection which Hegel took, at least implicitly, from Kant. In the mathematical method itself, regardless of the topic to which it is applied, we have at every stage concepts that are exhaustively defined, and propositions that are conclusively true, which we can neither correct nor reconsider. In philosophy, however, as Kant says, "the incomplete exposition [explication] precedes the complete one" (*Critique of Pure Reason*, A 730/B 758). Philosophy is the self-explication of reason which cannot proceed in a linear fashion, but only in recurring circles or loops by which reason modifies, reconsiders, and corrects its previous achievements. These previous statements, therefore, necessarily include a measure of vagueness and falsity. Hegel implicitly subscribes to this view, and develops it in the *Phenomenology* in a far-reaching way.

It is proper to mathematics: Mathematical method is unquestionably valid for its own special subject matter and its applications in empirical science and daily affairs and arguments. As mentioned above, Hegel does not challenge the validity of the forms of nondialectical understanding. His approach is critical in the Kantian sense; that is, he examines the capabilities and shortcomings of the nondialectical forms of thought, and limits each to the legitimate domain for which it is necessary. At the same time, though, he denies its pretension to transcend the domain

Conceptless relation of magnitude, and whose material is the dead space and the equally dead unit—and must be left to it. In a freer manner,° mixed with arbitrary and accidental elements, this method can also be maintained in ordinary life, in conversation, or in historical instruction, which aim to satisfy curiosity more than knowledge. In ordinary life, the content of consciousness is made up of cognitions, experiences, sensible concretions, also thoughts and basic principles,° and in general, such [items] that one considers to be given to consciousness beforehand, or to be a fixed and static being or essence. Sometimes consciousness follows those contents, and sometimes, by exercising free will [*die freie Willkür*],°

---

of its effective and legitimate application, and to serve as a model for philosophy.

In a freer manner: The method of argumentation, which belongs to the domain of the Understanding, has an important role in everyday discourse, in the acquisition of nonphilosophical knowledge, and in a philosophical introduction like the one before us. But in philosophy proper, truth cannot arise through argument and counterargument; for such a technique, like geometrical demonstrations, only manipulates the subject matter from without. In philosophy one must follow the internal evolution of the subject matter itself, and structure it according to the needs arising from the process. Therefore (we may add), philosophy also contains a quasi-narrative element, which does not deal with details, but rather follows the logically necessary transformations of the subject matter.

Also thoughts and basic principles: Hegel places sensory experience and the axioms of the understanding on the same dogmatic level. Rational axioms, when experienced as direct evidence, are "rigid thoughts," which, like sensory data, arise without mediation. As such, they belong to the noncritical consciousness and count among the mind's prejudices.

By exercising free will [die freie Willkür]: By way of arbitrary, and therefore dogmatic, decisions. According to Hegel, one is not necessarily liberated from dogmatism by making a decision to break one's attachments to the immediate contents of consciousness and subject them to critical scrutiny. Rather, dogmatism persists as long as we try to arrive at an explanation through an external and formal logical manipulation of the explained, which eventually is reduced to some other primary datum familiar to us and experienced as evident. This is so for two reasons: first, this knowledge, like mathematical demonstrations, is external to the subject matter;

it breaks the connection and relates to them as their external determination and manipulation. It leads the content back to something certain, be it even a momentary sensation, and when reaching a familiar resting point, conviction is satisfied.

Still, as we have mentioned, although the Concept's necessity banishes the loose march of the reasoning conversation as well as the rigidity of scientific pomposity,° their place should not be taken by the nonmethod of vague intuition [*Ahnung*] and enthusiasm, or by the arbitrariness of prophetic talk,° which disdain not only this, but any scientific approach.

When triplicity, which Kant had rediscovered° by instinct and still as something dead and Conceptless, was raised to its absolute

---

second, it is dogmatic in itself, since all it does is lead us from a sensible to an intellectual primary datum, that is, from one to another. It subsumes the first under the second without dismantling the idea of "primary" or "simple" data as such. I think that Hegel specifically has in mind Descartes, the father of geometrical method in philosophy, who demanded that sensible data be explained on the basis of the data of intellectual evidence. Descartes was also a philosopher who tried to break away from dogmatism through a major decision of the will. Hegel, like Spinoza, does not believe that one can overcome dogmatism through an arbitrary decision. One can only overcome dogmatism by the gradual development of consciousness.

Of scientific pomposity: Of those who use formal science as a philosophical method.

Arbitrariness of prophetic talk: Formal Understanding was also attacked by mystics, romantics, and prophetic visionaries, from whom Hegel separates himself. One should not interpret Hegel's critique of formal science as a critique of the very idea of scientific inquiry. Formal science is valid and necessary within the boundaries set for it by critical reason, as a product of the understanding. Beyond those boundaries, what is needed is not a mystical delusion, but a different kind of scientificity or scientific approach.

Which Kant had rediscovered: For Kant, the third category within each of the four groups making up the table of categories is a synthesis of its two predecessors. For example, totality is a synthesis of unity and plurality; limitation is a synthesis of reality and negation; and so on (*Critique of Pure Reason*, B111). Hegel views this as one of Kant's important philosophical

significance, the true form was placed in the true content,° and the Concept of Science emerged.° But here again, we should avoid considering as scientific that use of triplicity which degrades it to a lifeless schema, indeed to a phantom, and reduces scientific organization to a table. We discussed° this formalism above in general terms, and will now describe its manner more closely.

---

discoveries, which remained undeveloped until Fichte "raised it to its absolute significance," by deriving the triad from the complex structure of the Kantian "I think." Hegel's praise does not, however, subscribe to Fichte's formalistic use of the schema "thesis-antithesis-synthesis," which he applied indifferently and repetitively to any subject matter, and does not support the view that Hegelian dialectic can be captured by a formula, this or any other. The three-tiered structure of the dialectic can, and often must, take less expected, more flexible shapes at various stages of the system's unfolding. This is because the process is *structuring itself* in accordance with the diversity of the subject matter it traverses, rather than obeying, as in Descartes, some ready-made a priori rule. The three-tiered design is therefore an ex post facto result. It emerges from the process rather than controlling it in advance, and should be expected to yield a variety of particular forms, each responding to the context in which it arises. That the Berlin Hegel became somewhat more rigid and didactic as a system-builder does not change this analysis of his original position. The original position is sounder in terms of Hegel's other strong claims—and other views, concerning method, or the relation of form and content; and it is manifest in the quite unique texture of the *Phenomenology* and the *Logic*, the only Hegelian texts in which we see the dialectic actually at work (rather than merely summarized in retrospect).

True form was placed in the true content: Fichte, unlike Kant, derived the triadic form from the philosophical content itself—the I in relation to the non-I—rather than from an accidental and transient intuition.

And the Concept of Science emerged: Meaning Fichte's *Wissenschaftslehre*, which Hegel, despite his many ironic criticisms, credits as the beginning of true philosophical scientificity. From Kant arises the goal of establishing metaphysics as a science; Fichte, rather than Kant, opened the way to the realization of that goal by positing the triad as the principle of philosophical Science. Hegel, therefore, links himself to Fichte, and perhaps also to Schelling, as having gone decisively beyond their master,

This formalism believes it has conceived and expressed the nature and life of some shape by attributing to it one of the schema's determinations as predicate°—be it subjectivity or objectivity, magnetism, electricity, contraction and expansion, east and west, and the like.° This can be multiplied to infinity, since every determination and shape can be made to serve as another shape's form or moment according to that schema—and in gratitude, each will render the same service to the others: a circle of reciprocity in which it is impossible to experience what is the one, and what is the other, and what the matter itself is. These determinations are borrowed partly from ordinary sense perception [*Anschauung*]—in which case, of course, they are meant to signify something else from what they say—and partly they are taken from what has significance in itself,° namely, from pure thought-determinations like subject, object, substance, cause, the universal, and so forth. However, they are used

---

Kant. However, Hegel will soon argue that Fichte and Schelling failed to attain a truly scientific philosophy because they did not give it a living form. (Here again we have an example of a "dialectical" refutation in philosophy, which recognizes the great novelty in a thinker, yet exposes his failure to carry his own revolution out.)

We discussed: See text and commentary to pages 89 ff., which provide the background also for the following pages.

As predicate: The structure of Fichte's system is predicative. Each form which life and experience take serves as a rigid subject whose "nature and life" are purportedly explained by linking it to some new rigid predicate: "x is y." Fichte's procedure does not involve dismantling those rigid predicates and "setting them in motion" within a fluid system, as Hegel claims to do.

Magnetism, electricity, . . .: These examples are also discussed in Hegel's *Encyclopedia of the Philosophical Sciences*, a work which, ironically, is written in an even less "fluid" language than Fichte's *Wissenschaftslehre*. The *Encyclopedia* is a series of concise, compressed (and "frozen") paragraphs which are to be further developed by the lecturer.

What has significance in itself: An a priori category. The former (like "magnetism," or "east") are borrowed from empirical observation and artificially elevated to the rank of categories. Hegel argues that all are used uncritically, "as in daily life."

in the same uncritical and unexamined way as in ordinary life, or
as when speaking of strengths and weaknesses, expansion and contraction; so that this [rational] metaphysics is as unscientific as
those sensual images.

Such a simple determination, instead of being taken from the
inner life and self-movement of its existence, is drawn from intuition—which here means sensual knowing—and is expressed by
a superficial analogy;° and this empty, external application of the
formula is called a "construction." This formalism is like any other.
How dull must be the head which cannot be stuffed within a quar-
ter of an hour with the theory that there are asthenic, sthenic, and
indirectly asthenic diseases, and as many cures, and thus [expect
to] be transformed in that short time from a common healer [*Routi-
nier*] into a theoretical physician (for such instruction was considered sufficient until recently)? When the formalism of the philosophy of nature° teaches, for example, that the intellect is electricity,
or that the animal is nitrogen, or that it is equal to the south, to
the north, et cetera,° when it presents its teaching either in this
naked form, or brewed with further terminology—an inexperienced mind might stand in dazed wonder in front of such power,
which links together what seems to be so distant, and in front of
the violence done° to the immovable sensual image, to which that

Superficial analogy: Fichte's *Theory of Science*, like Schelling's *Philosophy of
Nature*, is constructed from the intuitive discovery of analogies and paral-
ogisms which obtain between phenomena, rather than on the deduction
or inner derivation of their contents.
The formalism of the philosophy of nature: This irony is also aimed at Schelling.
The intellect is electricity . . .: Examples of the "superficial analogy" mentioned above.
The violence done: The doctrine which Hegel attacks establishes connections between remote concepts by coercion, as if by an act of violence.
However, we must stress that Hegel does not find all such connections
between remote concepts to be violent or artificial. The crucial question
is whether we have followed through the inner development and mediation which obtains between them or not. A special kind of intellectual
violence occurs when a sensual image is given the dignity of a concept.
Hegel attributes this particular vice to Schelling, although he himself falls

linkage gave a false appearance of a Concept, while avoiding the main task—namely, the need to express the Concept itself, or the meaning of the sensual image. In all this an inexperienced mind will revere a profound genius. It will rejoice in the brightness of these definitions, which replace an abstract Concept with an observable ersatz and thus make it more attractive, and will congratulate itself for its soul-kinship with so splendid an enterprise. The trick of such wisdom is easy to learn and easy to exercise; but to repeat it when it has become known is as tiresome as repeating a pickpocket's sleight-of-hand whose secret has been exposed.

The instrument of this monotonous formalism is no more difficult to operate than a painter's palette which has two colors only, say red and green, one serving to color a historical picture, and the other a landscape. It is hard to decide which is greater: the facility with which everything in heaven, on earth, and under the earth is coated with this painter's-broth, or the conceited claim to excellence of this universal medium: the one supports the other. This method, which sticks to everything terrestrial and celestial, to every natural and spiritual shape, the few determinations of the universal schema, and thus labels and classes everything, yields nothing less than a "report as clear as daylight"° about the organism of the universe— that is, a table, resembling a skeleton on which paper-notes are stuck, or rows of closed boxes with labels in a spice dealer's shop.° That report is as clear as those two. In the example of the skeleton, the flesh and blood have been removed from the bones, and in the second example the boxes are hiding the matter [*Sache*], which itself is

---

prey to the same fallacy, as we can see in his *Philosophy of Nature* where empirical concepts like "air," "light," "electricity," "water," "disease," and the like appear as philosophical categories.

"Report as clear as daylight": A barb against the title of Fichte's work "A Report as Clear as Daylight to the General Public about the True Character of the New Philosophy: An Attempt to Force the Reader to Understand" (1801).

Closed boxes with labels in a spice dealer's shop: This is a deadly sarcastic attack on the formula "thesis-antithesis-synthesis," which is Fichte's (although it is attributed to Hegel himself by innumerable books and references, that fail to recognize his antiformalistic system).

not alive. Similarly, the report leaves out or hides the living essence of the matter. This approach, as we noted, culminates° in a totally monochromatic painting: ashamed of the schema's differences, it sinks them in the absolute's void as belonging to reflection, from which pure identity arises, the formless whiteness.° The schema's monochromatic character and lifeless determinations, like this pure identity and like the passage from the one to the other, are all alike a dead understanding and are all equally external knowledge.

Indeed, the most excellent thing cannot escape its destiny—to be deprived of its life and spirit and, thus abused, to see its flayed skin° adorning a lifeless and vain knowledge. But that is not the whole story:° in its very destiny we can recognize the power which the excellent thing exercises on people's hearts, if not on their minds, and also to notice the process of schooling it undergoes, a schooling toward [true] universality and the [true] specificity of form,° in which its fulfillment consists, and which alone makes it possible to use this universality also in the service of superficiality.

Science must organize itself° only through the Concept's own life. The determination, which others take from the schema and

---

Culminates: This way of thinking is liable to end in mysticism, because, ashamed of its schematic and frozen distinctions, it tries to dissolve them in the one indistinct absolute, that is, in the void.

Formless whiteness: This image is analogous to the "night in which all cows are black," above. In both cases, Hegel hints at the indistinctness of Schelling's absolute. Hegel argues that Fichte's failure to suggest real, live distinctions led to a dead, spiritless scheme. This prompted Schelling to abandon all distinctions and dissolve them in the empty One.

Its flayed skin: The scheme that replaced the set of living distinctions.

But that is not the whole story: There is also a positive side to this matter, because the truth of the new philosophy remains present even in the systems that force it into dead schemes, and the new philosophy is what actually makes those systems possible. The power and actuality of the new philosophy of idealism can be seen in the influence it exercises over people's hearts, for it continues to evolve even within those systems which falsify its message, and nevertheless strives towards its highest form, concrete universality.

stick to existence from outside [triplicity], is in Science the self-moving soul of the fulfilled content. That which is [*das Seiende*] goes through a movement° which becomes other, thus becoming its own immanent content, and on the other hand, takes this unfolding, or its existence, back into itself; namely, it makes itself into a moment and simplifies itself into a specific determination. In the former movement, negativity consists in the differentiation and positing of existence; and in the movement of return-to-self, negativity is the becoming of the determinate simplicity. This is how the content shows that it does not receive its specific determination from something else, as when stapling a label, but gives it to itself,° and ranges its own place out of itself as a moment of the whole. The table-like understanding keeps for itself the necessity and Concept of the content, [namely,] that which constitutes the concrete and living actuality of the matter it ranges. Or rather, it does not keep it, but simply does not know it; for if it had this insight, it would surely have manifested it. It does not even feel the need° for

Specificity of form: The form of triplicity.

Science must organize itself: In retrospect, the triad is the form organizing the philosophical Science, yet, that form must derive from "the Concept's own life," that is, from the evolution of its content. This form is thereby "the self-moving soul" of the content, rather than an a priori schema imposed upon it externally.

That which is [das Seiende] goes through a movement: Hegel reiterates the structure of dialectical movement—self-becoming in three stages—which he has already described several times before.

Gives it to itself: This is one of Hegel's most speculative ideas, that of self-particularization. The particular contents arise through a dialectical movement, neither as a mere catalog of sense contents or dogmatic thoughts, nor by "stapling a label." As I have suggested above, an element of empirical "being so" remains in Hegel's philosophy. Yet all particular contents are supposed to derive from spirit's recollection, namely from the internalized, historical form of its experience that has been interiorized in memory and become an organic part of spirit itself.

It does not even feel the need: This is the chief symptom of a frozen concept. Dialectic recognizes the necessity of the inferior forms of the understanding, but presumes that their deficiency creates a need that drives them beyond themselves. For this to happen, however, it is necessary that the

this, otherwise it would renounce its schematization, or at least view it as a Table of Contents° merely. Indeed, this understanding does not deliver the content, but only indicates its table.

Even a specific determination (say, magnetism) which is concrete or actual in itself, is cast down into something dead when it is only predicated of another entity,° but is not known as that entity's immanent life,° or as having in that entity its own native and genuine self-engendering° and exhibition. The formal understanding

---

lack be noticed, that the mind have a clear and strong awareness of it, or else the drive will be ineffective and a stalemate would arise, at least for the moment.

As a Table of Contents: I already mentioned the irony that Hegel's two final books are also written in such a style (the *Encyclopedia* and the *Philosophy of Right*). Each has the form of a compendium which succinctly crystallizes the Idea at its base, as a list of chapter headings which need oral development. In addition, both Hegel's followers and his opponents gave an even more schematic image to his later works than they actually deserved. Disciples, as is well known, tend to be more rigid and pedantic than their master, sometimes to the point of absurdity, and opponents rejoice in each absurdity they can denounce. Actually, from the logic of Hegel's system it follows that, since form follows content, the system cannot take on a rigid, monotonously repetitious form. Indeed, the two fully developed works Hegel wrote, the *Phenomenology* and the *Logic*, evolve in a rather free and flexible manner, and take various unexpected routes which cannot be enclosed in a rigid framework. The only uniformity they maintain is the circular, dialectical movement, that is, the triad taken in a broad, macro sense; but there is much freedom in how that movement proceeds, and where it turns each time.

Only predicated of another entity: See commentary on the problem of rigid predication, above.

Immanent life: Instead of linking rigid predicates which define one another in accidental strings, the philosopher should grasp the meaning of one predicate as belonging to the "self-movement" of the other, and as internally constituting that other.

Its own native and genuine self-engendering (also translatable as, "its original and unique way of self-generation."): The generation of each category from the dynamic context of all other categories involves a spontaneous element of emergence, or "self-engendering." It is not a mechanical or merely analytic deduction, and the necessity involved in this unique gen-

leaves to others the task of adding that main thing. Instead of penetrating into the matter's immanent content, the formal understanding overviews the whole and stands above the singular entity of which it speaks—that is, does not see it at all. Scientific knowledge, however, requires that we give ourselves up to the life of the Concept, or—which is the same—face and express its inner necessity. In so deepening its object, scientific knowledge forgets that overview, which is but the reflection of knowledge in itself outside of the content.° Rather, in being immersed in the content and following its movement, it returns to itself—not before the filling or content has taken itself back into itself, simplified itself into a specific determination, reduced itself to one side of an existence [*Dasein*] and passed into its higher truth.

---

eration is not automatic, as with an algorithm. Each step in this movement involves an original activity, a new or renewed act which cannot be reduced to its predecessor, although what has gone before it is a necessary condition for its generation. In other words, the dialectical progression is neither analytic nor synthetic (in the Kantian sense), but a synthesis of both. The movement of the other categories leads each particular category to the threshold of its emergence and definition, yet the last step is always the *original* "self-engendering" of that category. The ultimate content characterizing a particular category, and the act by which it emerges, cannot be derived from the prior movement of the other Concepts in a deterministic way. We rather have a novel element here, a "synthetic" element, in two senses: first, the ultimate emerging content cannot be reduced to what preceded it (but needs the participation of recollection); and second, the new, emergent Concept requires a specific activity of thinking or spirit. It follows that philosophical reason—as spirit's activity—cannot be represented by an algorithm, by a computer model, or by a formal scheme.

The reflection of knowledge in itself outside of the content: Hegel reiterates that philosophy is not an external reflection which observes the content of reality from outside its development, but is an inner reflection of the content of reality itself. As such, it must become immersed in the content, and allow it to guide its progress. No wonder that eventually it returns to itself within that content.

In this way, the simple,° self-overviewing° whole emerges from the richness, in which its reflection seems to have been lost. Since substance in general, as we put it above, is in itself subject, every content is its own reflection in itself. The subsistence or substance° of an entity [*Dasein*] is its self-identity, since its being nonidentical to itself would be its dissolution. However, self-identity is pure abstraction; and the latter is thinking.° When I say quality, I enunciate the [Concept of] a simple determination; through quality°

Simple: This is the tranquil result into which the series of negations, "the Bacchanalian whirl," eventually crystallizes, after all the contents and configurations have passed over into one another. Actually, the whole only appears to be simple, but is not actually so. One might say it has a kind of "second simplicity," which results from the fact that the circular movement has, in its full articulation, attained a state which appears to be rest, but is in fact full actuality.

Self-overviewing: Reflection returns to itself from the confusion and richness of the specific contents within which it seems to have been lost during previous stages. And through philosophical consciousness reality gains reflection of itself as one whole.

The subsistence or substance: The permanent element of being.

And the latter is thinking: Hegel reformulates an idea he expressed before. Being and thinking belong to one another within the same undeveloped and abstract beginning. This idea, in pages 97–99, 114–15, and elsewhere, was discussed primarily from one of its aspects, arguing that to take thinking in its immediate simplicity is to take it as simple being. Here, Hegel approaches the idea from its other aspect. To take being in its simplicity, namely as self-identical, without any difference and distinction, is to hold onto being as pure abstraction, and thus as an intellectual entity, or thought. Hegel's discussion here is too scanty and obscure to be compared with its full treatment in the *Logic*.

Quality: In Hegel's *Logic*, the category of "quality" presupposes being. Quality is qualified being, a being of such and such a character. Hegel calls this "being there" (*Dasein*). By this he means a particular and determinate being which exists on a rather low ontological level—like a particular color, a sound, a disconnected fact, a mere idea—and not yet as concrete substance. The determinate character of "being there" indicates, first, that it is no longer mere indistinct being (*Sein*), but qualified being, a particular entity. Second, it indicates that the entity possesses at least a minimal uniqueness ("being-for-itself"), for it is capable of referring to

one entity° is different from another, or is an entity, is for itself,
or subsists by virtue of that simplicity with regard to itself.° Yet it
is thereby essentially thought. Herein lies the [proper] conception
of being as thought; hereto belongs the insight which seeks to
avoid the ordinary, Conceptless talk° about the identity of thinking
and being.

---

itself as distinct from all the others. Third, the uniqueness of that entity
and its being-for-itself are the result of the reciprocal negations in and by
which it stands in relation to everything that coexists with it as different,
and by virtue of which it is what it is. It follows that what seems to be a
"simple and primary" quality or fact is not so in actuality, because it owes
its very simplicity to a mediating system of relations and negations. In
principle, the simple entity before us is only *relatively* simple; yet, within
the overall texture of being, "being there" is the simplest and most primitive entity: its very being is nothing beyond a simple quality. The red spot
persists in its being only as long as it remains red. Change its specific
shade, even in a slight degree, and you have abolished the very being of
that entity. This state of affairs persists until the category of substance is
attained, which allows an entity's individuality to be preserved while its
quality changes.

One entity: *Dasein* in the sense of entity or specific-being.

Simplicity with regard to itself: The content, or simple quality, by which the
entity is self-identical is, as said before, its element of being by virtue of
which that entity is and persists. Yet that simple quality is an abstraction.
As such, one must "abstract from it," too; and view the simple quality
as due not to the simplicity of being, but to the simplicity of thinking.
For an abstraction does not exist by itself; it always points towards something else.

The ordinary, Conceptless talk: Many misunderstandings, especially within
idealism, result from the idea that being and thought are identical, an
identity-principle attributed to Parmenides. Hegel accepts this identity as
true and profound, but under the following conditions. First, it must be
construed as dialectical identity, rather than as simple equality. Therefore,
being cannot be reduced to thinking, as has been done by various "subjective idealists" from Berkeley to Leibniz. Second, the identity in question
must be recognized as being still abstract and primary, and in need of
further development and actualization. In other words, the dialectical
identity of being and thought is the outcome and final end of the evolution of spirit, rather than an atemporal ontological state. That evolution

Now because the entity's subsistence consists in its self-identity or pure abstraction, it is its abstraction from itself,° or its non-identity with itself and dissolution—its own inwardness and return-to-self—it is its becoming. By virtue of this nature of that which is [*das Seiende*], and insofar as this nature is there for knowledge, the activity of knowledge does not manipulate the content as something foreign, and is not its own reflection outside of the content: Science is not that idealism° which replaces the dogmatism of assertions° with a dogmatism of [subjective] assurances; in other words, it is not the dogmatism of self-certainty. Rather, while watching the content return to its own inwardness, the activity of knowledge is no less immersed in the content, because it is the content's immanent self, and at the same time it returns to itself,° because it is pure self-identity within otherness. In this way, the activity of knowledge is the cunning° which, while seeming to abstain from

---

of spirit requires that thought remain internal to being, namely, that it accompany and drive the process of actualization from within itself, rather than observe it through an external method.

Its abstraction from itself: The abolition of its simplicity, or of its direct equality to Self. Its immediate being is dissolved and passes into becoming.

Science is not that idealism: Hegel believes there is dogmatic idealism just as there is dogmatic realism. Philosophical Science is indeed idealism, but not of the dogmatic kind known in the past, which Hegel views as the dogmatism of self-consciousness replacing the dogmatism of the thing-in-itself.

Dogmatism of assertions: Dogmatic realism, which makes direct assertions of being as a thing-in-itself. This is the famous position which Kant criticized as "dogmatism."

At the same time it returns to itself: Knowledge is engrossed within the content of reality as its self, but within the content of reality, it also returns to itself as knowledge. Thus we have reflection, specifically inner reflection. The process of knowledge, or thinking, is not identical with its object but retains a distance from it, an inner distance, as it is itself within its other.

The cunning: A central concept in Hegel's philosophy of history. Because consciousness is immersed within the process, it seems to be lost within the multiplicity of its figures. It is unaware of its own activity. Thus, an

all activity, watches° how the [specific] determination is living its
concrete life in the belief that it is promoting its own particular
interests and self-preservation, while actually doing the opposite,
namely, dissolving itself into a moment of the whole.

The importance of the understanding was indicated earlier with
respect to substance as having self-consciousness; now we see its
importance with respect to substance as having existence.° Exis-
tence° is quality, is a determinateness which is equal to itself, or is

---

ironic gap is formed between what consciousness thinks and knows about
its activity, and the motivation and true significance of that activity. This
ironic gap is a permanent feature of spirit's evolution which Hegel calls
"the cunning of reason." People act from motivations of passion, ambition, violence, and exploitation, and thereby unwittingly contribute to
historical progress and reason's development in the world. (This happens
not only to great "historical heroes," but also to the multitude of people
in their ordinary lives and actions.) In the text before us, Hegel provides
the ontological basis for the cunning of reason. By dialectical necessity,
reason must exist and act within its other, including the narrow egoism
which makes particular individuals persevere and strive to dominate others. But, it is equally necessary that Reason should return to itself within
them, and make those particular strivings a means for realizing its *own*
universal end.

Watches: Actually, a bird's-eye view of the system is only available to consciousness at the end of the road, not amidst the process within which it
moves both earnestly (without irony) and ambitiously, yet paradoxically,
and with a degree of inner awareness and self-deception. The ironic standpoint which is capable of recognizing the cunning of reason in history is
born retrospectively, when consciousness reconstitutes its past movements, and observes how it had been furthering universal goals while
striving merely to further its own particular objectives.

As having existence: In most of the foregoing text, the intellect's major role
has been seen from the standpoint of "subjective logic"—that is, of the fact
that being has the character of a subject. Here, however, Hegel stresses
the role of the intellect as the principle of objective external being. In other
words, so far we have primarily stressed that substance is also an intellectual subject; now we stress that the intellect itself is a kind of object.

Existence: Although *Dasein* in this context is used more closely to its technical sense in the *Logic* (best translated as "being there"), it is not quite so;
a little later it is linked to substance and to genus, which are more devel-

determinate simplicity, determinate thought; this is the Understanding of existence.° Thereby it is *Nus* [*sic*]. The first one to have
recognized the essence [of existence] as *Nus* was Anaxagoras. His
followers conceived the nature of existence more precisely as *eidos*
or idea, that is, as a specifically determined universality,° or kind
[genus]. The term "kind" sounds common and a little too low for
the ideas—for the beautiful, the sacred, the eternal which today
reign supreme. But in fact, an idea expresses neither more nor less
than a kind. People nowadays often despise a term which expresses
a Concept with precision; they prefer a term which—if only because it is a foreign word—wraps the Concept in fog, and thereby
gains an edifying ring. Precisely because existence is determined as
kind, it is simple thought; *Nus*, simplicity, is the substance. Because
of its simplicity or self-identity, substance appears° as rigid and en-

---

oped categories than the simplest particular determination of being,
called *Dasein*. So even here, Hegel uses *Dasein* in the nontechnical sense
of "existence," and thus I translate it.

The understanding of existence: This is the objective intellect, or Understanding as immersed within the object, in outer being. The Greeks, for example Anaxagoras, expressed this idea when speaking of *nous* (intellect) as
a kind of natural power which dominates and guides the cosmos. For
Anaxagoras, intellect was a kind of being or object. Plato refined this
view by conceiving the objective intellect as a Form or Idea. Aristotle
interpreted this view in terms of genus and species. In all these transformations—including Plato's Ideas, Aristotle's genera, and the Aristotelian
nous operating at the outter limit of the cosmos, as unmoved mover—
the intellect has always been understood as an object, a thing (*res*). This is
the principle which underlies the first part of Hegel's *Logic*, the "Objective
Logic" (= *logos*, taken as object). Accordingly, this part of the book places
the concept of substance, and not subject, at its center. It not only accounts for Greek philosophy, but also the modern "dogmatic" metaphysics of Descartes, Spinoza, and Leibniz.

Specifically determined universality: As distinguished from determinate particularity (being there, *Dasein*), and from mere universality, or indeterminate universality (being, *Sein*). The Platonic idea or the Aristotelian genus
is specific universality, a unity of universality and particularity.

Because of its simplicity . . . substance appears: What has been said previously concerning being (*Sein*) in general and being there (*Dasein*) is

during. Yet this self-identity is likewise negativity; thereby the rigid existence passes into dissolution. At first° it seems that the determinateness is what it is by virtue of its relation to another, and that its movement is forced upon it by a foreign power. Actually, however, it has its being-other within itself, and is self-movement: this is implied in the very simplicity of thinking. For that simplicity is the self-moving and self-differentiating thought, and is genuine interiority, the pure Concept. In this way, understandability [*Verständigkeit*] is a becoming [a process], and as becoming it is rationality [*Vernünftigkeit*].°

---

now said about substance, the highest form of objective *logos*. Substance stands higher than mere particular existence, and also higher than its characteristics, quantity, and quality, because substance allows particular existence to pass away, while maintaining the thing's individuality. Substance is a complex and highly mediated system which finally "returns to itself" as the pure and self-identical being by virtue of which a permanent existent endures. However, in the next stage, it turns out that substance also lacks ontological stability. The element of simplicity in substance must produce self-negation and be dissolved into a system of relations. It is only as subject—as "Concept"—that an entity can gain ontological stability.

At first: At the stage of primary, undeveloped individuality, that of particular quality or being there (*Dasein*). At that stage of the *Logic*, it seems that the particular entity, identified with its determinate quality, is what it is only by virtue of the external relations of negation which it maintains with all the others: red is not green, not yellow, also not sweet, and so on, and all these negative relations constitute its being red. Because no substance is yet present, all the other entities are foreign to the first entity, and the negative relations which constitute its specific existence are viewed by the first entity as an external and foreign power. But in the next stage—that of substance—the multiplicity of those qualities turns out to belong to the identity of one and the same existing system, and the negative relations are grasped as internal to its identity. This provides the basis for further development, in which self-negation produces reflection and subjectivity as a further dimension of substance.

Understandability [Verständigkeit] is a becoming . . . is rationality [Vernünftigkeit]: The rigid, objective intelligibility of substance enters a dialectical process, and therefore moves from "Understanding" to "Reason."

This nature of that which is—to be, in its being, its own Concept—constitutes logical necessity° in general. It alone is the rational; it is the rhythm of the organic whole; it is as much the knowing of the content as the content is essence and Concept—in other words, it alone is the speculative. The concrete shape, in moving itself, makes itself into a simple determinateness; thereby it raises itself to logical form and is in its essentiality;° its concrete existence is only this movement, and is immediately a logical existence. There is no need, therefore, to impose formalism on the content from without; the content itself is a passage to formalism, which ceases to be external formalism, since the form is the native becoming of the concrete content.

This nature of scientific method—to be unsevered from the content, and to determine autonomously its own rhythm—receives its authentic exhibition in speculative philosophy. As for our present text, although it expresses the Concept,° it must not be taken as anything more than an anticipatory assurance. Its truth does not lie in its partly narrative presentation. Therefore, it cannot be refuted by a counterassurance which claims that things are not so, but different, or by reciting and recalling conventional opinions as if they were established and well-known truths; or again by dishing up some innovation from the shrine of inner divine intuition. Such is the usual [negative] reception which [the world of] knowledge reserves to what is unfamiliar—it reacts with resistance to it, in order to save its own freedom, its own insight and authority, from

---

Logical necessity: For Hegel, necessity is not a property of assertions, propositions, sentences, or speech acts, but a dimension of being in its evolution. Necessity means that being itself is shaped as Concept. Thus, there is no mere being, opaque and "in itself," upon which thinking projects necessity through external discourse. Rather, empirical reality is itself the embodiment of a Concept which operates within it, and gives it its structure. This is the origin of logical necessity to Hegel.

Is in its essentiality: In following logical necessity, philosophical knowledge grasps reality not in its crude manifestation as being, but in its essential manifestation as Concept (see "the pure essentialities," above).

Although it expresses the Concept: Of true philosophy.

the authority of a foreigner (since those we meet for the first time are perceived as foreigners); and also in order to remove the appearance of a certain kind of shame which supposedly lies in learning something. Likewise, when the unfamiliar is received with applause,° this reaction is of the same kind which, in another sphere, constituted ultrarevolutionary° talk and action.

The important thing in the study of Science is that we should take upon ourselves the exertion of the Concept. Science requires attention to the Concept as such, to simple determinations like being-in-itself, being-for-itself, equality-with-itself [= self-identity], and so forth. These are self-movements which we might have called souls, had not their Concept indicated something higher than the soul. When the habit of following representations is broken by the Concept, it suffers as much stress° as does the formal thinking which reasons here and there in nonactual thoughts. The former habit° should be called material thinking,° an accidental consciousness which is so absorbed in its material that it finds it very painful at the same time to lift its self [*sein Selbst*] out of the material in a pure way, and be with itself. Reasoning, on the contrary, is freedom

With applause: Even though the unknown usually produces anxiety and resistance, at times it provokes superficial enthusiasm. Both cases point to an immature mind.

Ultrarevolutionary: Hegel wrote at the time of Napoleon, with the French Revolution still reverberating in the air. He viewed the revolution as bringing about great progress, but objected to the ultrarevolutionaries' abstract approach to it. The applause which they received from a sector of the public, including, at times, the young Hegel himself, was the fashionable applause with which a new, but immature, idea is often received.

Suffers as much stress: A dialectical mode of thinking disturbs the ordinary course of both sense images and formal conceptual thinking. Therefore each objects to it to the same degree.

The former habit: The sense images and ordinary life-beliefs.

Material thinking: The mode of thinking which is attached to matter, without liberating itself from its coercive power. Hegelian philosophical thinking resides immanently within its matter, whereas formal or analytical thinking is liberated from matter in being external to it. Thus it loses its matter and ends in abstraction.

from the content and the arrogance° which treats the content from above; of it is required the effort to renounce that freedom, and instead of acting as the arbitrary moving principle° of the content, to submerge its freedom in it, let the content move itself by its own nature—that is, through the self as its own self [*durch das Selbst als das seinige*]—and to contemplate that movement.° In the immanent rhythm of the Concept, one must get rid of one's own occurring ideas, and abstain from interfering in it with an arbitrary act [*durch die Willkür*] or wisdom acquired elsewhere. This restraint is an essential moment of paying attention to the Concept.

We should notice two further aspects in which the reasoning [argumentative] attitude is opposed to conceptual thinking:

(1) On the one hand, argumentative reasoning takes a negative relation to the content it apprehends; it knows how to refute and

Arrogance: Analytic thinking regards matter as something given to it for manipulation, and thus experiences its freedom from it as a kind of arrogance. The "subject matter itself"—the content of reality—becomes something passive, dead, which moves only when set in motion by the analytical understanding through acts of inference and external organization. The understanding is the active moving power which manipulates the content of reality, and is considered superior to that content. (This is "vanity.")

The arbitrary moving principle: In acts of inference. Although they look necessary from the standpoint of a formal, logical language game, acts of inference are arbitrary from the standpoint of reality's content. The order of inference and demonstration is not necessarily the order of being. However, the act of inference is here the only power that sets the content in motion. Therefore, from its own standpoint, the content is being moved arbitrarily.

To contemplate that movement: The philosophical method demands that the philosopher be absorbed by the subject matter, that his thinking mind be assimilated with, or to, the thought that activates the subject matter itself. It thus follows the immanent movement of the subject matter—which becomes its own movement—and finally contemplates the structure that emerges from this process. This contemplation, as we have seen, is therefore retrospective or a posteriori. "The method is nothing but the structure of the whole as it is constituted in its pure essentiality" (p. 156).

demolish it.° To see that things are not so is a merely negative insight; it is a final point which does not go beyond itself to a new content; rather, in order to have a content, something else must be picked up somewhere. This [negative reasoning] is a reflection into the empty I, the vanity of its knowing.° This means that not the content alone, but also the insight is vain; for that insight is the negative which fails to see the positive within itself. Because that reflection fails to win its own negativity as content,° it never resides in the matter itself but is always outside and beyond it; hence, it deludes itself into believing that when it asserts the void, it always reaches farther than a content-rich insight does. By contrast, as indicated above, in conceptual thinking the negative belongs to the content itself, and is the positive—both as the immanent movement and specific determination of the content, but also as its totality. Grasped as a result,° it is the determinate negative, and thereby equally a positive content.

(2) But considering that such thinking has content°—a content of representations, thoughts, or a mix of the two—there is something else which keeps it from being treated conceptually. This is

---

To refute and demolish it: In formal argumentative thinking, a refutation is conclusive. An argument is annihilated and nothing is preserved of it. There is no continuity of negation and affirmation. In order to retain something positive, we must turn to a new argument taken from elsewhere. Not so with a dialectical refutation, which preserves an essential ingredient of that which has been negated, and makes it a moment of a new affirmation.

The vanity of its knowing: See "arrogance," above.

Fails to win its own negativity as content: Negation does not lead here to a definite new affirmation. The only thing one can see here is nothingness, the void which has been left after something had been refuted.

Grasped as a result: Within the totality, the positive system of truths results from the system of negations.

Such thinking has content: This is the positive side of its thinking; but its content is made of sense images and rigid thoughts. Therefore, it is precisely the positive side of that thinking which provides an obstacle to true comprehension.

an extraordinary impediment, whose nature is connected to the essence of the Idea° as mentioned before; more precisely, it expresses the Idea's appearance as a movement of apprehension by thought [*denkendes Auffassen*].

In its negative attitude° just discussed, argumentative reasoning is itself the self into which the content returns;° whereas in its positive knowledge,° the self is a represented subject, to which the content relates as accident and predicate.° This subject is the basis to which the content is tied, and on which the movement back and forth takes place. Conceptual thinking is different.° Because the Concept is the

The essence of the Idea: Hegel seems here to be using "Idea" in the systematic sense he will employ in the *Logic*: the dialectical unity of being and conceiving (whose movement he has outlined above).

In its negative attitude: When using negative sentences.

The self into which the content returns: The self (*Selbst*) in general, or at least in the logical sense, is that to which the content "returns" as a result of its movement and evolution. In the case of argumentative thinking, because the negative sentence negates the content utterly and completely, it returns it to negation itself as the ironic "self" of that content.

Whereas in its positive knowledge: In using positive assertive sentences.

As accident and predicate: Hegel returns to his analysis of predicative language. In positive assertions, the self to which the content of the sentence is returned is its rigid subject, standing motionless at its base, while the predicates hang unilaterally on it, as accidents. Note that Hegel speaks interchangeably of the subject in the logical or grammatical sense (the subject of a sentence or proposition) and the mental sense (the knowing, or mental subject). The equivocation could be based on Hegel's assimilation of Kant's view, that the knowing subject stands behind the unity of a judgment, as the principle that links its predicates. This is why Hegel says that in a merely analytic mode of thinking, the "motionless" logical subject results in a "motionless" (merely abstract) human subject. But even if he meant to allude to this important implication, his practice of the equivocation (the two senses of "subject") is likely to confuse.

Conceptual thinking is different: In Conceptual (dialectical) thinking, negation does not abolish the content; affirmation does not create a rigid, unilateral link between subject and predicate; and movement is not external to the subject but rather is its own movement—that is, it is the movement of the whole system of its predicates, which is identical with the subject.

object's own self which presents itself as its becoming, it is not an immobile subject that upholds the accidents without moving, but is a self-moving Concept which takes its determinations back into itself. The immobile subject disintegrates in this movement; it passes over to the distinctions and content, and rather than continuing to confront the determinateness, that is, the differentiated content and its movement, it constitutes them. The solid ground which reasoning had in the immobile subject falters,° and only that movement itself becomes the object. The subject which fills its content ceases to go beyond it, and can have no further predicates and accidents.°

Thereby, on the other side, the content's dispersion is connected by the self;° the content is not something general that, free of the subject,° would fit many others. Indeed, the content is no longer the

The solid ground . . . falters: This is the Hegelian doctrine of the "collapse of the subject," an idea that gained currency in postmodern thinking of the late twentieth century. Still, Hegel abolishes only the *fixed* subject, whom he replaces with a different, flowing subject, patterned as a circular system.

No further predicates and accidents: All its predicates, and only they, constitute its specific peculiarity. To that extent the predicates are not accidents, but are all equally essential. Thereby, the entity in question is not a particular token of some universal form, but a true individual—a specific *singular* system. Incidentally, this idea has roots in Leibniz (whom Hegel had studied in Jena). Leibniz conceived of the predicates of a complex substance (even those describing its history as a singular entity) as being included in it a priori. In Hegel's interpretation, the substance *is* that system of predicates; but he argues that this way of thinking can hold water only if substance is understood as subject.

The content's dispersion is connected by the self: Its being an individual subject unifies its diverse contents into that specific singular system.

Free of the subject: The element of generality is here shaped not as a *universal* (a genus, a species), but as a *totality* (a whole), which is a singular entity. A universal predicate (e.g., "animal") is not attached specifically to some singular subject but can freely adhere to many different entities (subjects)—an elephant, a Tyrolean dog, Napoleon's horse, and so forth. But in a totality, all the predicates refer exclusively to this one entity, as their single subject. God, world history, the spirit, are singular totalities. All the contents characterizing such an entity and its evolution belong to

subject's predicate° but its very substance, it is the essence and Concept of what is being spoken about. The representing mode of thinking, by its nature, follows the predicates and accidents and goes beyond them—and does so with right, since they are only predicates and accidents. But its progress is arrested° when that which in the proposition has the form of a predicate, is the subject itself. Here it suffers, so to speak, a countershock. It starts from the subject as if the subject remained the ground; but since the predicate is actually the substance, it discovers that the subject has passed into the predicate and has thereby been sublated. Thus, because what had appeared to be a predicate turned out to be the whole independent mass, thinking cannot roam around freely° any longer, but is held fast by this weight.

---

that singular subject only, in precisely the manner in which they have actually appeared and found their place in it.

The content is no longer the subject's predicate: Thus understood, the predicate is no longer a rigid content hanging on the subject as accident. Rather, the predicate (when taken in its dynamic relation to all the other predicates), is *the essence and subject matter itself*—it is the actual subject; and it discloses itself not as a fixed particular item, but as a detailed and comprehensive (yet singular) system.

Its progress is arrested: The ordinary understanding starts from the subject as a rigid particular whose meaning is finished and given, and hangs on it some general predicate, which also fits many other subjects. But when pondering the matter more thoroughly, it is astonished to discover that the subject is the very substance, the issue at hand itself. Thereby its freedom of navigation between many possible predicates is suddenly restrained, and from sheer generality the mind is driven to think a comprehensive (holistic) *individual*. (Of course, for that arresting blow to occur, the thinking mind must have already digressed from its ordinary course: the inner blow accelerates a process whose nucleus already exists.)

Roam around freely: In philosophical discourse we cannot attach *any* predicate to a subject, or refer the predicate to several different subjects. In moving from sheer generality to a comprehensive (holistic) individual, we gain a subject to which certain predicates, and no others, are specifically bound, and they alone are necessary from its standpoint. Thus the "arrogant" freedom of the analytic Understanding is restrained. Also, the history of the subject acquires a necessary dimension, as belonging to

Usually° one starts by (a) taking the subject as the ground and as the fixed and object-like [*gegenständliche*] self,° from which the necessary movement proceeds to the manifold of determinations, or predicates. At this point° (b) the knowing I enters and takes the place of that subject, constituting the connection between the predicates and the subject which hold them together. (c) But since the first subject passes into the determinations and constitutes their soul, the second, namely, the knowing subject, continues to find in the predicate that which it wants to be through with,° and beyond

---

that same subject's singularity. For example, one can no longer say that humans are characterized by rationality in general; one may only refer to the specific rationality that has been embodied in the life of humanity in its various periods and civilizations, which have actually evolved and taken shape. They all acquire a necessary status, not as mere "accidents" of the subject (in this case: the human spirit), but as *necessary* attributes of it—a series of predicates constituting its very substance.

Usually: From here to the end of the paragraph Hegel reviews the failure of ordinary thinking. The prime mover in its collapse was Kant's idealism. Despite its failure to draw all the necessary conclusions from its own principle, Kant's philosophy has nevertheless set rational thinking in a process that eventually overcame the limitations of both dogmatism and Kant himself.

The fixed and object-like [gegenständliche] self: This is the phase of dogmatic realism. Substance is here understood as a rigid object-like entity, in which thinking plays no role; and the dominant unit of discourse—the propositional form—is understood as imitating the object-like relation between substance and accidents.

At this point: The point at which Kant entered the scene. This is the stage of idealism. Here the knowing subject (the I) emerges as the power linking together the predicates in the proposition, or linking the subject and its predicates. (See the "Transcendental Analytic" in *The Critique of Pure Reason*, especially the section "On the Guideline for the Discovery of all the Pure Concepts of the Understanding.") Yet Kant still maintained a rigid relation between subject and predicates, even though self-consciousness became their connecting principle.

That which it wants to be through with: In turning to the predicate, the mind turns away from the subject (whose meaning it believes to possess as "a minted coin," p. 139), and is surprised to rediscover that subject in the predicate which it had expected to be quite different from. This surprising discovery starts the move from Kantian to speculative idealism.

which it wants to return to itself. Thus, instead of being able° to set the predicate in motion by an activity of reasoning, which checks whether this or that predicate fits the first subject, it now has to deal with the self of the content; it cannot be [any longer] for-itself, but must be together with that content.

The above can be expressed formally by saying that the nature of a judgment° or a proposition in general, which contains the difference between subject and predicate, is destroyed by the speculative proposition.° The first turns into an identity-proposition,

Instead of being able: In Kant, the knowing act still consists in examining whether a rigid predicate conforms to a rigid subject; even though the examination is now based on the subject's forms of thought rather than on object-like relations presumably existing in a "thing in itself." The knowing subject fails in its attempt to merely engage in such comparisons, because it discovers *itself* in the object, and discovers the logical subject within its predicates. In this way, the predicative mode of thinking breaks down and calls for a speculative mode.

The nature of a judgment: According to Hegel, judgment (*Urteil*) performs a separation between subject and predicate. This may be indicated by the German word *Ur-Teil*, "primary division." (Hölderlin also made this a major point in his early thought; see the introduction.)

The speculative proposition: A rare and rather enigmatic term in Hegel. Its meaning is widely debated. Actually, by the logic of Hegel's position, no single proposition of *any* form can express a speculative content. Hegel, therefore, cannot possibly be demanding that a speculative proposition replace the predicative proposition as the proper way of expressing philosophical truth. That demand would project an ideal that can be neither realized, nor even exemplified, in the Hegelian system. I therefore tend to think that in speaking of "a speculative proposition" Hegel does not intend to establish a new, presumably dialectical form of discourse, but to indicate the collapse of the usual predicative sentence as a philosophical instrument. Proper philosophical discourse must consist in a whole system of sentences, some of which are contradictory, whose mutual relationships are supposed to express the inner movement of the Concept. As for the examples Hegel gives later (sentences like "God is Being," and "The actual is the universal"), I think they illustrate a special kind of predicative proposition, those expressing identity or equivalence. The one-sided predicative form is incongruent in such a sentence with the intended content, and therefore prepares the ground for the collapse of

which contains the countershock to that relation [of subject and predicate]. This conflict,° between the form of a proposition in general and the unity of the Concept which destroys it, resembles the conflict which takes place in rhythm between meter and accent. Rhythm results from their unification and floating center. Similarly, the identity of subject and object in the philosophical proposition must not nullify their difference,° which the form of the proposition expresses; rather, this unity must emerge as harmony. The form of the proposition is the appearance of the determinate sense, or the accent which specifies its filling; whereas the fact that the

---

this form of thinking and expression. Yet Hegel cannot regard such sentences as a proper expression of philosophical truth. At best they may count as a means of transition, a lever leading from predicative to speculative thinking, which neither attains nor even illustrates the latter.

Since no single sentence can capture the process of speculative thinking in Hegel's sense, we may conclude that Hegel's examples serve to illustrate how a truly dialectical content *cannot* be forced into the ordinary propositional form. If so, it follows that, as levers of transition, "speculative propositions" have relatively low standing in the process of Knowing. Hegel goes on to stress that his examples are identity-propositions lacking a sense of novelty. Their service to Knowledge consists in upsetting its ordinary way and hinting at a different way which they themselves are unable to realize. The speculative proposition heightens the sense of dissatisfaction we get from the subject/predicate proposition, and urges our thinking to go beyond it—not to another *form* of proposition but to the complete process of dialectical thinking, which no single sentence of *any* form can express. In addition, the speculative proposition has relative value at the end of the road, as an abbreviated heading that summarizes a speculative process which it cannot, however, contain in a live and meaningful way. The speculative process will be an explication of that abbreviation, orally or in writing.

This conflict: Referring to the conflict between the speculative-conceptual content which breaks away from ordinary language, and the predicative form of that language. Hegel idealizes that conflict as harmony, comparing it to music or poetry; yet it looks more like an unresolved difficulty in his system, that is, an antinomy.

Must not nullify their difference: The predicates must have distinctive differences which add specificity and filling to the subject, rather than simply repeating it in general terms (as in "God is Being").

predicate expresses the substance, and that the subject itself falls into the universal, is the unity in which the accent fades out.

Let us clarify this with examples. In the proposition *God is being*,° the predicate is being; it has a substantive meaning in which the subject dissolves. Being is not meant to be a predicate here, but the essential thing; thereby God seems to cease to be that which he is by virtue of his place in the proposition, namely, the rigid subject. And since the subject is lost, thinking no longer moves from subject to predicate, but feels arrested and pushed back to the thought of the subject, because it misses that subject. In other words, since the predicate itself is expressed as subject, as being [*als das Sein*], as the essence which exhausts the subject's nature, thinking therefore finds the subject immediately also in the predicate. Hence, instead of moving within itself in the predicate° and reaching the free attitude of reasoning, thinking now becomes absorbed in the content—or at least, is called upon to be so absorbed. Similarly, in saying *the actual is the universal*, the actual as subject vanishes in its predicate. The universal must not only have the meaning of a predicate, such that the proposition pronounces the actual to be universal, but the universal must express the essence of the actual.

God is being: As mentioned, Hegel chose a special kind of proposition. He dubs it an "identity proposition," which defines something by its highly generalized essence. The predicate is so general and essential that in passing from subject to predicate we actually remain within the subject, and feel that no predication has been performed, but that the subject itself was reiterated as predicate. This sense of tautology embarrasses the mind, which fails to hold on to a specific predicate. Having left the subject behind, the mind comes upon it again in the place where it no longer expects to find the subject (but expects to find the predicate instead)— and thus the subject ceases to be fixed for it in one rigid place.

Instead of moving within itself in the predicate: By being thrust back from the predicate to the subject, the ordinary understanding cannot maintain its superior position: it cannot continue to compare different predicates with a rigid subject-term given in advance, and decide in the usual way whether they conform to it (analytically, synthetically, or not at all). Wherever it turns, it has the same general content. It is therefore unable to extract itself from the essential content but remains attached to it (one might say, arrested by it), and cannot escape to the arbitrary freedom it possessed before.

In this way, thinking loses the fixed object-like [*gegenständlich*] ground it had in the subject, each time that it is thrust back to it in the predicate; and in the predicate it returns not to itself, but to the subject of the content.

This unusual arrest is the main cause when people complain° that philosophical writings are unintelligible, a complaint we hear even from those who otherwise possess the cultural prerequisites for understanding these works. This also accounts for a very specific reproach often made against philosophical texts—that many passages must be read over again before they can be understood—a reproach that is supposed to assert something so improper and final that, if well grounded, there is no defense against it. What we said above clarifies the issue. The philosophical proposition, because it is a proposition, invokes the opinion that here is the usual relation of subject and predicate and the usual attitude of knowing. The philosophical content of the proposition destroys this usual attitude and the opinion which comes with it. Opinion [*Meinung*] discovers that things are meant [*gemeint*] differently than in the way it has opined [*meinte*]; and this correction of its opinion requires of Knowing that it return to the proposition and apprehend it differently.

A difficulty to be avoided is to confuse the speculative and the argumentative mode [of philosophizing]. This confusion arises when what we say of the subject is meant at one time in the sense of its Concept, and at another time in the sense of its predicate or accident. One mode stands in the other's way; and only a philosophical exhibition which strictly excludes the usual relation between the parts of the proposition will attain plasticity.°

Complain: The arrest (or inner blow) described above is the reason why philosophy is hard to understand. The difficulty is not intellectual, but mental and educational. Ordinary thinking encounters impediments that shatter its routine expectations, and force upon it the need of adjusting to unexpected change.

Plasticity: Lefebvre explains "plastic" as "attached to the content," inseparable from it. But one can also understand this adjective as the contrary of "rigid."

Actually, nonphilosophical thinking also has its right,° which is valid, although the speculative propositional mode fails to observe it. The [usual] form of the proposition must be sublated not only immediately, not merely by the content of the proposition; rather, the opposite movement must be verbalized [*ausgesprochen*]. An inward arrest is not enough: the return of the Concept to itself must also be exhibited.° This [textual] movement, which fulfills [in speculative thinking] the task formerly assigned to the demonstration,° is the dialectical movement of the proposition itself. It alone is the actually speculative, and only the [verbal] expression of that [whole] movement is a speculative presentation. As proposition, the speculative is merely an inward arrest and a retreat of essence into itself which lacks existence. Indeed, philosophical presentations often relegate us to that inward intuition, and spare them-

Nonphilosophical thinking also has its right: This is a current motif in Hegel. Speculative thinking does not invalidate the other modes of thinking as long as they are confined to their own domain.

Must also be exhibited: The passage to dialectical thinking requires a new mode of writing. One cannot make do with the inner arrest caused by predicative sentences whose form is incongruent with their intention, and one cannot overcome the limitations of predicative language by some inner light. The overcoming must find its own literary expression—by using language differently than in traditional philosophy. Hegel's unique kind of writing in the *Phenomenology* is, I think, intended to overcome both the argumentative mode of thinking and the mysticism that pretends to replace it. His difficult, yet mostly intelligible, mode of writing, which unsympathetic critics called "foggy" and even "mystical," was actually fashioned against mysticism. Overcoming argumentative thinking should yield a Concept, not a mystical experience, and must have a rational expression open to all, even if the language we possess can do this only in roundabout ways while offending the common understanding.

The task formerly assigned to the demonstration: Having sublated the argumentative mode of thinking, philosophical discourse grounds itself in dialectical circles, which negate their own point of departure and return to it on a new level. This dialectical circularity replaces the role that has formerly been assigned to demonstrations and formal proofs in philosophy.

selves the exhibition of the dialectical movement of the proposition which is required.°

The proposition is supposed to express what the true is; but the true is essentially subject, and as such is but the dialectical movement—that self-engendering march which leads itself forward and returns into itself. In nondialectical knowledge, it is the demonstration which fulfills this role—to verbalize the inwardness. But ever since dialectic and demonstration were separated, the Concept of a "philosophical demonstration" has actually been lost.

Someone might call to our attention that dialectical movement, too, has propositions which form its own parts or elements. So it seems that the difficulty we mentioned above always recurs,° and belongs to the matter itself. This resembles what occurs in ordinary demonstrations, whose grounds need to be grounded in their turn, and so on to infinity. But this form of grounding and conditioning belongs [specifically] to the demonstration, which [we saw to be] different from dialectical movement, and thus belongs to external knowledge. As for dialectical movement, it has the pure Concept for its element and therefore has a content which, in its very self, is a subject through and through. Here no content occurs,° which acts as an underlying subject and receives its meaning

The dialectical movement of the proposition which is required: Hegel fulfilled this requirement only in the *Phenomenology* and the *Logic*, whose mode of writing is indeed unique.

The difficulty . . . always recurs: Hegel practically admits he has no way of overcoming this problem. Dialectical thinking cannot use an artificial technical language, because philosophy must arise from the historical culture and language. Yet historical languages are irremediably predicative in the inadequate sense. (The defect of predicative propositions is raised again by Hegel in *The Science of Logic*, book 1, part 1, chapter 1 ["Being"], note 2).

Here no content occurs: In cases like those cited (of very general primary propositions), the subject term has no predetermined fixed meaning to which one then adds predicates, but is a mere name. Its entire meaning comes from the series of predicates which give it content and particularization.

by way of a predicate; the proposition here is only an empty form.°
Apart from the self which is intuited or represented by the senses,°
it is above all the name° as name which marks the pure subject—
the empty Conceptless One. We may therefore find it useful to
avoid the name *God*,° because this word is not directly also a Concept but is a genuine name, a rigid stillness of an underlying subject; whereas other words, for example, *being* or the *one, singularity,
subject*, and the like immediately also signify Concepts. About this
subject [God], many speculative truths are indeed pronounced; but
because the subject is given as static, these truths lack an immanent Concept and easily assume the form of mere edification.° In

Only an empty form: The propositional form, connecting a rigid predicate
to a pregiven fixed subject, is empty because it does not conform to any
true philosophical content. (Indirectly, Hegel also takes aim at Kant, who
deduced fundamental philosophical contents—the categories—from the
forms of judgment).

The self which is intuited or represented by the senses: The merely subjective
sense of self.

The name: An empty name, analogous to the empty I of sense certainty.
(As is usual with him, Hegel speaks interchangeably of the knowing subject and the logical subject of the proposition.)

To avoid the name God: No subject is more fixed and predetermined than
the reference of the name "God." Tradition has packed into that name
so many meanings and connotations, that almost no way exists to overcome its predetermination. This situation is highlighted by the ontological proof, which starts from a richly predetermined sense of "God" and
explicates what it already contains. (Another example is Descartes' guar-
antee of evident knowledge, based upon God's goodness.) Hegel says he
prefers terms like "being" or "subject" to "God," because they are more
conceptual; but his reason is not clear. Is he saying these are general
terms while "God" is singular? But Hegel also prefers the term "one,"
which is no less singular. Hegel seems wavering on this question, perhaps
because he is writing here in a polemical vein, which sometimes leads
him to rhetorical exaggerations.

Edification: Hegel said above that philosophy should beware of edification,
that is, of creating a pious state of mind by elevated talk and uplifting
exhortation rather than knowledge. And since the name "God" calls for this
mood, it had better be avoided as the subject of philosophical explication.

this respect, the obstacle due to the habit° of grasping a speculative predicate according to the [ordinary] propositional form (rather than as Concept or essence) can be decreased or increased by [fault of] the philosophical discourse we use. In order to faithfully express its insight about the nature of speculation, the [philosophical] presentation must maintain a dialectical form, and include nothing that is not a Concept and is not Conceptual.

The study of philosophy is hampered not only by the reasoning attitude, but also, and equally, by the unreasoning conceit of ready-made truths, whose owner feels no need to go back to [and examine], but uses them as the ground and believes he can assert and use them for judging and condemning. From this direction a pressing need is felt to make philosophy a serious matter again. In every science, art, skill, and handiwork, it is evident that a manifold effort of learning and exercise is needed in order to master them. But when it comes to philosophy, the following prejudice seems to reign today, namely, that although not everyone can make shoes just because he has fingers and eyes and was given tools and leather—yet everyone possesses an immediate understanding and judgment of philosophy, because he carries its measure in his natural reason—as if he did not carry the measure of a shoe in his

---

The obstacle due to the habit: Hegel here summarizes the issue. Since no way exists of avoiding subject/predicate sentences, the philosophical mind should be trained to treat those sentences in a new way. It must learn to grasp the predicates not "according to the propositional form"— not as one-sidedly attached to a subject that has a fully determined meaning—but "as Concept and essence," namely, as a process that unfolds in a detailed dialectical manner and thereby constitutes its own essence. As such, the process of predication *contructs* the subject and becomes identical with it. The predicates' relation to the subject is one of dialectical equivalence rather than unilateral dependence. Such thinking disrupts intellectual habits and opposes the structure of ordinary language, so it must be illustrated by new literary means that break the atomic appearance of singular propositions and set them "in movement." Educating the mind to dialectical thinking depends therefore in large measure on the way in which philosophy is presented, orally and in writing.

foot! Mastering philosophy is made to depend today on the lack of learning and cognitions, so that philosophy ceases where they begin. Often philosophy is considered to be devoid of content, a formal knowledge only; and the insight is badly lacking that [on the contrary,] if there is something true in a science or body of knowledge also with respect to content,° it deserves this name only when it has been engendered by philosophy. Let the other sciences argue and reason without philosophy as much as they will: without it they can have neither life, nor spirit, nor truth.

Regarding genuine philosophy, we see that instead of the long road of cultural education, instead of the rich and profound movement by which spirit attains to Knowing, there steps forward today a direct revelation of the divine, accompanied by a common sense that has never toiled and educated itself either in other sciences or in genuine philosophy, and presumes to offer an instant equivalent and a perfect substitute to the road of cultural education—as some people praise chicory as a substitute for coffee. It gives [me] no pleasure to remark, that ignorance—indeed, the most formless and tasteless crudeness,° which cannot frame its thinking in a single abstract proposition, let alone a string of propositions—assures us at one time that it is freedom and tolerance of thought, and at another time that it is genius. That genius which today rages in philosophy° has

---

With respect to content: Hegel (with due modification) adopts Fichte's idea that every science—mathematics, physics, law, political science—is based on a special Concept or category determined in philosophy. The system of these basic Concepts forms an "Encyclopaedia of Philosophical Sciences."

The most formless and tasteless crudeness: These adjectives refer to the philosophy of common sense and the philosophy of genius—two opposites pretending to grasp philosophical truth immediately, without the necessary philosophical formation and evolution. The superficiality of common sense and the alleged profundity of crude romantic genius are similar in that respect, except that common sense is open to everyone, while genius conceives of itself as the gift of a few.

That genius which today rages in philosophy: "Genius" was a current category in German aesthetics of the end of the eighteenth century. Kant described any worthwhile artist (not only the towering ones) as possessing the faculty of genius. A genius (= true artist) exhibits "aesthetic

previously, as we know, raged in poetry. But when its products made any sense,° genius did not produce poetry but only trivial prose; and when it went beyond the latter, it produced crazy speeches. Similarly, today a natural philosophizing° steps forward, for which the Concept is not good enough; and because it has the virtue of lacking the Concept, it takes itself to be poetic and intuiting thinking,° and dispatches to the market arbitrary combinations of the imagination which thought has only mixed up—creatures that are neither fish nor meat, neither poetry nor philosophy.

On the other hand, when natural philosophizing flows in the more peaceful bed of common sense, it provides, at best, a rhetoric of trivial truths; and if reproached because of the insignificance of those truths, it assures us that it bears their meaning and filling in its heart° (so they must be present in others, too), and thinks that

---

ideas" combining intuition, imagination, and reason in a work of art that is a singular embodiment of a universal principle, which can neither be generalized nor repeated and imitated. This theory established a link between genius and a *kind* of intellectual intuition. Later thinkers, including Hegel's friends Hölderlin and Schelling, and his later rival Schopenhauer, gave this idea a romantic turn, as intuitive profundity which penetrates into the root of being. Schelling linked a form of genius to philosophy itself, thus giving philosophy the character of art, or of a semimystical disclosure. Varieties of this view of genius were "raging" in Hegel's time (and, indeed, persisted in German thought up to Heidegger).

Any sense: Any cognitive sense (other than as poetry).

Today a natural philosophizing: Hegel assails the fashionable trend of relying on the simple person's naïve or natural wisdom, as embodied in popular proverbs, common truths and conventions, and the like. Hegel rejects that wisdom not in itself, but as substitute philosophy, that is, as crude images which profess to be immediately true.

Poetic and intuiting thinking: Using the style of the romantics who compose philosophical poetry, or who philosophize in poetic language. In his private notes Hegel chided a few writers, now forgotten, who composed romantic philosophies of nature. Whether he also meant greater figures, like Hölderlin, is unclear. (While Hölderlin's poetry is often powerfully philosophical, he also wrote philosophy directly.)

It bears their meaning and filling in its heart: In response to the charge that they utter banal truths, the partisans of sound, though trivial, common

by invoking the "innocent heart" and the "purity of conscience" and the like, it says final things which are immune to challenge and of which nothing further can be demanded. However, the best should not be left behind in the pits of inwardness, but called out to light. One could have long ago since spared oneself the trouble of putting forth ultimate truths like these, because they are already found in catechism, or in popular proverbs, and the like. It is not difficult to see the ambiguity and slant in these truths, and, quite often, to show to the consciousness holding them that it also holds the opposite truths.° In attempting to pull itself out of the embarrassment into which it has fallen, consciousness is prone to fall into new disconcertments, and finally to explode and say decidedly that things are such and such, and the rest is sophistry—a slogan used by common sense against cultivated philosophy, just as ignorance uses the word *reveries* to stigmatize philosophy once and for all.

In relying on feeling as its inner oracle, common sense has finished with whomever disagrees with it. It must declare that it has nothing to say to those who do not feel the same and cannot find the same things in themselves; in other words, it tramples on the root of humanity. For the nature of humanity is to press for concord with others, and it exists only within an actualized community of minds. Whereas the antihuman, the bestial, consists in persevering [in the mode of] feeling and communicating only through it.

Whoever asks for a royal road to Science° will find it most comfortable to rely on healthy common sense; and, in order to keep

---

sense claim that originality does not reside in the content of a statement, but in the heart and subjective sincerity of those holding it.

The opposite truths: A person holding fast to the views of common sense can be brought to realize—as Socrates has done—that he also holds opposite views with the same solid confidence. The resulting embarrassment might liberate certain persons from their dogmatism. However, the majority (again, as the Socratic example shows) will become irritated and aggressive, and dig even deeper into their entrenched dogmatism.

A royal road to Science: In the last part of the preface, Hegel again tries to show that there are no shortcuts to philosophical science. Hegel paraphrases the saying attributed to Euclid that "there is no royal road to geometry." Philosophy, too, requires effort, labor, and many intermediary

in step with the times and philosophy, to go over reviews of philosophical works, and even read the prefaces and first paragraphs
of such works. For these offer the general principles on which
everything depends, while the reviews provide not only a historical notice but a judgment which, being a judgment, stands higher
than what it judges. This common road can be followed while
wearing a housedress, whereas the lofty feeling of the eternal, the
sacred, the infinite, wears the apparel of a high priest as it strides
a road which is [not really a road but] already the immediate Being
at the center,° the genius of profound, original ideas and of elevated flashes of insight. Nonetheless, just as this profundity is not
a revelation of the source of essence,° so those fireworks are not
the empyrean.° True thoughts and scientific insights are gained
only through the work of the Concept. The Concept alone can
generate the universality of Knowing which [on the one hand]
does not suffer from the deficiency and obscurity of ordinary [or,
the crude, *gemein*] common sense,° but is cultivated and complete
knowledge; and on the other hand is not the extraordinary universality of a gift of reason that corrupts itself by the laziness and

---

stages, not as a technical but as an essential condition. Those seeking a
royal road in philosophy fail to see that the process of discovery is equally
a process of mental formation and education, in which the mind is transformed and becomes more capable of the next stages of its understanding. On the other hand, truth itself is a development; therefore the need
to undergo a process on the way to truth is an objective requirement,
deriving from the nature of truth itself, and not only from the limitations
of the human mind. Whoever seeks a leap to philosophical truth shows
she does not understand the nature of the truth she is seeking.

The center: Hegel reiterates the same critique of Schelling expressed on
pages 62, 93–94, and 164 above.

Essence (Wesen): in the dual sense mentioned (of essence and being).

The empyrean: The mythological residence of the gods and the sphere of
fire.

Ordinary [or the crude, gemein] common sense: *Gemein* means "the commonly shared," and also "crude" or "vulgar." Hegel forms a pun with
ungemein, meaning the "not commonly shared," and also the "not vulgar"
(rather, the "esoteric" or "aristocratic"). His critique—in the name of
universality—is aimed at both the vulgar and the esoteric.

conceit of genius. Rather, this universality is truth which has matured to its native° form, and can be possessed by every self-conscious reason.

⇥⇤

According to me, that by which Science exists is the self-movement of the Concept. Yet current opinions about the nature and shape of truth are different from my position and even opposed to it, both in the ways discussed above and in more external respects. So an attempt to exhibit the system of Science according to my standpoint cannot expect to be favorably received. Meanwhile I can ponder° the fact that while the excellence of Plato's philosophy was placed in his scientifically worthless myths,° there were also other times° (even called times of enthusiasm), when Aristotle's philosophy was revered on account of its speculative depth,° and Plato's *Parmenides*, no doubt the greatest artwork of ancient dialectic,° was considered the positive expression and true disclosure of divine life; and despite the frequent obscurity which ecstasy° generated, this

Native: In the sense of authentic, originally destined.

Ponder: And find comfort in this awareness.

Placed in his scientifically worthless myths: That was a worthless period in the history of philosophy.

There were also other times: Better philosophical times. Hegel seems to be thinking of the neoplatonic school and perhaps of its renewal during the Renaissance.

On account of its speculative depth: Rather than on account of its formal logic (which, for Hegel, misses the dialectic), or its doctrine of natural science. Hegel betrays the hope that his own speculative depth will also gain recognition.

The greatest artwork of ancient dialectic (or: "the greatest achievement of the art of ancient dialectic"): Is Hegel suggesting that his *Phenomenology* should count as "the greatest achievement of the modern art of dialectic"?

Ecstasy: A key concept in religious mysticism originating in neoplatonic teaching and its concept of being-outside-oneself. Besides the words *Enthusiasmus* and *Begeisterung*, Germans often use (as Hegel does here) the word *Schwärmerei*, which received a negative connotation when Kant used it to denote an irrational delusion. Hegel has taken the same nega-

misunderstood ecstasy° was supposed to be nothing but the pure
Concept. And I also bear in mind that what is excellent in contemporary philosophy derives its value from being scientific; and even
if other people construe that scientificity in a different way [than I
do], philosophy still gains its validity from this. I therefore can hope
that my attempt to vindicate Science for the Concept° and expose
it in this element° will pave its way by virtue of the inner truth of
the matter itself. We ought to have the conviction that the nature
of truth is to break out when its time comes, and to appear only
when its time has come. Therefore it never appears prematurely,°
nor does it find the public unprepared for it. Also, the individual
[author] needs a [public] effect in order to ascertain for himself°

---

tive attitude when speaking against the "effervescent enthusiasm" (*Begeisterung*) which replaces in Schelling the "cool progress" of the Concept
(see page 78 above). However, changing his mood, Hegel now hints that
some kind of ecstatic enthusiasm can be compatible with the Concept,
as the spiritual energy stored in it. And, as we have seen (in the "Bacchanalian whirl" and elsewhere), the dialectical Concept translates the ecstatic form into the language of rationality.

This misunderstood ecstasy: One must distinguish between ecstasy as a conceptual structure expressing truth, and ecstasy as an emotional experience
resembling drunkenness and consisting in the obliteration of all distinctions. The adequate philosophical interpretation of ecstasy (self-transcendence, or being-oneself-outside-of-oneself) means that every particular
element in thought transcends itself toward another in a mutual process
of negations, in virtue of which each of them regains its distinctive character. This is also the structure of the dialectical system. Ecstasy, like the
Bacchanalian whirl mentioned above, signifies a *logical* system which embodies the pure Concept and is accessible to every thinking person.

To vindicate Science for the Concept: To vindicate the philosophical science
in the [dialectical] way characteristic of the Concept.

In this element: Within the dialectical Concept.

Therefore it never appears prematurely: Ironically, Hegel himself here starts
tossing in a series of proverbs of folk wisdom, some grounded in his
philosophy or his personal hopes as an author.

To ascertain for himself: Hegel puts on a philosophical shield even while
speaking personally. Although he is personally convinced that his system
is true, subjective certainty is not sufficient for truth; it must be universalized and objectivized in culture and the spirit of the time. Who would

that which is still his solitary affair—and to experience as universal the conviction which so far has been his own particular experience. But often we have to distinguish° between the public and those who act as its representatives and spokespersons. In certain respects the public acts differently than these people, even in opposition to them. When a philosophical work fails to find an echo, the public, in a good-natured way, blames itself; whereas those people who are so sure of their competence shift the blame to the author. The effect on the public is quieter than the activity of these dead when they bury their dead.° The general outlook today has indeed become more cultivated,° its curiosity more vivid and its judgment quicker, so that the feet of those who are to carry you out° already

---

believe that Hegel is seeking recognition only because of this metaphysical reason, and not as a simple human? Still, one must admit that for a philosopher like Hegel, the sociology of reception presents a real issue. And remembering his far-reaching ambition—to become the philosopher of the last historical era, and help bring it to consummation—we see the thirty-six-year-old Hegel identifying his personal aspirations with the central needs of mankind as he understands it.

To distinguish: Anticipating a remedy to a possible literary failure, Hegel draws a line between the public and those who profess to speak in its name—the critics. If his book should be killed by the critics, that would not necessarily indicate that time and the public have not matured to it.

These dead when they bury their dead: The critics who kill books while they themselves are spiritually dead (and usually so are the books, too). The allusion is to the Matthew 8:22: "But Jesus said unto him, follow me; and let the dead bury their dead." Knowingly or not, Hegel implies that those who will not follow the truth expounded in the *Phenomenology* are as good as dead and, like those who had rejected Jesus, will remain an empty historical shell.

More cultivated: More sophisticated. The somewhat provincial Hegel seems to be concerned about a certain kind of urbane wit of literati who react superficially to novelties in the life of the mind.

The feet of those who are to carry you out: Referring to Acts of the Apostles 5:9: "Then Peter said unto her, how is it that ye have agreed together to tempt the spirit of the Lord? Behold, the feet of them which have buried thy husband are at the door, and shall carry thee out" (King James Ver-

stand at the door. Nevertheless, one must often distinguish between this, and the slower action° which makes amends for the [initially] dismissive rebuke,° and corrects the course of [public] attention, which has been forced° by impressive assurances. By this slow action, one person wins his public world [*Mitwelt*] only after a while, whereas the other has no other world [*Nachwelt*] beyond the present.°

In addition, we live in a time in which the universality of spirit has been greatly enhanced, and singularity° [= the individual], as is appropriate,° is correspondingly treated with indifference. This

---

sion). Hegel fears that the critics who kill everything will also probably bury his book.

The slower action: An action which affects the true spirit of the time and corrects the distortions of fashion.

The [initially] dismissive rebuke: Of which Hegel is afraid.

Which has been forced: An allusion to Schelling, Fichte, and other fashionable philosophers who have "forced" the public's attention by groundless impressive assurances—their extortion should be corrected by the deeper evolution of the spirit of the time.

No other world [Nachwelt] beyond the present: Hegel is playing with the idea of posterity as kind of a "next world," perhaps even in the consoling sense of granting reward and doing justice. Incidentally, the critics neither killed nor praised the *Phenomenology* but rather ignored it, especially for the first two years. The *Phenomenology* has since become a classic, one of the most influential works of modern philosophy.

Singularity: Hegel seems to be referring to himself as an individual within his time.

As is appropriate: Throughout this finale, Hegel changes his former assertive mood and takes a rather modest turn of accepting his lot in advance. This is very far from the outspoken statements we have read in the beginning, when he declared his goal to help replace the love of knowledge with actual knowledge. Hegel is caught in a natural tension between his grandiose ambition, his concern of failure, and the critical understanding which restrains his ambitions and reminds him of the individual's limited power. This conflict shows that Hegel was no fanatic founder of religion, but a lucid critical thinker, very ambitious but nonetheless balanced.

universality clings to its cultural richness and demands its full range for itself.° In a time like that, the individual's action can count as only a minute part in spirit's overall work; so he must forget himself even more—which already occurs anyway, because of the nature of Science. Of course, the individual must do whatever he can, and become that which he can become; yet one must demand less of him, as he must also reduce his expectations and demand less from himself.

Demands its full range for itself: Spirit claims for itself all the ingredients which make it up: all the significant individuals, historical movements, and cultural traits—and holds onto them as part of itself. Hence no single individual can claim a monopoly over the spirit of the time; and certainly that spirit cannot be reduced to one of its trends. This conception is at the base of Hegel's dialectical pluralism. At the same time, Hegel takes a much too modest position (or pose) here, because his *Phenomenology* claims to be not one more trend or shade *within* the totality, but rather a clarified reformulation of the totality as a whole. In that respect, it claims to stand higher than any particular shape, shade, or trend.

Works on Hegel

><

THE FOLLOWING bibliographical survey and annotated selection of books in English are meant to illustrate some of the approaches to Hegel interpretation. Works published in the last decade or so are mentioned in greater proportion, so as to illustrate the recent revival of interest in Hegel in the English-writing world.

><

Hegel in English had been at first dominated by the more spiritualist (and religiously inspired) nineteenth-century appropriations of German idealism linked to the names of T. M. Greene, J.M.E. McTaggart, and J. Royce, among others. At the beginning of the twentieth century, this was the current image of Hegel, accepted also by G. E. Moore and Bertrand Russell who, on its account, rejected Hegel so strongly and ridiculed him so poignantly that an anti-Hegel myth—indeed, a ritualistic Hegel-bashing and derision—has accompanied the growth of Anglo-American analytic philosophy through much of the twentieth century. A notable exception in America was John Dewey, who had been rather receptive to a version of Hegel stripped of the religious dimension and the notion of the absolute, and appropriated from Hegel—as he did from Darwin—a secular, this-worldly notion of historicality and a "philosophy of change."[1]

Hegel came into disrepute in Angolophone academia also because he has been used and abused—and wrongly associated with—the two despotic revolutions of the twentieth century, communism and fascism. This explains part of the literature after World War II—and again after the demise of communism—that insists on Hegel's image as a rationalist liberal.

In France, a "new Hegel" was discovered between the two world wars through landmark works by Jean Hyppolite, Jean Wahl, and especially Alexandre Kojève. Hyppolite's commentary of the *Phenomenology* remains

[1] See, among other things, Richard Rorty, "Dewey between Hegel and Darwin," in *Rorty and Pragmatism*, ed. Herman J. Saatkamp Jr. (Nashville, TN: Vanderbilt University Press, 1995).

very helpful today, and Kojève's lectures, while sometimes overstated, are
still fresh and thought-provoking. The "French" reading—this-worldly,
nondogmatic, more historical, psychological, and existential in its orientation (rather than speculative or religious)—was opposed not only to the
lofty British Idealists, but also to dogmatic Marxism, which saw in Hegel
an upside-down precursor of Marx whose merit was to provide the Revolution with a "scientific" method; and to the many romantic conserva-
tives and antidemocrats (and liberals, too) who misread Hegel's doctrine
as German-nationalistic, and as culminating in an authoritarian, semi-
totalitarian state.[2]

The "French" reading centered on the richer and pregnant *Phenomenology* rather than the more rigid systematic works. It saw Hegel's main
protagonist in the individual consciousness generating history through
its drive to attain recognition and freedom, to overcome its inevitable
self-splitting and alienation, and to be reconciled to society, the universe,
and the universal element in both, in a way that enhances rather than
suppresses its individuality. This and other emphases—the more "down-
to-earth" approach, avoiding a rigid, formalistic rationality, and recognizing the important role of contingency and particularity—made the
"French" Hegel appealing to existentialist thinkers like Sartre, Jean Wahl
(who had started as a student of Kierkegaard's reaction to Hegel), and
Maurice Merleau-Ponty, and their respective generations. Sartre, in *Being
and Nothingness*, combined Kojève's Hegel with his own appropriations
of Husserl, Heidegger, and Freud—all modifying each other.

Beside Sartre, an impressive number of intellectuals who made their
mark on the French scene after World War II had attended Kojève's seminars on the *Phenomenology* in the 1930s. They absorbed part of its vocabulary and philosophical dynamic even when they weren't Hegelians. Furthermore, excepting the structuralists, who rejected Hegel's historicism
en bloc, Hegelian themes and modes of thought continued to inform—
critically, as background for inner debate and "deconstruction"—the next,
poststructuralist French generation of Deleuze, Derrida, and Foucault.
The accusation of "imperialism" they made against Hegel makes them
rebels, but not foreigners. Thus, while Foucault thought of himself as a
Nietzschean, actually his genealogy of social and cultural institutions is
historicist in the Hegelian sense (while rejecting progress) rather than in
Nietzsche's psychological sense. And Derrida, who attacks the Hegelian

---

[2] This view was famously imported to the Anglo-American scene by Karl
Popper's 1945 treatise, *The Open Society and Its Enemies*.

bias which gives priority to unity, universality, and identity over their opposites, is nevertheless operating in a philosophical space that was made possible by Hegel and came into existence once Hegel was stripped of his claims of synthesis, closure, and alleged "necessity."[3]

Three further trends in France should be mentioned. One is the non-dogmatic, Marxian inspired left-Hegelian reading of Jacques d'Hondt (*Hegel, philosophe de l'histoire vivante*, 1987, and *Hegel in His Time*, listed below), which portrays Hegel as a philosopher of historical change and transformation, a far more radical social critic than his heavy image suggests; as well as related works by Guy Planty-Bonjour (*Le Projet Hegelien*, 1993) and others. Recently d'Hondt also published a Hegel biography, not yet translated into English (but there is a new English biography by Terry Pinkard [*Hegel*, Cambridge University Press, 2003]). Another French approach, led by Eric Weil (*Hegel et l'État; Philosophie politique*) and echoed in E. Fleischmann's *La philosophie politique de Hegel* (Paris: Plon, 1969), linked Hegel to the realist, somewhat harsh political rationalism of Hobbes and Machiavelli, stressing that politics has its own logic independently of other domains. A third, quite different line in France presents Hegel as primarily a religious thinker, for whom absolute spirit was the Christian God fashioned in Lutheran terms, and whose Christology was meant more seriously than as mere metaphor of philosophical truth. The stronger versions of this view are contained in works like Claude Bruaire's *Logique et religion chrétienne dans la logique de Hegel*, 1964, and Albert Chapelle's massive *Hegel et la Religion* (4 vols., 1964–1971), and more recently, in Marie-Dominique Goutierre, *Hegel*, 1997; and Bernard Bourgeois, *Études hegeliennes*, 1992; *Hegel à Francfort ou Judaisme, Christianisme, hégélianisme*, 1970). Varieties (mostly softer) of this approach have certain English-language counterparts in the works (listed below) by Fackenheim, Yerkes, Quentin Lauer, Crites, and, to some degree, Houlgate and Taylor (though Taylor's reading has other distinctive dimensions).

---

[3] Notice also that, alone among the philosophers of reason, Hegel insists *that difference and self-severance are vital moments of identity*: therefore, Derrida, Deleuze, and other philosophers of difference radicalize a moment that Hegel was the first to highlight (Derrida, indeed, recognizes his debt to Hegel on several occasions). Similarly, existential thinkers from Kierkegaard to Sartre have radicalized the moment of *contingent particularity*, which Hegel also made important; although in the end, so they complained, contingent particularity is trivialized by the broader universality that mediates the emergence of the Hegelian singular individual.

In Germany, the nineteenth-century right- and left-wing Hegelianism took extreme varieties in the next century. Left-Hegelianism was overtaken (also outside Germany) by organized Marxism (the Marxist church), which subordinated its study of Hegel to the project of unearthing and justifying the genesis of its official truth (much as some Protestants study the Jewish "Old Testament"); while the right wing's nationalist Hegel, the political romantic and alleged deifier of the authoritarian state, emerged as a protofascist dressed in brown.

After World War II, this Hegel image receded, giving way to a variety of more sober approaches, too diverse to all be mentioned here—including critical-Marxist, hermeneutical (in Dilthey's sense, renewed by Gadamer), liberal-protestant, historicist, and purely logical. In the 1950s, Joachim Ritter and his disciples repainted Hegel in liberal colors. Hegel's influence on the Frankfurt School is particularly evidenced in works by Adorno (as in *Drei Studien zu Hegel*) and Herbert Marcuse (whose *Hegel and Revolution* remains a brilliant classic), and following them, Jürgen Habermas and Axel Honneth. Habermas stresses reason's embodiment in historical and linguistic forms, and reads Hegel's "absolute spirit" as the horizon of universal reason looming beyond them; while Honneth and Ludwig Siep, following Kojève, work out the diverse shapes of the desire for recognition, understood as driving and underlying all human life and society.

It is noteworthy, however, that German scholarship turned away from the *Phenomenology*, which has remained central in France, and today dominates in the United States. (Notable exceptions that highlight the rule are Werner Becker's *Hegels Phänomenologie des Geistes*, and a collection about the *Phenomenology* edited by H. F. Fulda and D. Henrich, *Materialien zu Hegels Phänomenologie* with interpretations by Kojève, Hyppolite, Gadamer, and Pöggeler. Part of the reason of the relative neglect of the *Phenomenology* may be the wish to distance the political Hegel in favor of a purely logical or hermeneutical reading. This is noticeable in works by Hans Friedrich Fulda, Klaus Hartmann,[4] and others of this generation, who (like the older British school, but with an opposite aim) preferred the *Logic* and the *Encyclopedia* as their dominant texts. Their opposite aim consists in reading the *Logic* nonmetaphysically, as a system of thoughts about pure thought, or a chain of hermeneutical categories, and also—

---

[4] In the essay "Hegel, a Nonmetaphysical Reading," whose title speaks for itself, and which became influential in the United States.

as did Fulda—in giving metaphysics a new and different meaning (which explains why Hegel insisted that the *Logic is* a metaphysics).

Fulda (especially in *Das Problem einer Einleitung in Hegel's Wissenchaft der Logik* [Frankfurt a. M.: Klostermann, 1965/1975]) sees Hegel's *Logic* as the core of his philosophy and as "genuine metaphysics." By this Fulda understands not a theory of beings or of being in general, but a pure "theory of meaning," designed to assess and recast our basic concepts in a way that transcends the fallacies of Western metaphysics, and can be applied to different modern domains of discourse and action. Fulda then links this "genuine metaphysics" with what he calls "an immanent theology"—one that has little in common with ordinary theology since it does not describe the divine as a special being, but rather as a system of meaningfulness, of meaning-endowing forms.

The "flight from politics" in German scholarship was only partial, however. Frankfurt thinkers from Adorno to Habermas were pointedly political, seeking to replace metaphysics not by another form of cognitive philosophy, but rather by concrete social thought. And many scholars in West Germany (not to mention the DDR) studied the Hegel-Marx relationship, either approvingly or in the attempt to debunk the Marxist trend. Then there were theological readings of Hegel, notably heterodox Protestant, which stressed the "becoming of God" and the inherence of the divine in human ethical life (now liberally conceived). And there was the complex and interesting attempt by Michael Theunissen to link all three dimensions—logic, politics, and theology—by reading the *Logic* as a theologico-political treatise. He did this in *Hegels Lehre vom absoluten Geist als theologisch-politischer Traktat* whose title deliberately evokes Spinoza and also alludes to Carl Schmitt. (Later he partly revised his interpretation.)

A major interpretative voice, also centering on speculative rather than social philosophy, is Dieter Henrich, whose life-long work sheds new light on Hegel's early years and Hölderlin's impact on Hegel's emerging views of being and consciousness (see the introduction). Unlike many others, Henrich seems to be much more committed to the historical Hegel and his milieu rather than to some contemporary agenda.

It may be illustrative to compare some of the distinctive readings above. Both Fulda and Theunissen see Hegel's *Logic* as the core, and as summarizing and overcoming Western metaphysics. Philosophy after Hegel can be transcended only by a kind of secularized, immanent theology, free of the old religious connotations. But Fulda sees this philosophical theology as broadcasting meaning equally to every domain, while in Theunissen it specifically creates the conceptual framework for a new *social ethics*, a modern transformation of Protestant theology. This transformation of speculative metaphysics (declared to have reached its end) into ethical practice recalls a similar move by Marx and the Frankfurt thinkers; but the parallel does not go much farther. Theunissen adopts a Marxist pattern yet rejects Marx's specific content and proposals; instead, he seeks, via Hegel, to inform the modern social and ethical scene with a message recast from theology.

Theology is absent from the work of most of the other socially concerned scholars who, inspired by the Frankfurt program, are interested in Hegel's concept of "ethical life" per se, without the broader speculative context. (They therefore place special value on Hegel's Jena lectures prior to the *Phenomenology*.) The systematic context comes into play only—or mainly—in the form of Hegel's critique of the merely epistemological subject of the Descartes-to-Kant tradition. This critique denies that an actual subject can be constituted by knowledge alone, or through merely abstract categories, as in Kant; it places primary importance, as conditions of individuality, on social media that have from the outset an intersubjective constitution—like language (Habermas accepts the "linguistic turn" and reads part of it into Hegel), work, family, rights, and various other forms of personal and institutional recognition. Thereby, social rationality takes the role of metaphysical reason in this mode of reading, which became influential also in parts of the Anglophone literature.

WORKS ON HEGEL IN ENGLISH: AN ANNOTATED SELECTION

The following annotated list is offered for the purpose of initiation and illustration. It is but a fraction of what is currently available on Hegel. Substantial bibliographies can be found in some of the works mentioned below.[5]

Avineri, Shlomo. *Hegel's Theory of the Modern State*. London: Cambridge, 1972.

> Refuting Hegel's authoritarian and nationalist image, and stressing the elements of a classic modern liberal in him, this book helped revive interest in Hegel's political thought among English-language readers.

---

[5] A bibliographical essay (until about 1990) is given in Stephen Houlgate's listed book.

Crites, Stephen. *Dialectic and Gospel in the Development of Hegel's Thinking*. University Park: Penn State University Press, 1998.

A massive treatise on the early Hegel, stressing the role of Christian idiom, and the Gospel drama of Creation, Fall, Covenant, Incarnation, Crucifixion, and other major themes, as the "template" forming Hegel's thought in other areas, too, and as the "subtext" of absolute Knowing. About half the book concerns the underlying role of religion in the *Phenomenology.*

Dickey, Laurence Winant. *Hegel: Religion, Economics, and the Politics of Spirit 1770–1807*. New York: Cambridge University Press, 1987.

An influential study of one main aspect of Hegel's development and cultural milieu before the *Phenomenology,* focusing on religion and economics (but not on cognitive philosophy). The book stresses the influence of Protestant (and Pietistic) trends in the process of liberalization, and (like Lukács) of Hegel's reading of Adam Smith and other Scottish economists.

Fackenheim, Emil. *The Religious Dimension in Hegel's Thought*. Chicago: University of Chicago Press, 1967.

A tone-setting book which, as the title suggests, analyzes the underlying religious aspects of Hegel's thinking, and (similarly to Taylor) brings out this important dimension without explicitly giving it precedence.

Findlay, John. *Hegel: A Re-Examination*. 1958. Reprint, Oxford: Oxford University Press, 1976.

The first book in English after World War II calling for a new look at Hegel. Its merit was to revise the rigid academic systematization favored by pious Hegelians (and by Stace and Mure). Hegel's dialectic cannot be construed as inflexibly as formal logic; its broad-lined necessity leaves room for contingency, accidental features, and alternative secondary routes.

Forster, Michael. *Hegel's Idea of a Phenomenology of Spirit*. Chicago: University of Chicago Press, 1998.

Opposing the selective singling out of one aspect of Hegel's project in neglect of others, Forster studies the *Phenomenology* as a complex whole, stressing the "extraordinary" coherent integration of its several goals and moves. These include pedagogical, epistemological, and metaphysical tasks: preparing the modern mind for the new science; justifying this science against the skeptics; and recasting truth and knowledge as a communal enterprise. Thereby, the *Phenomenology* is coherent both in its own terms, and as part of the overall system.

Franco, Paul. *Hegel's Philosophy of Freedom*. New Haven: Yale University Press, 1999.

A commentary on *The Philosophy of Right* and other texts. The Hegelian state is the modern realization of human autonomy, Hegel's driving theme. Reuniting morality and legality, Hegel is a liberal who overcame the atomism and self-interest of liberalism. Franco also insists that Hegel's social theory is inseparable from his logic and metaphysics.

Hardimon, Michael O. *Hegel's Social Philosophy: The Project of Reconciliation*. Cambridge: Cambridge University Press, 1994.

Hegel's social philosophy sets to resolve the problem of alienation by reconciling modern man to his society (and making him at home in it), thereby also realizing the rationality that defines us. Hegel's *Philosophy of Right* is read from this important angle. (The author does not, however, recognize the same problem in our relation to being and the universe.)

Harris, H. S. *Hegel's Ladder*. Vol. 1, *The Pilgrimage of Reason*. Vol. 2, *The Odyssey of Spirit*. Indianapolis: Hackett Publications, 1997.

A monument of learning and analysis, treating the *Phenomenology* as a living philosophy with existential, social, and religious dimensions, and richly situating it in its cultural context. In trying to make sense of the work as a whole, Harris offers (a) a concise paragraph-by-paragraph commentary, and (b) a free flowing, multisided discussion of the main issues (and many side ones). The conclusion stresses that, beyond social activism, Comprehension (Harris' capitalization) is the highest form of self-realization in Hegel.

Heidegger, Martin. *Hegel's Phenomenology of Spirit*. Bloomington: Indiana University Press, 1988.

An ontological interpretation of the *Phenomenology* (in part). There is no epistemology in the *Phenomenology*. Hegel's aim was to bring the question, what is being? which drives Western philosophy, to completion. In the part on "Consciousness" he inquires into the objectivity (real being) of objects; and in "Self-Consciousness" he inquires into the being of the self—and finds it must be explicated as independence, or freedom (hence the transition to "practical philosophy"). Yet Hegel erred in trying to categorize being. (Heidegger's teaching lectures, here as elsewhere, offer strikingly accurate insights alongside his typical idiosyncrasies.)

Henrich, Dieter. *The Course of Remembrance and Other Essays on Hölderlin.* Stanford, CA: Stanford University Press, 1997.
Henrich's important work on Hegel and Hölderlin is described in detail in the introduction.)

Hondt, Jacques d'. *Hegel in His Time: Berlin 1818–1831.* Peterborough, Ontario: Broadview Press, 1988. First published in French in 1968.
A left-Hegelian portrait of Hegel and his milieu in the Berlin years. Joined to the author's French *Hegel secret* and his recent Hegel biography, it pictures a more lively, critical intellectual and social reformer hiding behind the established Herr Professor and heavy writer, a thinker more at odds with his time, and incapable of speaking his mind too plainly.

Houlgate, Stephen. *Freedom, Truth, and History: An Introduction to Hegel's Philosophy.* London: Routledge, 1991.
An introduction (with a bibliographical essay) covering truth and its history, dialectic, logic and ontology, rights and freedom, art, philosophy, and religion, with a strong emphasis on Hegel's Christianity (understood as the teaching of the church more than Christ's).

Hyppolite, Jean. *Genesis and Structure of Hegel's Phenomenology of Spirit.* Evanston, IL: Northwestern University Press, 1974. First published in French in Paris, 1946.
A masterly section-by-section commentary, the most influential French interpretation next to Kojève's. The structural analysis of the changing shapes of consciousness and their relative collapses is conducted from the dual viewpoint of "for itself" and "for us"—the experiencing consciousness undergoing the process, and the investigating philosophical consciousness that already knows the end.

Kaufmann, Walter. *Hegel: A Reinterpretation.* Garden City, NY: Doubleday, Anchor Books, 1966.
Following Findlay in a different approach, Kaufmann offers a cultural mapping of Hegel that makes him fresh and interesting despite his flaws, a European intellectual in the line of Goethe and Nietzsche, and superior to Kant. Philosophically, however, Hegel emerges somewhat diffuse. The brief commentary to the Preface of the *Phenomenology* is mostly valuable for its decoding of cultural allusions to Hegel's milieu.

Kojève, Alexandre. *Introduction to the Reading of Hegel*. New York: Basic Books, 1969.

Secular and left-leaning, Kojève's lectures were most influential in stressing the drive for recognition that has become dominant in Hegel interpretations since. History is the comprehensive human horizon, and the motor generating history—the struggle for recognition with its asymmetrical results—creates the two alienated classes of masters and servants. Hegel's philosophical knowledge became possible only after the French Revolution, when mutual recognition came to be embodied in modern institutions.

Lukács, George. *The Young Hegel*. Cambridge, MA: MIT Press, 1975.

A study of the early Hegel by a prominent European intellectual who had turned from idealism to Marxism when already wellknown; stressing the problem of alienation as central to the young Hegel; his exposure to economic writers like Smith and Ferguson; and the historical dimension of the *Phenomenology*, with its complex allusion to concrete historical periods.

Marcuse, Herbert. *Reason and Revolution*. Boston: Beacon, 1960.

A clear, instructive, overall review of Hegel serves Marcuse as starting point for creating, against Hegel's own conclusion, a critical theory in the Frankfurt style, suggesting that sociology and empirically oriented social thought replace philosophy in its classic, atemporal orientation.

Marx, Werner. *Hegel's Phenomenology of Spirit*. New York: Harper and Row, 1975.

Although described as a "commentary [on the *Phenomenology*] based on the Preface and Introduction," this short book is a series of related essays rather than a textual commentary. Marx's reading tends to be Schellingian; world history realizes preestablished structures and ends, and spirit guides the process from the start, rather than being constituted by it.

Mure, G.R.G. *A Study of Hegel's Logic*. Oxford: Clarendon Press, 1950.

A standard commentary, in the general systematic tradition of the British Idealists, going beyond Stace in using the greater *Logic* in addition to the *Encyclopedia*, and stressing the dynamic nature of the categories as forms of a living process. The book elaborates on Mure's earlier, approachable introductory, *The Philosophy of Hegel* (1940, reprint, London: Oxford University Press, 1965).

Neuhouser, Frederick. *Foundations of Hegel's Social Theory: Actualizing Freedom*. Cambridge, MA: Harvard University Press, 2000.

Portraying Hegel as a liberal (against communitariansm), the author leans on Rousseau (who can, however, be read in two ways), and on Kant. Hegelian autonomy ("social freedom") requires free institutions recognized by individuals as emanating from their will. And Hegel valued personal morality and "subjective freedom" not much less than Kant.

Patten, Allan. *Hegel's Idea of Freedom*. Oxford: Oxford University Press, 1999.

An interpretation of Hegel passages explicitly dealing with freedom, especially in *The Philosophy of Right*, arguing that civic freedom depends on the ethical elements embodied in historical institutions.

Pinkard, Terry. *Hegel's Phenomenology: The Sociality of Reason*. Cambridge: Cambridge University Press, 1994.

A jargon-free redescription of the *Phenomenology* (and briefly the *Philosophy of Right*), in the post-Kantian trend in which the social dimension prevails. In detaching itself from Hegel's running text and several core ideas (with their ontological import), it constructs a revised *Phenomenology*, which the author thinks fit for our time. The main focus is on how changing historical communities conceptualize and justify their forms of life and sources of authority. Self-consciousness is not an inner mental state but a participant in a "social space," to which "spirit" and "absolute Knowing" are also translated.

Pippin, Robert. *Hegel's Idealism: The Satisfaction of Self-Consciousness*. Cambridge: Cambridge, 1989.

This influential study triggered the reading known as "post-Kantian" which views Hegel as a nonmetaphysical thinker who mainly set out to complete Kant's idealist move in the Transcendental Deduction and the Paralogism. Kant's problems and failures in dealing with self-consciousness drove Hegel to a more coherent variety of idealism. Hegel also shared Kant's attack on the metaphysics of transcendence and of substance.

Redding, Paul. *Hegel's Hermeneutics*. Ithaca, NY: Cornell University Press, 1996.

The author sees Hegel as "post-Kantian" and as a hermeneutical thinker (following K. Hartmann). Hegelian subjectivity is shaped hermeneutically; and since it involves diverse forms of recognition, it is by "hermeneuticizing" Kant that Hegel completes Kant's revolution in the political domain. Hegelianism is "postmetaphysical Kantianism."

Smith, Steven B. *Hegel's Critique of Liberalism*. Chicago: Chicago University Press, 1989.

As against the formal view of rights, this study, relying on Kojève's emphasis on recognition, attributes to Hegel a "substantive" view of rights whose centerpiece is a "right to recognition." This allows Hegel's version of liberalism to appear as a middle ground between the deontological (Kant, Rawls) and the communitarian.

Solomon, Robert. *In the Spirit of Hegel*. New York: Oxford University Press, 1983.

Stating that the *Phenomenology* is disordered in structure, and describing its aim as a personal journey of an individual toward the self-reshaping that enables truth to emerge, this vivid study, which is often discussed polemically, treats Hegel's work in a secular left-Hegelian vein which discounts his theological claims and has little room for the "religious dimension."

Stace, W. T. *The Philosophy of Hegel*. 1924. Reprint, New York: Dover Publications, 1955.

A classic in the older style, presenting the whole of Hegel's philosophy (logic, nature, and spirit, following the *Encyclopedia*) as a chain of categories that derive from each other as if deductively, and trying to make sense of their transition. Though some moves are ingenious, Hegel emerges as an overly systematized and rigid dialectician—a more elaborate Fichte.

Taylor, Charles. *Hegel*. Cambridge: Cambridge University Press, 1975.

A groundbreaking study that helped legitimize Hegel to Anglophone academia. Taylor covers the whole system. Opposing Kojève's secularist reduction of spirit to history, he insists on spirit's transhistorical, ontic, and religious dimension. And, linking Hegel to Herder and the romantics no less than to Kant, he suggests an "expressivist" view of nature and a "communitarian" view of politics as correction to nonhistoricist, atomist liberalism.

Westphal, Merold. *History and Truth in Hegel's Phenomenology*. Atlantic Highlands, NJ: Humanities Press, 1979. Reprint, Bloomington: Indiana University Press, 1998.

A short, readable commentary to the *Phenomenology,* stressing the historicality of transcendental subjectivity and of absolute Knowing. Following Henrich, love rather than recognition (or as another form of it) is a key concept in understanding how Hegelian spirit is meant to surpass abstract rationality.

Wood, Allen. *Hegel's Ethical Thought.* Cambridge: Cambridge University Press, 1990

Against the belief that Hegel had no specific ethics (given his fierce attack on Kant's Ought), this study explores the ethical views underlying Hegel's social, political, and historical thought as an alternative to utilitarianism and Kantian deontology. Wood brackets the speculative and metaphysical context of these views and examines them as ethics per se.

Yerkes, James. *The Christology of Hegel.* Albany: SUNY Press, 1983.

A rich treatment of Hegel's religious Christian symbols, understood as "images' (*Vorstellungen*), in relation to theology and philosophy.

Yovel, Yirmiyahu. *Dark Riddle: Hegel, Nietzsche, and the Jews.* Cambridge: Polity Press; University Park: Penn State University Press, 1998.

The book's first half is a comprehensive study of the evolution of Hegel's interpretation of Judaism and the Jews. The matter is approached philosophically, as a problem *within* the Hegelian system as well as *for* it. The analysis shows the issue to be more central than meets the eye. It also provides a prism through which other Hegelian themes—like *Aufhebung,* alienation, the absolute-as-subject, the unhappy consciousness, or political modernity—acquire additional light and context.

Index

><

absolute: empty romantic conception of, 93–94; as result, 102–4; as subject (*see* absolute as subject). *See also* truth

absolute as subject: central role in Hegel's philosophy of, 16–17; objections to notion of, 95–97; ontological significance of, 22; predicative language and, 107–10; as rejection of Hölderlin, 48–49; as a result, 102

absolute Knowing: criticism of, 61; as historical need, 73n; as living experience, 4–5, 7–8; objective idealism and, 137n; path to, 4, 8–9, 25; role of mediation in, 104; significance of, 24; systematic nature of, 110. *See also* Knowing

absolute spirit: expressed as philosophy, art, and religion, 26, 112n; narrow versus universal sense of, 10; as subject versus as person, 13n.10. *See also* spirit

abstraction, formal logic and, 30

acorn analogy, 84

actuality (*Wirklichkeit*): "actual is rational," 33; Aristotle versus Hegel on, 67n; development of being into, 18; existence versus, 66n, 85n; spirit as, 112; unity of being and thought, 69n

adequatio rei et intellectus, 32

alienation (*Entfremdung*): being and, 24; defined, 101n; experience and, 135; otherness versus, 101n; philosophy as cure for, 6–7

analogy, in interpretation of Hegel, 13

analytic philosophy, 61

Anaxagoras, 172

Anaximander, 154n

antinomy of language, 108–9n

aphorisms: inadequacy of, 14; paradox of, 14–16; value of, 14–16

appearance (*Erscheinung*), 138, 153

argumentative reasoning, Conceptual thinking versus, 176–80, 185–89

Aristotle: on actuality, 67n; ancient appreciation of, 194; categories in, 23; on ethical life, 7; genus and species in, 172n; God for, 18; Hegel's incorporation of, 14; on nature and teleology, 106; as rational philosopher, 4; soul in, 136n; unmoved mover in, 106n

art: absolute spirit and, 26; Hegel on history and essence of, 40 nn. 23 and 24

assertion (*Behauptung*), 63, 170

Aufhebung (sublation): absolute and, 95n; dialectical, 86n, 155n; history of philosophy and, 32; *Phenomenology of Spirit* as, 82n; reflection and, 105; of religion, 3, 28; of representation, 124–30; science and, 39; of social and political institutions, 25; spirit and, 10, 25, 135; of thought, 15, 43

autonomy, defined, 6

Bacchanalian whirl: ecstasy and, 195n; positive dialectic as, 39, 67n; the true as, 153–54; the whole as, 168n

Bacon, Francis, 78n

beauty: versus kitsch, 128n; powerless, 128n
becoming: being as, 18, 23–24, 104n;
of God, 3; mediation as, 104
Begriff. See Concept
being (*Sein*): as becoming, 18, 23–24,
104n; development of, 18; essence
versus, 145n; Hölderlin on, 47; immediacy and, 96n, 114–15, 131; in
Logic, 9; mathematics and, 145n,
152n; in *Phenomenology of Spirit*, 9;
philosophy's role in development
of, 24, 27–28; predicative language
and concept of, 184; as starting
point for philosophy, 47–48; subject-like character of, 48–49, 53;
substance and, 96, 168n; thought
and, 169. *See also* ontology
Berkeley, George, 125n, 148n
Berlin period in Hegel's thought,
41n, 160n
Bestimmung (determination), 68n, 131,
139, 152, 154, 161, 168
Bible: Acts 5:9, 196n; Matthew 8:22,
196n
Bildung. See education
binaries. *See* opposites
Burbridge, John, 52n.37

Calvinism, 5
categories: a priori, 161n; Aristotle
and, 23; Fichte and, 90n, 126n,
190n; Hegelian, 133n; identity of
subject and, 21; Kantian, 32, 52,
54n, 71n, 90n, 159n; ontological, 22
certainty (*Gewissheit*): defined, 116n;
truth versus, 116n
child development, as metaphor for
development of spirit, 83–84
Christianity: God of, 10; Hegel's dialectical version of, 3; spirit versus
nature in, 27

civil society, 5; as objective spirit, 25–
26. *See also* social world
coherence theory of truth, 31
common sense, philosophy of, 125n,
126n, 189–93
Concept (*Begriff*): conceptual thinking
versus argumentative reasoning,
176–80, 185–89; defined, 132n,
137n; definitions versus, 64n; intuition and, 74n; knowing without,
80–81; life of, 164–67; pure, 113–
14n; relation to things of, 32–34; Science as expression of, 174–76; in *Science of Logic*, 148n; simple, 85n; two
senses of, 84n; universality of, 65n
consciousness: development of, 85–
88; and dualism, 116–17n; experiencing versus philosophical, 112–
13n; philosophy and development
of individual, 88n; as protagonist of
Phenomenology, 115n, 134n; Science
in relation to, 116–18; standpoint
of, 116–17n; substance and, 95–97;
two moments of, 134
Copernican revolution, Kantian, 9,
12, 50–54, 132n
critical philosophy, 57
Croce, Benedetto, 58–59
cultural education. *See* education
culture: as development of being, 19,
24–25; individuals in relation to,
119–24; as substance, 76n. *See also*
social world
cunning of reason: 170–71; Kant's anticipation of, 55

Darstellung. See exhibition
Dasein, 66n, 85n, 152n, 171–72n, 173n
death: as metaphor for negativity,
128n; spirit and, 128–29
definitions, Concepts versus, 64n
Descartes, René: concept of subject
in, 20, 115n, 131n; mathematical

model for reasoning in, 143n, 147n; philosophical method of, 70n, 159n; and simplicity, 85n; truth for, 42 desire, 60

determination. See *Bestimmung*

dialectic: demonstration versus, 187–88; exhibition in Hegel's writings of, 160n, 165n, 166–67n, 187n; formal logic versus, 29; general characteristics of, 35–38; and interiorization, 86n; language appropriate for, 15, 187n, 189n; as logic, 36; love compared to, 100n; monism and, 26; negativity inherent in, 12n.9, 36; no a priori rules for, 37; not a thesis-antithesis-synthesis formula, 29, 46, 92n, 160n, 163n; philosophy conducted through, 30–31, 189; of Plato versus Hegel, 38–39; role of moments in, 67n; role of opposites in, 37; self-reflection and, 99n; significance of, 60; spiral movement of, 14; as subjective education, 41–42; as teleological, 37; unification as problem addressed by, 48

dialectic-as-journey: dialectic-as-Science versus, 38–40; and individual's education, 41–42; *Phenomenology of Spirit* as, 39–41

dialectic-as-Science: dialectic-as-journey versus, 38–40; *Science of Logic* as, 39–41

Difference between Fichte's and Schelling's Systems, The, 46n

Dilthey, Wilhelm, 142n

discourse. See theory of discourse

divine, and development of spirit, 78–79

dogmatism, 142, 158–59n, 170

dualism, 116–17n, 141n

Ebreo, Leone, 100n

Eckhart, Meister, 100n

economics, 5

ecstasy, 78, 194–95

edification (*Erbauung*): defined, 77n; philosophy versus, 77–78n, 79, 100n, 188

education (*Bildung* [also cultural education]): ancient versus modern, 130; beginning of, 71; philosophy and, 190; as retracing development of spirit, 119–24, 121n; self-certainty transformed through, 132n; self-education of human race, 119–20n

eidos, 172

Einstein, Albert, 150n

empiricism: and Berkeley's idealism, 125n; dogmatism of, 131n; one-sidedness of, 79n, 89n; and simplicity, 85n

Encyclopaedia of Philosophical Sciences, 40, 118n, 133n, 161n, 166n, 190n

energeia, 18

Enlightenment: education and, 130; Hegelian philosophy and, 3, 82n, 89n, 117n; and meaning of being, 2

enthusiasm, 78, 79n, 93n, 119, 159, 194

epistēmē, 39, 110n

equality. See *Gleichheit*

Erinnerung. See recollection

essence (*Wesen*): being versus, 145n; consciousness and, 76

eternity, end of philosophy and, 72n

ethical life: defined, 7; as presupposition of absolute spirit, 25–26; role of, 7–8, 25–26

Euclid, 192n

evil, 139–40

excluded middle, law of, 38. *See also* non-contradiction, law of

exhibition (*Darstellung*): of cultural education, 121–22; defined, 63n; Kant versus Hegel on, 70–71n; of philosophical truth, 71n, 95, 155 existence: actuality versus, 66n, 85n; defined, 66n; substance versus, 173n; Understanding and, 171–73

Existentialism, 98n

Existenz, 66n, 85n. *See also* existence

experience: consciousness and, 135; post-medieval philosophy on, 78–79n; role in development of spirit of, 79

externalization, dialectic of inwardness and, 80n

falsity: defined, 37; role of, 138–41, 146n

familiar, the (*Bekannte*), 88, 125–26

Fichte, Johann Gottlieb: categories in, 90n, 126n, 190n; concept of subject in, 16, 21n; and fusion of Kant and Spinoza, 46; Hegel's criticism of, 45–46, 89–92, 99n, 126n, 127n, 163n; Hegel's incorporation of, 16; Hölderlin and, 47; influence of, 45–46, 160n; nationalism of, 82n; and practical reason, 7; subject in, 53, 90–91n, 95n, 97n; system of, 90n, 91n, 110n, 190n; thesis-antithesis-synthesis formula of, 29, 46, 92n, 160n, 163n

finitude, Kant versus Hegel on, 57

formalism: critique of, 92–94, 161–64; in method, 161–64; as stage in development of content, 174

freedom: and being in-and-for-itself, 112n; ontological and sociopolitical senses of, 24

French Revolution, 82n, 175n

Fulda, Hans Friedrich, 52n.37

Galileo Galilei, 78n

generalization, 64n

genius, 163, 190–91

geometrical method, 143–44 nn, 146n, 147n

German Idealism, 90n, 112n

geschichtlich, 142n

Gleichheit (equality): 94, 95, 98, 140, 149

God: Aristotle versus Hegel on, 18; becoming of, 3, 23–24; complex nature of, 100–101; Hegelian synthesis of Christian and Spinozan, 10; immanence in human history of, 17, 18, 27, 56–57; for Kant, 56; and love, 100; as name versus Concept, 188; in Spinoza, 10, 20, 28

Goethe, Johann Wolfgang von, 27

Harris, E. H., 52n.37

Hegel, G.W.F.: Berlin period of, 41n, 160n; Jena period of, 7, 41n, 179n; misconceptions about, 58; "old," 58–62; significance of, 59–62

Heidegger, Martin, 10n.4, 24n, 47, 109n, 191n

Henrich, Dieter, 45n, 48

Herder, Johann Gottfried von, 119n

historisch, 142n

history: dialectical structure of, 36–38; empirical aspect of, 63n, 65n; God as embodied in, 17; historical truths, 142–43; Kant on, 55; role of, 12, 25, 60, 119n, 122–23; world-spirit and world, 122–23

history of philosophy: refutation in, 111n, 138–39n; system of philosophy and, 31–32, 73n

Hölderlin, Friedrich: cosmic love in, 100n; as Hegel's classmate, 45; Hegel's criticism of, 45–46, 74–75n, 99n, 105n, 191n; influence of, 45n, 47–49; and language, 109n

Husserl, Edmund, 70n

idealism: empiricist, 125n; Hegelian, "objective," 12, 112n, 136n, 137n; identity of being and thought in,

169n; subjective, *33, 46. See also*
German Idealism

identity: mathematics and, 149; of
subject versus substance, 20, 29.
See also *Gleichheit*

image. *See* representation

immanence: of God, 17, 18, 27, 56–
57; Hegel as philosopher of, 18, 27,
78n; in Spinoza, 96n; transcendence versus, 53

immediacy: becoming and, 104n; of
being, 96n, 114–15, 131; coerced,
123; defined, 84n; of subject, 129

in-and-for-itself (*an und für sich*), 112

incommensurability, 150n

individuals: defined, 44n.26; development through Science of, 115; education of, 119–24; freedom of, 115–
16; in relation to spirit, 197–98;
true, 179n; as universal, 119–20

infinity, good versus bad, 150n

intellectual intuition: criticism of, 97;
genius and, 191n; Hegelian rationalist interpretation of, 49–50, 70n,
74–75n; Kant on, 49–50, 74–75n,
93n; Schelling on, 49, 74–75n, 93n,
97n

intention, meaning versus, 34–35

interests of reason, Kant on, 55

interiority. *See* inwardness

interiorization, 38, 67n, 86n, 123–24n,
154–55n, 165n

intuition, 74–75, 79–81, 159. *See also*
intellectual intuition

inwardness, dialectic of externalization and, 80n

Jacobi, Friedrich Heinrich, 47, 74–
75nn, 99n, 105n

Jena period in Hegel's thought, 7,
41n, 179n

judgment: Hölderlin on, 47; and predicative language, 182

Judgment and Being (Hölderlin), 47,
182n

Kabbala, 100n

Kant, Immanuel: and being, 9; categories, 23, 132n; concept of subject,
16–17, 20–21; critique of religion,
3; derivation of categories, 90n;
dogmatism critiqued, 131n, 181n;
on enthusiasm, 79n; exhibition as
concept, 63n, 70–71n; as founder of
modern philosophy, 17; Hegel and,
14, 16, 50–57; on history of philosophy, 66n; on intellectual intuition,
49–50, 74–75n, 93n; mathematical
versus philosophical reasoning,
143n, 149n, 157n; and metaphysics,
51, 160n; and modernity, 82n; and
nature, 11, 12n.7; and philosophical
method, 70n, 156n; and practical
reason, 7; and rationalism and empiricism, 89n; role of Concepts in,
33; role of interest in, 55; self and
other in, 54n.40; space in, 148n;
subject in, 95n; and system, 90n,
110n; thing-in-itself of, 135n; and
triplicity, 159–60n; and universal individual, 119n. *See also* Copernican
revolution, Kantian

Kaufmann, Walter, 139n

Kierkegaard, Søren, 43–44, 115n,
13n.9

kitsch, 128n

Knowing (*Wissen*): defined, 118n; familiarity versus, 125–26. *See also* absolute Knowing

known. *See* familiar (*Bekannte*)

Kojève, Alexandre, 83n

Krug, Professor, 22, 44n.27

language. *See* theory of discourse

law, interpretation in, 59

Lectures on the History of Philosophy, 17

Lefebvre, Henri, 94n
Left Young Hegelians, 17
Leibniz, Gottfried Wilhelm, 92n, 106n, 179n
Lessing, Gotthold Ephraim, 139n
Locke, John: on experience, 78n; philosophical method of, 70n, 156n
Logic. See *Science of Logic*
logic: dialectical, 36; formal, validity of, 30; philosophical method and, 156; subject-like character of, 29–30; transcendental, 52–53
logos: as constitutive versus descriptive, 70n; dialectic and, 36; logic and, 29, 53, 138n; significance of Hegel's view of, 60; as structure of reality, 17, 29, 53, 87n, 138n; as universal thought, 4
love: defined, 100n; dialectic compared to, 100n; God as, 100
Luther, Martin: on ethical life, 7; on spirit in relation to world, 5

magnitude, 148–49
Maimonides, 18n
Marx, Karl: and nature, 11; and union of substance and subject, 17
mathematical knowledge, 143–52, 156–58; limitations of, 147–51
matter, thinking in relation to, 175–76
meaning (*Bedeutung*): Enlightenment undermining of, 2; of existence, 61; intention versus, 34–35; modern rationality and, 6, 12; of statements, 34–35, 108
mediation (*Vermittlung*): as becoming, 104; role in absolute Knowing of, 103–4
memory. *See* interiorization
mental image. *See* representation
metaphor, 3
metaphysics, 2, 51; critical, 53; dogmatic (pre-Kantian), 9, 17, 33, 51–

53; history of, 54; idealist, 17; Kant's Copernican revolution and, 51; of morals, 52n.36; as science, 51; of substance, 53; of transcendence, 53
method. *See* philosophical method
modernity: experience as significant concept in, 79n; Hegel and, 82–83n, 111–12, 112n, 196n; Kant versus Hegel on, 57; negative aspects of, 5–6; and reconstruction of meaning, 2, 6, 12; subject-centered ontology and, 54
moment(s): of consciousness, 134; defined, 67n; falsity as, 153n; of knowing, 141; mutual necessity of, 68n; pure thinking as, 131
monism, dialectical, 26
morality, Kant on, 55–56
multiculturalism, 37n
mysticism: emptiness of, 79–81, 164n; Hegel and, 4, 27–28, 81n, 186n

Napoleon, 82n, 175n
Nathan the Wise (Lessing), 139n
nationalism, 46, 82n
Nativity of Christ, 83–84n
nature: dialectic and, 86–87n; pantheism and, 26–27; social mediation and, 26; spirit in relation to, 11–12, 27; teleology of, 106
necessity: historical, 43; logical, 174n
negation: double, 29, 38; and retention of negated stage, 36, 86n, 155n; the subject and, 19–20; Understanding as, 127n, 128n. *See also* negativity
negative dialectic. *See* dialectic-as-journey
negativity: death as metaphor for, 128n; and falsity, 138–41; as mover, 136; permanence of, 12n.9; significance of, 60; spirit and, 129; subjec-

tivity as, 98n; substance as, 98. *See also* negation

Nietzsche, Friedrich, 57, 59, 154n

"night in which all cows are black" metaphor, 94, 164n

noncontradiction, law of, 29, 38, 68n, 91n, 103–4n

nostalgia, Hegel versus, 76–77n

nous (Nus), 172

oak tree analogy, 84

objective spirit: defined, 111n; socio-political world as, 25–26

ontology: existence and actuality, 66n; journey of, 9; of infinite being, 22; Kant's Copernican revolution and, 50–54; Kant versus Hegel on, 12n.7; in *Logic*, 22, 52n.37, 168n, 173n; monism and, 26–27; and social philosophy, 1–4; of subject, 22–23; truth and, 19, 32–33. *See also* being

opinion (*Meinung*), 65, 185

opposites, non-exclusiveness of, 37

organic model of development, 66–67

other: alienation versus, 101n; multiculturalism and, 37n; role in truth of, 37; self and, 54; self-identity achieved through, 20, 21

pantheism, 26–27

Parmenides, 127n, 169n

Parmenides (Plato), 39

particularization: 20, 68n, 90n, 108n, 124n, 187n

particulars: spirit and, 124n; subject in relation to, 22–23, 42, 44; universals in relation to, 65n, 165n

phenomenology, Husserlian, 70n

Phenomenology of Spirit: consciousness as protagonist of, 115n, 134n; dialectic-as-journey and, 39–41; as historicization of Plato's theory of ed-

ucation, 72n; and individual's education, 41–42, 43–44, 115n; purpose of, 119n; role in Hegelian system of, 40–41; summary of, 8–9

philosophical method, 155–64; guided by subject matter, 69–70n; logic and, 155; mathematical versus, 156–58, 157n; triplicity in relation to, 159–60

philosophy: absolute spirit and, 26; as actual versus love of knowing, 71–73, 72n; ancient versus modern, 130; conflicting doctrines in, 65–68; critical, 57; critique of contemporary, 190–98; as development of being, 24, 27–28; development versus result of, 68–70; dialectical logic as method of, 30–31; discourse appropriate for, 15, 63–65, 102–3n, 107–8, 108–9n, 182–83n, 185–89n; edification and, 77–78n, 79, 100n, 188; education and, 190; end of, 71–72n; Hegel on history and essence of, 40 nn. 23 and 24; historical diversity of, 65–68; history of, 31–32, 73n, 111n; and immanence, 18, 27; individual conscience's development and, 88n; interpretation of past of, 59; justification of, 72–73n; mathematics versus, 143n, 145, 147, 149n, 152–53, 156–58, 157n; method of (*see* philosophical method); ordinary perception of, 189–90; and other sciences, 190; path to, 41–42, 192–94; principles in, 110; as Science, 71–73; speculative (*see* speculative philosophy); subjective nature of absolute and, 28–31; system and history of, 73n

philosophy of unity. *See* unification philosophy

Pico della Mirandola, Giovanni, 100n

Plato: actual knowledge for, 72n; "appearances" in, 30; on becoming, 104n; cosmic love in, 100n; dialectic of, 38–39; education in, 120n; Forms in, 49, 133n, 172n; and mysticism, 81n; opinion in, 65n; as rational philosopher, 4; reception of philosophy of, 194; recollection in, 124n

poetry: Hölderlin on being and, 47; philosophy and, 109n

polemics in preface, 45–50

politics: Hegel on history and essence of, 40 nn. 23 and 24; Kant on, 55. *See also* objective spirit

positing (*Setzung*): defined, 97n; Hegel and contemporaries on, 97–98n

positivism: Hegel versus, 30; illusions of, 61; and simplicity, 85n

postmodernism, 179n

predicative language, 15–16, 103n, 107–10, 178–85, 187–89

presentation. *See* exhibition

pre-Socratic philosophers, 154n

principles: critique of basic, 110, 134n, 158; derivation of system from, 89–90n

propositions, 15, 34, 107–8, 182–85, 187, 190

public, philosophy and, 195–97

quality, 168–69n

rationalism: dogmatism of, 131n; Hegel and, 4; one-sidedness of, 89n; rationality versus, 74n

rationality: development of, 42–43; freedom of, 42–43; modern, 6, 89; other of, 36; "rational is actual," 33; versus rationalism, 74n; science and, 89; as substantive, 60

reality, relation to Concepts of, 32–34

Reason (*Vernunft*): Concept in relation to, 175–76; cunning of, 55, 170–71; teleology of, 106; Understanding versus, 27, 36, 64n, 65n, 87–88

recollection (*Erinnerung*), 38, 86n, 123–24n. *See also* interiorization

reflection: internal versus external, 98–99n; non-conscious, 99n; role in development of absolute of, 105. *See also* self-reflection

refutation, 110–11, 138–39n, 176–77

Reinhold, Karl Leonhard, 21n

religion: absolute spirit and, 26; as background for Hegel's philosophy, 4, 22; Hegel on history and essence of, 40 nn. 23 and 24; Hegel's transcendence of, 4; history of, 3–4; illusions of, 61; interpretation in, 59; modernity and, 112; philosophy in relation to, 2–4

representation (*Vorstellung*), 14n, 64, 65n, 74, 82, 124–25, 127–28

representational theory of truth, 33

representational thinking, 8

Republic (Plato), 38, 39

romanticism, 46–47, 76n, 93–94, 103–4n, 159n, 190–91

Rorty, Richard, 58, 78n

Rousseau, Jean-Jacques, 43

Sache, 69n

Sartre, Jean-Paul, 11, 98n

Schelling, F.W.J. von: concept of subject in, 16; cosmic love in, 100n; as Hegel's classmate, 45; Hegel's criticism of, 45–46, 74–75n, 89–90n, 93–94, 162n, 164n, 191n, 193n, 195n, 197n; and intellectual intuition, 49, 74–75nn, 93n, 97n, 191n; and nature, 27; subject in, 53, 97n; and teleology, 12

schematism, 71n, 166

Schopenhauer, Arthur, 17, 59, 191n

Schwärmerei, 79n, 194n. *See also* enthusiasm

Science (*Wissenschaft*): Concept expressed through, 174–76; consciousness in relation to, 116–18; contemporary dilemma of, 89; defined, 110n; first part of, 134; versus formalism, 164–67; knowing as, 110; misapplication of, 89–91; necessary movement of, 133–34; path to, 118–24; and philosophy, 71–73, 190; as spirit knowing itself, 114. *See also* dialectic-as-Science; truth

Science of Logic (*Wissenschaft der Logik*): as conceptual skeleton, 13; dialectic-as-Science and, 39–41; and existence, 171n; history and, 54; and Kant's transcendental logic, 52; as metaphysics, 53–54; and method, 155–56n; and ontology, 9, 22, 52n.37, 168n, 173n; and predicative propositions, 187n; role of subject in, 17; spiritual essences in, 133n

self: absolute in relation to, 81n; development of, 7–8, 107; ordinary conception of, 181; other of, 54

self-alienation. *See* alienation

self-certainty, 117, 131, 170

self-consciousness: development of, 9, 129–32; as result of process, 36

self-conscious spirit, current situation of, 75–78

self-identity, 20–22; Fichte versus Hegel on, 90–91n; Kant and, 20–21; as result of process, 36, 98n; substance and, 168–69

self-particularization, 22–23, 124n, 165n

self-reflection, 98n. *See also* reflection

sense perception: 22, 124n, 129n, 137–38n, 149, 161

senses, relation to Understanding of, 130–32

simplicity, 85n, 96n, 114–15, 168, 172

social world, 1–2, 5, 7–8, 9–10, 25, 28, 44. *See also* civil society; culture; objective spirit

Socrates, 38, 192n

sophia, 72n

Sophist (Plato), 39

space, 148, 148n

speculative philosophy: defined, 49–50; in Hegel and contemporaries, 93n, 138n; scientific method and, 174

speculative proposition, 182–83n

Spinoza, Baruch: and being, 9, 47; *causa sui* in, 34, 113n; comparative thinking critiqued by, 69n; concept of substance in, 16–17; God for, 10, 20, 28, 96, 100n; Hegel's incorporation of, 14, 16, 112n; and "intellectual love of God," 28; on knowledge and being, 137n; mathematical model for reasoning in, 143n, 147n; on method, 156n; and mysticism, 81n; naturalism of, 27; and negation, 127n; as premodern, 112n; as rational philosopher, 4; substance in, 95n

spiral: evolution of spirit as, 37; as model for dialectic, 14

spirit: civil society as objective, 25–26; current situation of, 75–78, 82–84; death and, 128–29; defined, 10–11; development of, 83–85; as hallmark of modern era, 111–12; impoverishment of, 78–79; nature in relation to, 11–12, 27; and negativity, 129; Science as development of, 114; self-conscious, 75–78; worldly embodiment of, 4–5, 13. *See also* absolute spirit; objective spirit

spiritual essentialities (*geistige Wesenheiten*), 132, 133n
spiritual substance, 113n
statements, truth and meaning of, 34–35
subject: absolute as, 16–17, 22, 95–97; absolute spirit as, 13n.10; collapse of, 179n; as constituted, 60; knowing, Hegel versus Fichte on, 90–91n; ontological versus epistemological perspective on, 22; in predicative language versus conceptual thinking, 178–80; self-negation of, 19–20; substance and, 97–99, 129, 136, 171n
subjective idealism, 33, 46
subject-like (structure, system, logic, character, etc.): 12, 27, 29, 30, 36, 37, 86n, 106n, 108n, 132n, 136n, 150n, 157n
subject/object, 22, 24, 25, 26, 95n, 136n, 141n, 161
sublation. See *Aufhebung*
substance: existence versus, 173n; logic of, 20, 29; self-identity of, 168–69; Spinoza on God as single, 96; spiritual, 113n; subject in relation to, 95–97; subjective aspect of, 97–99, 129, 136
System of Science, The, 40

teleology: of absolute, 99–100n; of being, 12; dialectic and, 37; of Reason, 106; of subject, 98n; of world, 55–56
theodicy, 101n
theory of discourse, 34–35; philosophy and, 15, 63–65, 102–3n, 107–8, 108–9n, 182–83n, 185–89; predicative language, 107–10, 178n, 182–85; and speculative proposition, 182–83n

thesis-antithesis-synthesis formula, 29, 46, 92n, 160n, 163n
thing-in-itself (*Ding an sich*), 33, 69n, 99n, 131n, 135n, 136n
things, relation to Concepts of, 32–34
thought (*Gedanke*): 75, 127, 130, 131, 133n, 134, 139, 154, 158
time, 150–52; philosophy and, 72n, 73n; spirit's development in, 85n
transcendental logic, 52–53
triplicity, 159–60
"true is the whole": result versus development and, 64n, 102; three senses of, 31–32
truth: certainty versus, 42, 116n; coherence theory of, 31; as conformity of thing and intellect, 19, 32–33; dialectical structure of, 36–38; discourse appropriate for exhibiting, 63–65; evidence and, 42; falsity in relation to, 138–41, 153; form of, 137–38; historical, 142–43; mathematical, 143–52; ontic character of, 19, 32–33; philosophical versus non-philosophical, 142–54; representational theory of, 33; as science versus intuition, 73–75; of statements, 34; timeliness of, 195. *See also* absolute

Understanding (*Verstand*): as absolute power, 127; defined, 3; existence and, 171–73; formalism of, 164–67; logic and, 30; and negation, 127n, 128n; pure I and, 88n; Reason versus, 27, 36, 64n, 65n, 87–88; relation to senses of, 130–32; as "wondrous power of dissolution," 127
understanding, process of, 35
unification philosophy, 48, 127n

universals: concrete, 84n; emptiness of, 102, 130; immediate, 95; individuals as, 119–20; modernity and, 197; particulars in relation to, 65n
unsociable sociability, Kant on, 55

Vorstellung. See representation
Wesen. See essence

will: centrality of, 60; Kant on, 55, 56; subject in relation to, 12
Wirklichkeit. See actuality
Wolff, Christian, 143n
world, goal of, 55–56
world-spirit, as subject of world history, 122–23

Zeitgeist, 25, 38, 43, 122n